每天读一点英文

Everyday English Snack

那些无法拒绝的名篇

The famous masterpieces you never say no

章华◎编译

陕西师范大学出版社

图书在版编目（CIP）数据

那些无法拒绝的名篇：英汉对照 / 章华编译 .—西安：
陕西师范大学出版社，2009.8
（每天读一点英文）
ISBN 978-7-5613-4786-7

Ⅰ.那… Ⅱ.章… Ⅲ.①英语—汉语—对照读物
②文学欣赏—世界 Ⅳ.H319.4：I

中国版本图书馆 CIP 数字核字（2009）第 146813 号

图书代号： SK9N0799

上架建议： 英语学习

那些无法拒绝的名篇（经典卷）

作　　者： 章　华
责任编辑： 周　宏
特约编辑： 辛　艳　刘宇圣
封面设计： 张丽娜
版式设计： 风　筝
出版发行： 陕西师范大学出版社
（西安市陕西师大 120 信箱　邮编：710062）
印　　刷： 北京嘉业印刷厂
开　　本： 880*1230　1/32
字　　数： 300 千字
印　　张： 11
版　　次： 2009 年 9 月第一版
印　　次： 2012 年 9 月第五次印刷
ISBN 978-7-5613-4786-7
定　　价： 29.00 元

目录
Contents

浮生若梦
Life is like a dream

你们必须努力寻找自己的声音
You must strive to find your own voice

为你，千千万万遍

For you，a thousand times over

爱之光芒，驱走生命的黑暗

Love will consume all the darkness

那些无法拒绝的名篇

The famous masterpieces you never say no

浮生若梦

Life is like a dream

Dr. Faustus
浮士德博士的悲剧

[英] 克里斯托夫·马洛（Christopher Marlowe）

《浮士德博士的悲剧》取材于德国传奇。浮士德是一位伟大的学者，渴求各领域的知识。他对中世纪一成不变的学科深感厌恶，开始转向一种黑色魔法。通过咒语他结识了魔鬼的仆从。浮士德与魔鬼签订了协议，他将自己的灵魂卖给魔鬼，作为回报魔鬼则要在此后的 24 年中满足浮士德所有求知的愿望。在魔鬼的帮助下，他尽情施展魔法，见到了教皇、亚历山大大帝以及绝代佳人希腊王后海伦。与此同时，浮士德经历了内心的矛盾与斗争。以下选段出自该剧的第一幕，是有关与魔鬼签协议的情节。

Faust. Now that the **gloomy** shadow of the night,
Longing to view Orion's drizzling look,
Leaps from the antarctic world unto the sky
And dims the welkin with her pitchy breath.
Faustus, begin thine incantations
And try if devils will obey thy hest,
Seeing thou has prayed and sacrificed to them.
Within this circle is Jehovah's name
[He draws the circle on the ground.]
Forward and backward anagrammatized,
The **breviated** names of holy saints,
Figures of every adjunct to the heavens
And characters of signs and erring stars,
By which the spirits are enforced to rise.
Then fear not, Faustus, but be resolute
And try the uttermost magic can perform.
[Enter MEPHISTOPHILIS in the shape of a dragon.]
I charge thee to return and change thy shape;
Thou art too ugly to attend on me.
Go, and return an old Franciscan friar;
That holy shape becomes a devil best.
I see there's virtue in my heavenly words:
Who would not be proficient in this art?
How pliant is this Mephistophilis,
Full of obedience and humility!
Such is the force of magic and my spells.
Now, Faustus, thou art conjurer laureate
That canst **command** great Mephistophilis:
Quin redis, Mephistophilis, fratris imagine!

[Re-enter Mephistophil is like a Friar.]

Meph. Now, Faustus, what wouldst thou have me do?

Faust. I charge thee wait upon me whilst I live
To do whatever Faustus shall command,
Be it be make the moon drop from her sphere
Or the ocean to overwhelm the world.

Meph. I am a servant to great Lucifer
And may not follow thee without his leave:
No more than he commands must we perform.

Faust. Did not he charge thee to appear to me?

Meph. No, I came now hither of my own accord.

Faust. Did not my **conjuring** speeches raise thee?
Speak!

Meph. That was the cause, but yet per accident,
For when we hear one rack the name of God,
Abjure the Scriptures and his Saviour Christ,
We fly in hope to get his glorious soul;
Nor will we come unless he use such means
Whereby he is in danger to be damned;
Therefore the shortest cut for conjuring
Is stoutly to abjure the Trinity
And pray devoutly to the prince of hell.

Faust. So I have done, and hold this principle,
There is no chief but only Belzebub
To whom Faustus doth dedicate himself.
This word "damnation" **terrifies** not me
For I confound hell in Elysium;
My ghost be with the old philosophers!

But leaving these vain trifles of men's souls—
Tell me, what is that Lucifer thy lord?

Meph. *Arch-regent and commander of all spirits.*

Faust. Was not that Lucifer an angel once?

Meph. Yes, Faustus, and most dearly loved of God.

Faust. How comes it, then, that he is prince of devils?

Meph. O, by aspiring pride and insolence,
For which God threw him from the face of heaven.

Faust. And what are you that live with Lucifer?

Meph. Unhappy spirits that fell with Lucifer,
Conspired against our God with Lucifer,
And are forever damned with Lucifer.

Faust. Where are you damned?

Meph. In hell.

Faust. How comes it, then, that thou art out of hell?

Meph. Why, this is hell, nor am I out of it:
Thinkst thou that I who saw the face of God
And tasted the eternal joys of heaven
Am not tormented with ten thousand hells
In being deprived of everlasting bliss?
O Faustus, leave these frivolous demands
Which strike a terror to my fainting soul!

Faust. What, is great Mephistophilis so passionate
For being deprived of the joys of heaven?
Learn thou of Faustus manly fortitude
And scorn those joys thou never shalt possess.
Go, bear these tidings to great Lucifer:
Seeing Faustus hath incurred eternal death
By desperate thoughts against Jove's deity,

Say he surrenders up to him his soul
So he will spare him four and twenty years,
Letting him live in all voluptuousness,
Having thee ever to attend on me:
To give me whatsoever I shall ask,
To tell me whatsoever I demand,
To slay mine enemies and aid my friends,
And always be **obedient** to my will.
Go, and return to mighty Lucifer,
And meet me in my study at midnight
And then resolve me of thy master's mind.

Meph. I will, Faustus.

Faust. Had I as many souls as there be stars
I'd give them all for Mephistophilis!
By him I'll be great emperor of the world,
And make a bridge thorough the moving air
To pass the ocean with a band of men;
I'll join the hills that bind the Afric shore
And make that country continent to Spain,
And both contributory to my crown;
The Emperor shall not live but by my leave,
Nor any ***potentate*** *of Germany.*
Now that I have obtained what I desire
I'll live in speculation of this art
Till Mephistophilis return again.

第一幕　第三场

浮士德：现在阴郁的夜色
欲呈现出猎户座多雨的样子，
从那南极的世界跃向天空，
以墨色的呼吸涂黑了整个苍穹，
浮士德，开始做法吧，
看看魔鬼们是否能听从你的符咒，
你已经为他们奉献了祭品、还向他们祈求。
这个圈里是耶和华的名字，
[他在地上画了个圈]
前前后后字符颠倒，
圣贤名号掐尾去头，
天宫诸宿相关等等
颗颗流星黄道诸宫
个个魂灵唯命是从。
无需惧怕什么，浮士德，坚决一些
把魔力发挥到极致吧。
[麦菲斯托菲利斯以龙形现身]
我命你回去换一副模样来；
你这么丑陋怎么来侍奉我。
回去，变成一个圣芳济教派的老修士来；
那副神圣的模样最适合一个魔鬼了。
我看到了我咒语中神秘的力量，

谁能如此精通这种技巧？
这麦菲斯托菲利斯是如此听话，
真是服服帖帖、毕恭毕敬。
现在，浮士德，你真是魔法界的魁首，
竟然可以使唤起麦菲斯托菲利斯来；
快来，麦菲斯托菲利斯，变作修士的样子！
[麦菲斯托菲利斯扮修士重上]

麦　菲：来了，浮士德，你想让我做些什么？

浮士德：我命你在我有生之年侍奉我，
听我的差遣去做任何事情，
不论是让你摘天上的月亮，
还是用大海淹没整个世界。

麦　菲：可我是魔鬼撒旦的奴仆，
没有他的许可是不能为你做事的；
没有他的命令我们什么都不能做。

浮士德：他命令你到我这里来了吗？

麦　菲：没有，我到这里来是因为自己的缘故。

浮士德：难道你不是听到了我的咒语而出现的？
老实说！

麦　菲：是因为这个，可这也是很偶然的。
因为我们只要一听到有人在诅咒上帝的名字，
要放弃圣经和他的救主基督，
我们就会飞来，希望得到他荣耀的灵魂；
如果他不是使用这样的手段，我们是不会来的，
由此他正处在可能遭到上帝惩罚的危险之中；
因此最快捷的做法

就是勇敢地放弃对圣父、圣子和圣灵的信仰，
转而虔诚地膜拜地狱的王子。
浮士德：我正是凭着这个信仰来做的，
只有一个主神就是魔鬼撒旦，
我愿将一切奉献给他。
那“上帝的惩罚”几个字吓不倒我，
因为我已经分不清地狱和福地的区别了；
让我的灵魂去和那些古时的哲人在一起吧！
可现在先把这些有关鬼魂的琐事放一放，
给我讲讲你们的主子撒旦吧。
麦　菲：他是所有魂灵至高无上的统治者。
浮士德：撒旦原来不也是天使吗？
麦　菲：是的，浮士德，他是上帝最宠爱的一个。
浮士德：可怎么回事呢，他竟然成了魔鬼的王子？
麦　菲：噢，是因为他对尊严的渴望和他的傲慢，
上帝把他逐出了天堂。
浮士德：可你们为什么跟他在一起呢？
麦　菲：都是些心怀不满的天使们，
跟着撒旦密谋反对上帝，
然后随撒旦一起受到了永久的惩罚。
浮士德：他们在哪里呢？
麦　菲：在地狱。
浮士德：怎么回事呢，你是怎么逃出地狱的？
麦　菲：嗨，这里就是地狱，我并没有逃出去：
你想想我是见识过上帝容貌的人，
也品尝过天堂中永恒快乐的滋味，

现在被剥夺了享受无尽福祉的权利，
难道不像是在万重地狱里受着折磨？
浮士德，别再用这些琐碎的问题折磨我了，
它们在我脆弱的心里.引起了恐慌。

浮士德：啊，难道麦菲斯托菲利斯也会如此感伤，
因为被剥夺了天堂中的快乐？
从我这里学一学男人的坚强吧，
把这些你永远不会再有的快乐抛在一边吧。
去，把这些消息告诉伟大的撒旦：
说我愿意死后不得复生，
因我已经彻底放弃了上帝具有神性的想法，
说我愿意将我的灵魂与他做个交换，
让他给我 24 年的时间，
让我在你的服侍下，
享遍人世间的奢华，
给我一切我所想得到的，
告诉一切我所想知道的，
毁灭我的敌人，帮助我的朋友，
总是按我的意志行事。
去，转告强大的撒旦。
午夜时分在我的书房见，
然后告诉我他的决定。

麦　菲：好的，浮士德。

浮士德：如果我的灵魂能和天上的星星一样多，
我会全部拿它们去和麦菲斯托菲利斯交换！
有了他，我会成为世上最伟大的君主，

我会在狂风中建造一座桥梁，
带着我的人马跨越大海；
我会扫清那些固守着非洲沿岸的山脉，
使它们与西班牙连成一体，
再都臣服于我；
没有我的许可，皇帝也活不下去，
还有德国的当权者。
现在我已得到了我想要的，
我得去好好想想这魔法的事了，
直到麦菲斯托菲利斯回来。

When you want knowledge like you want air under water then you will get it.

——Socrates

当你需要知识就像你在水底需要空气时，你准能得到它。

——古希腊哲学家　苏格拉底

实战提升 Practising & Exercise

作者介绍

克里斯托夫·马洛（1564–1593）是英国文艺复兴时期的杰出代表，被称为“大学才子”。在他短暂的一生中，他完成了6部剧本的创作。其中最负盛名的有《帖木儿》、《浮士德博士的悲剧》、《马耳他岛的犹太人》和《爱德华二世》。除剧本外，马洛还写下了《海洛与勒安得耳》和《激情的牧人致心爱的姑娘》两首诗。

单词注解

gloomy ['glu:mi] *adj.* 阴暗的；阴沉的

breviate ['bri:viit] *n.* 摘记

command [kə'mɑ:nd] *v.* 命令 指挥

conjuring ['kʌndʒəriŋ] *n.* 魔术

terrify ['terifai] *v.* 使害怕，使恐怖

obedient [ə'bi:djənt] *adj.* 服从的，顺从的

potentate ['pəutənteit] *n.* 君主；统治者

名句大搜索

我命你回去换一副模样来；你这么丑陋如何侍奉我。

______

他是所有魂灵至高无上的统治者。

______

没有我的许可，皇帝也活不下去，还有德国的当权者。

______

Hamlet
哈姆雷特

［英］威廉·莎士比亚（William Shakespeare）

《哈姆雷特》是莎士比亚最负盛名的一部悲剧。丹麦王子哈姆雷特深陷在厌世情绪中，因为他父王的去世和他母后仓促地改嫁新任国王——他的叔叔克劳迪斯。随后哈姆雷特的父王在他面前显灵，并告诉他自己是克劳迪斯谋杀的。克劳迪斯还篡取了王位并霸占了王后，同时激励王子为自己不该发生的惨剧而复仇。可是哈姆雷特不具备当时复仇者那种头脑简单而嗜血成性的品格，他多疑而又好沉思，因此每当他采取行动时，总是以失败告终。以下节选的片段是剧中最负盛名的王子独白，细腻地揭示了哈姆雷特内心的思想与复仇的行动所产生的矛盾。

Ham. *To be, or not to be—that is the question;*
Whether'tis nobler in the mind to suffer
The slings and arrows of **outrageous** fortune,
Or to take arms against a sea of troubles,
And by opposing end them? To die, to sleep—
No more, and by a sleep to say we end
The heart-ache and the thousand natural shocks
That flesh is heir to'tis a consummation
Devoutly to be wish'd. To die, to sleep;
To sleep, perchance to dream. Ay, there's the rub;
For in that sleep of death what dreams may come,
When we have shuffled off this mortal coil,
Must give us pause. There's the respect
That makes calamity of so long life;
For who would bear the whips and scorns of time,
Th'oppressor's wrong, the proud man's contumely,
The pangs of despis'd love, the law's delay,
The insolence of office, and the spurns
That patient merit of th'unworthy takes,
When he himself might his **quietus** make
With a bare bodkin? Who would these fardels bear,
To grunt and sweat under a weary life,
But that the dread of something after death—
The undiscover'd country, from whose bourn
No traveler returns—puzzles the will,
And makes us rather bear those ills we have
Than fly to others that we know not of?
Thus conscience does make cowards of us all;
And thus the native hue of **resolution**

Is sicklied o'er with the pale cast of thought,
And enterprises of great **pith** and moment
With this regard, their currents turn awry
And lose the name of action.

哈姆雷特：生存还是毁灭，这是一个问题；
一个高贵的灵魂是该去承受
狂暴命运的无情摧残，
还是该挺身去反抗那无边的烦恼，
并将它们一扫而净？死了，睡了——
不再有了；如果睡眠能结束我们心灵的创伤和
肉体所承受的上百种痛苦，这结局倒也圆满
倒也得偿所愿。死了，睡了；
可睡着了或许还会做梦。这就麻烦了；
当我们蜕去了这尘世的躯壳后
在那死亡之眠中又会有怎样的梦呢
得好好想想。可就是这点顾虑
使人终身受折磨；
有谁愿意去忍受时光的鞭打与嘲弄
压迫者的不仁，高傲者的鄙夷
忍受那失恋的痛苦，正义遥不可期
官员们的傲慢，辛劳奉献后却换来多少凌辱
而只要一把小小的匕首他就可以

解脱了。谁愿意去肩负重担，
在烦劳生活的压力下呻吟、流汗，
可是对死后又感到恐惧
从来没有任何人从死亡的
国土里回来——因此动摇了，
使我们宁愿忍受目前的苦难
而不愿投奔向另一些未知的痛苦？
于是顾虑使我们变成了懦夫；
那决断时无畏的血色
染了层思想多虑的病容
那许多伟大的事业与时刻
就是在这顾虑之下
改变了初衷
丧失了行动的能力。

Don't believe that winning is really everything. It's more important to stand for something. If you don't stand for something, what do you win?

——Lane Kirkland

不要认为取胜就是一切，更重要的是要有信念。倘若你没有信念，那胜利又有什么意义呢？

——柯克兰

实战提升
Practising & Exercise

作者介绍

威廉莎士比亚（1564-1616）是世界上最杰出的戏剧家和诗人之一。他一生共创作了 38 个剧本，154 首十四行诗及两首长诗。他是世界文学史上的巨擘。他认为文学应该是真、善、美的结合，应该反映人性与现实。

单词注解

outrageous [aut'reidʒəs] *adj.* 可憎的；可耻的

quietus [kwai'i:təs] *n.* 最后的一击；死；清偿

resolution [ˌrezə'lju:ʃən] *n.* 决心；决定

pith [piθ] *n.* 精髓；要旨；核心

名句大搜索

生存还是灭亡，这是一个问题。

___

于是顾虑使我们变成了懦夫。

___

就是在这顾虑之下，改变了初衷，失去了行动的意义。

___

The Pilgrim's Progress
天路历程

[英] 约翰·班扬（John Bunyan）

《天路历程》开始是作者的一个梦，梦中有个“基督徒”在诵读《圣经》，当他从书中得知他的城市将要毁于大火时，他将这个灾难告知别人，但是人们都不予理睬。最后他和“柔顺”先行逃走，在路上，他们跌入“绝望深渊”。“柔顺”无法坚持，打道回府了。后来，“基督徒”被“万事通”误导，被“福音传道”带回正路。后来他又与“忠诚”一同前行。在经历一番激烈的搏斗后，他们来到名利场，在这里“忠诚”被判处死刑，“基督徒”想办法逃了出来，并得到“希望”的帮助，由于厌倦了艰辛的旅途，他们选择了一条轻松的路，却不幸落入“绝望”之手。最后他们终于抵达天国，永享长生不老和上帝的福音。

Then I saw in my dream, that when they were got out of the wilderness, they presently saw a town before them, and the name of that town is Vanity ; and at the town there is a fair kept, called Vanity Fair ; it is kept all the year long ; it bearth the name of Vanity Fair because the town where it is kept is lighter than vanity ; and also because all that is there sold, or that cometh thither, is vanity. As is the saying of the wise, "All that cometh is vanity" .

This fair is no new-erected business, but a thing of **ancient** standing ; I will show you the original of it.

Almost five thousand years agone, there were pilgrims walking to the Celestial City, as these two honest persons are ; and Beelzebub, Apollyon, and Legion, with their companions, **perceiving** by the path that the pilgrims made, that their way to the city lay through this town of Vanity, they contrived to set up a fair ; a fair wherein should be sold all sorts of vanity, and that it should last all the year long. Therefore at this fair are all such merchandise sold, as houses, lands, trades, places, honors, preferments, titles, countries, kingdoms, lusts, pleasures, and delights of all sorts, as whores, bawds, wives, husbands, children, masters, servants, lives, blood, bodies, souls, silver, gold, pearls, precious stones, and what not.

And, moreover, at this fair there is at all times to be seen jugglings, cheats, games, plays, fools, apes, knaves, and rogues, and that of every kind. Here are to be seen, too, and that for nothing, thefts, murders, adulteries, false swearers, and that of a blood-red colour.

And as in other fairs of less moment, there are the several rows and streets, under their proper names, where such and such wares are vended ; so here likewise you have the proper places, rows, streets (viz. countries and kingdoms), where the wares of this fair are soonest to be found. Here is the Britain Row, the French Row, the Italian Row, the Spanish Row, the German Row, where several sorts of vanities are to be sold. But, as in other fairs, some one **commodity** is as the chief of all the fair, so the ware of Rome and her merchandise is greatly promoted in this fair ; only our English nation, with some others, have taken a dislike thereat.

Now, as I said, *the way to the Celestial City lies just through this town where this lusty fair is kept* ; and he that will go to the city, and yet not go through this town, must needs go out of the world. The Prince of princes himself, when here, went through this town to his own country, and that upon a fair-day, too, yea, and as I think, it was Beelzebup, the chief lord of this fair, that invited him to buy of his vanities ; yea, would have made him lord of the fair, would he but have done him reverence as he went through the town. Yea, because he was such a man of honour, Beelzebub had him from street to street, and showed him all the kingdoms of the world in a little time, that he might, if possible, allure the Blessed One to cheapen and buy some of his vanities ; but he had no mind to the merchandise, and therefore left the town, without laying so much as one farthing upon these vanities. This fair, therefore, is an ancient thing, of long standing, and a very great fair.

Now these pilgrims, as I said, must needs go through the fair. Well, so they did ; but behold, even as they entered into the fair, all the people in the fair were moved, and the town itself as it were in a hubbub about them ; and that for several reasons: for First, The pilgrims were clothed with such kind of raiment as was diverse from the raiment of any that traded in the fair. The people, therefore, of the fair, made a great gazing upon them: some said they were fools, some they were bedlams, and some they were outlandish men.

Secondly, And as they wondered at their apparel, so they did likewise at their speech ; for few could understand what they said ; they naturally spoke the language of Canaan , but they that kept the fair were the men of this world ; so that, from one end of the fair to the other, they seemed barbarians each to the other.

Thirdly, But that which did not a little amuse the merchandisers was that these pilgrims set very light by all their wares ; they cared not so much as to look upon them ; and if they called upon them to buy, they would put their fingers in their ears, and cry, "Turn away mine eyes from beholding vanity," and look upwards, signifying that their trade and traffic was in heaven.

One chanced mockingly, beholding the carriages ot the men, to say unto them, What will ye buy? But they, looking **gravely** upon him, said, "*We buy the truth*" . At that there was an occasion taken to despise the men the more ; some mocking, some taunting, some speaking reproachfully, and some calling upon others to smite them. At last things came to a hubbub and great stir in the fair, insomuch that all order was confounded. Now was word presently brought to the great one of the fair, who quickly came down, and deputed some of his most trusty friends to take these men into examination, about whom the fair was almost overturned. So *the men were brought to examination* ; and they that sat upon them asked whence they came, whither they went, and what they did there, in such an unusual garb? The men told them that they were pilgrims and strangers in the world, and that they were going to their own country, which was the Heavenly

Jerusalem ; and that they had given no occasion to the men of the town, nor yet to the merchandisers, thus to abuse them, and to let them in their journey, except it was for that, when one asked them what they would buy, they said they would buy the truth. But they that were appointed to examine them did not believe them to be any other than bedlams and mad, or else such as came to put all things into a **confusion** in the fair. Therefore they took them and beat them, and besmeared them with dirt, and then put them into the cage, that they might be made a spectacle to all the men of the fair.

接着，我在梦境中看到他们走出荒原。不久，他们就看到了前面的一个小镇，小镇的名字叫浮华镇。在这个小镇，有个常年不散的集市，名为“浮华集市”。起此名字，是由于这个小镇比浮华还要轻浮，同时，也是由于集市上所买卖的东西都是奢侈浮华的东西。正如智者所言：“所要来的都是虚空的。”

这个集市并不是刚刚建立的，而是由来已久了；接下来，我就给你讲一讲它的由来。

大约五千年前，有一批朝圣者，就像这两个忠实的人一样，要到天国去朝拜。恶魔亚玻伦、魔鬼比埃兹巴伯以及众喽啰们，对朝觐者去天国的路进行了研究后发现，他们在朝觐的途中，必然要取道浮华镇，于是他们谋划在这里建立一个集市；在这个集市上出卖各种浮华的东西，并常年开放。因此，在这个集市上所经营的商品就包括：房子、土地、职业、地盘、荣耀、特权、名位、国家、王国、欲望、幸福以及各种快乐；比如，妓院、老鸨、老婆、丈夫、孩子、主人、奴仆、生命、血液、肉体、灵魂、银子、金子、珍珠、宝石等。

而且，在这个集市上，你不时地会看到变戏法的人、骗子、赌博、游戏、傻子、模仿者及各色人等。在这儿，不用花一个子儿，你就会看到，偷盗、谋杀、通奸、虚假的宣誓，每一样都令人触目惊心。

有一些不是很重要的集市也有大大小小的各种街道，通过名字就知道他们所经营的东西，这个集市和其他集市一样，也有自己固有的地方、道路和街市（比如，国家街市或王国街市），在这儿，这些东西更容易被找到。这个集市里有英国街、法国街、意大利街、西班牙街还有德国街，这些街上卖好多种浮华的东西。但是，正如在其他街上看到的一样，这条街上也有某种商品特别畅销，比如，罗马的货物及其商品在这里就备受推崇，仅有英国人和少数几个国家的人不太喜欢他们。

正如刚才我所提到的，通往天国的道路恰恰要穿过这个拥有浮华集市的小镇。那些想要到天国朝觐却又不经过这个小镇的人是必须“离开这个世界的。”当初，耶稣本人也是取道此镇而回到自己的国家。耶稣到的那一天，正是赶集的日子。是的，我想，是这个集市的主要创办人，魔鬼比埃兹巴伯，邀请耶稣去购买他的浮华商品；他还许诺，只要耶稣在路过集市的时候，向他表示敬意，他就会让耶稣成为集市的主人。当时，魔鬼带他走遍了集市所有的街道，不一会儿的工夫，就向他展示了世界各国的领土。是的，耶稣是一个如此荣耀的人，倘若可能的话，魔鬼就会引诱他同自己讨价还价，并买走他的某些浮华商品；

但是耶稣并没有把这些放在心上，一分钱没花便离开了那个小镇。由此可见，这个古老的集市，可谓是由来已久，规模庞大。

正如刚才我说的，现在，这两个朝觐者必须要穿过这个集市。而且，他们也这样做了。但是，当他们走进集市的时候，集市上所有人都骚动了起来，整个小镇也好像因他们的到来而开始了一片喧哗！这是为什么呢？

第一，两位朝圣者身上穿的衣物和集市上所卖的任何一件都不同。因而，集市上人便盯着他们看，有人说他们是傻子，有人说他们是疯子，也有人说他们简直就是外地来的怪人。

第二，当他们在大街上闲逛的时候，他们不仅服饰奇异，而且他们的语言也与集市上的人不同；因为几乎没人能够听懂他们的话。他们很自然地操着应许之地的迦南语，但是，集市上的经营者们，他们却是生活在这个凡俗的世界，根本听不懂这两个人的话。因而，当这两个人从这个集市走向另一个集市时，他们在这些经营者眼里，仿佛都是蛮荒之人。

第三，但是，令那些商人所不高兴的是这两位朝觐者对他们所卖的物品并不感兴趣；这俩人在看那些商人的时候，也是不屑一顾的样子。假若商人要招呼他们买东西，他们便用手指堵住自己的耳朵，喊道，“我们不看虚假的东西。”然后，便抬头看天，好像他们的生意是在天上。

一个商人看着朝觐者手里的烟卷，想碰碰运气，便操着愚弄的口气对他们说：“你们想要买什么？”他们却表情严肃地看着他说：“我们要买真理。”这好像又给了商人们嘲笑他们的机会，有人讥讽他们，有人奚落他们，有人责备他们，甚至有人招呼别人来揍他们一顿。终于，集市上突然一阵喧哗，因为他们想要的东西实在是令人迷惑不解。很快这些话就传到了集市首领的耳朵里了，他立刻赶了过来，并委托他最信任的几个朋友对这两人进行了审问。因为正是他们使整个集市几乎闹翻了天。于是，这两人就被带去接受审问。审理他们的人问他们从哪里来，要到哪里去，穿着这种奇怪的服饰在那里做什么。他们回答，他们是朝觐者，是寄居在这凡俗世上的，他们要回自己的国家去，他们的国家是天上的耶路撒冷；他们还说，镇上的人和集市上的人没有理由这么羞辱他们，还妨碍他们的旅程。在有人问他们想买什么的时候，他们说要买真理。但是，审讯他们的人根本就不相信这些，认为他们不是疯子就是傻子，抑或，他们根本就是存心来捣乱的。于是，他们逮捕了这两个朝觐者，还殴打了他们，给他们身上涂满脏兮兮的泥土，还把他们关进笼子里，让集市上所有人都来羞辱他们。

Whom the gods destroy, they first make mad.

——Euripides

上帝要谁灭亡，必先让他疯狂。

——欧里比德斯

作者介绍

约翰·班扬（1628–1688），他于 1647 年加入了不奉国教的新教，开始传教生涯，因在传教时没有获得国教教会的批准，先后两次入狱。他的代表作、英文作品中最成功的宗教寓言《天路历程》就是在狱中完成的。班扬的语言具体生动，情节鲜明真实，简单易懂。

单词注解

ancient ['einʃənt] *adj.* 古代的

perceive [pə'siːv] *v.* 察觉；感知

commodity [kə'mɔditi] *n.* 商品；日用品

gravely [greivli] *adv.* 严肃地，庄重地

confusion [kən'fjuːʒən] *n.* 混乱；骚动

名句大搜索

通往天国的道路恰恰要穿过这个拥有浮华集市的小镇。

____

我们要买真理。

____

于是，这两人就被带去接受审问。

____

A Tale of Two Cities

双城记

[英] 查尔斯·狄更斯（Charles Dickens）

年轻医生梅尼特因故被关进巴士底狱，18 年后获释。这位精神失常的白发老人被旧日的仆人得伐石收留。在和女儿路茜去英国的旅途上，他们邂逅了侯爵的儿子查理·代尔纳。他憎恨自己家族的罪恶，毅然放弃财产的继承权和贵族的姓氏，移居伦敦。1789 年巴黎人民攻占了巴士底狱。远在伦敦的代尔纳为了营救管家盖白勒，冒险回国。但他一到巴黎就被捕入狱了。梅尼特父女闻讯后出庭作证使代尔纳回到妻子的身边。很快，代尔纳又被逮捕并被判处死刑。爱慕路茜的卡尔登来到巴黎，买通狱卒，顶替了昏迷中的代尔纳，梅尼特父女带着代尔纳顺利地离开了法国。卡尔登为了爱情，从容献身。

It was the best of times, it was the worst of times, it was the age of wisdom, it was the age of foolishness, it was the epoch of belief, it was the epoch of **incredulity**, it was the season of Light, it was the season of Darkness, it was the spring of hope, it was the winter of despair, we had everything before us, we had nothing before us, we were all going direct to Heaven, we were all going direct the other way—in short, *the period was so far like the present period, that some of its noisiest authorities insisted on its being received, for good or for evil, in the superlative degree of comparison only.*

There were a king with a large jaw and a queen with a **plain** face, on the throne of England; there were a king with a large jaw and a queen with a fair face, on the throne of France. In both countries it was clearer than crystal to the lords of the State preserves of loaves and fishes, that things in general were settled for ever.

It was the year of Our Lord one thousand seven hundred and seventy-five. Spiritual revelations were **conceded** to England at that favoured period, a sat this. Mrs. Southcott had recently attained her five-and-twentieth blessed birthday, of whom a **prophetic** private in the Life Guards had heralded the sublime appearance by announcing that arrangements were made for the swallowing up of London and Westminster. Even the Cock-lane ghost had been laid only a round dozen of years, after rapping out its messages, as the spirits of this very year last past (supernaturally deficient in originality) rapped out theirs. Mere messages in the earthly order of events had lately come to the English Crown and People, from a congress of British subjects in America: which, strange to relate, have proved more important to the human race than any communications yet received through any of the chickens of the Cock–lane brood.

France, less favoured on the whole as to matters spiritual than her sister of the shield and trident, rolled with exceeding smoothness down hill, making paper money and spending it. Under the **guidance** of her Christian pastors, she entertained herself besides, with such humane achievements as sentencing a youth to have his hands cut off, his tongue torn out with pincers, and his body burned alive, because he had not kneeled down in the rain to do honour to a dirty procession of monks which passed within his view, at a distance of some fifty or sixty yards. It is likely enough that, rooted in the woods of France and Norway, there were growing trees, when that sufferer was put to death, already marked by the Woodman, Fate, to **comedown** and be sawn into boards, to make a certain movable framework with a sack and a knife in it, terrible in history. It is likely enough that in the rough outhouses old some tillers of the heavy lands adjacent to Paris, there were sheltered from the weather that very day, rude carts, be spattered with rustic mire, snuffed about by pigs, and roosted in by poultry, which the Farmer, Death, had already set apart to be his tumbrils of the Revolution. But that Woodman and that Farmer, though they work unceasingly, work silently, and no one heard them as they went about with muffled tread: *the rather, for as much as to entertain any suspicion that they were awake, was to be atheistical and traitorous.*

那是最美好的时代，那是最糟糕的时代；那是个睿智的年月，那是蒙昧的年月；那是信心百倍的时期，那是疑虑重重的时期；那是阳光普照的季节，那是黑暗笼罩的季节；那是充满希望的春天，那是让人绝望的冬天；我们面前一无所有；我们大家都在直奔天堂，我们大家都在直下地狱——简而言之，那个时代和当今这个时代是如此的相似。以致当年有些显赫一时的权威人士坚持认为，无论对它说好说坏一概只能使用最高级的比较词语来评价它。

当时，在英国的王位上，是一个大下巴的国王和一个相貌平常的王后；在法国的王位上，是一个大下巴的国王和一个容貌姣好的王后。在这两个国家里，那些坐享利禄的王公贵族，觉得天下大势永久安定，这是比水晶还清楚的事。

那是纪元 1775 年。在那得天独厚的时代，如同现代一样，英国也屡屡出现神灵的启示。索斯科特夫人过了 25 岁华诞，据禁卫军中一个士兵的先知宣称，伦敦和威斯敏斯特将遭毁灭，在劫难逃，即预示她的神驾降临。即使公鸡巷的幽灵在咄咄逼人地发出它的预言之后销声匿迹整整 12 年，去年的精灵们咄咄逼人发出的预言仍跟她差不多，只是少了几分超自然的独创性而已。前不久英国国王和英国百姓才得到一些人世间的消息。那是从远在美洲的英国臣民的国会传来的。说来奇怪，这些信息对于人类的影响竟然比公鸡巷魔鬼的子孙们的预言还要巨大。

总的来说，法国的灵异事物大体不如她那以盾牌和三叉戟为标志的姐妹那么受宠。法国正在一个劲儿地往坡下滑，她滥发纸币，大肆挥霍。除此之外，法国在教士们的指导下，建立了些仁慈的功勋,寻求了点乐趣。譬如判处砍掉一个青年的双手，用钳子拔出他的舌头，然后把他活活烧死，因为他看见一队满身污泥的修道士在离他五六十码远的地方经过时，他没有跪倒在雨地里向他们致敬。当这个受难者被处死时，生长在法国和挪威森林里的某些树木很可能已被“命运之神”的伐木人做上标记，要砍倒它们，锯成木板，做成某种活动的框架，里面装有一只袋子和一把刀，这就是历史上引起恐怖的装置。就在这一天，在巴黎近郊贫瘠的土地上，某些农户的简陋的小披屋里，很可能有一些大车在那儿躲避风雨。那些车很粗糙，车身溅满了郊野的泥浆，猪群在旁边呼哧呼哧转悠，家禽在它上面歇息，这些东西也极有可能被“死神”这个农民看中，要在革命时作为押送死刑犯的囚车。但是,那个伐木人和农民,尽管忙个不停,却总是默不作声，蹑手蹑脚不让人听见。因此若是有人猜想到他们已在行动，反倒会被看作是无神论和大逆不道。

作者介绍

查尔斯·狄更斯（1812–1870），英国小说家，出生于海军小职员家庭。他只上过几年学，全靠刻苦自学成为知名作家。狄更斯一生共创作了14部长篇小说，许多中、短篇小说和杂文、游记、戏剧、小品。其中最著名的作品是描写劳资矛盾的长篇代表作《艰难时代》和描写1789年法国革命的另一篇代表作《双城记》。其他作品有《雾都孤儿》、《老古玩店》、《大卫·科波菲尔》和《远大前程》等。 狄更斯是19世纪英国现实主义文学的主要代表。马克思把他和萨克雷等称为英国的“一批杰出的小说家”。

单词注解

incredulity [ˌinkri'dju:liti] *n.* 不轻信；不相信；怀疑

plain [plein] *adj.* 简朴的；朴素的；

concede [kən'si:d] *v.* 让给，给予；容许

prophetic [prə'fetik] *adj.* 预言的，预言性的

guidance ['gaidəns] *n.* 指导；引导；领导

comedown [kʌmdaʊn] *n.* 衰落；丧失；落魄

名句大搜索

那是最美好的时代，那是最糟糕的时代；那是个睿智的年月，那是蒙昧的年月。

以致当年有些显赫一时的权威人士坚持认为，无论对它说好说坏一概只能使用最高级的比较词语来评价它。

因此若是有人猜想到他们已在行动，反倒会被看作是无神论和大逆不道。

Life of Pi

少年Pi的奇幻漂流

[加] 扬·马特尔（Yann Martel）

《少年Pi的奇幻漂流》讲述的是帕特尔的父亲决定全家带着动物移民加拿大，他们所乘坐的日本货船在太平洋失事，帕特尔侥幸生存下来，在海上漂泊了227天。期间最危险的就是与一只成年孟加拉虎理查德·帕克的斗争。他曾想了6种对付这只虎的计策。最后终于明白，只要保证了理查德·帕克的饮食，他就不会有危险。后来他利用老虎的一些弱点开始了驯虎的过程。这驯虎的过程也是少年帕特尔演变成成年男人的过程。

When we reached land, Mexico to be exact, I was so weak I barely had the strength to be happy about it. We had great difficulty landing. The lifeboat nearly capsized in the surf. I streamed the sea anchors — what was left of them — full open to keep us perpendicular to the waves, and I tripped them as soon as we began riding a crest. In this way, streaming and tripping the anchors, we surfed in to shore. It was dangerous. But we caught one wave at just the right point and it carried us a great distance, past the high, collapsing walls of water. I tripped the anchors a last time and we were pushed in the rest of the way. The boat hissed to a halt against the sand.

I let myself down the side. I was afraid to let go, afraid that so close to deliverance, in two feet of water, I would drown. I looked ahead to see how far I had to go. The **glance** gave me one of my last images of Richard Parker, for at that precise moment he jumped over me. I saw his body, so immeasurably vital, stretched in the air above me, a fleeting, furred rainbow. He landed in the water, his back legs splayed, his tail high, and from there, in a few hops, he reached the beach. He went to the left, his paws gouging the wet sand, but changed his mind and spun around. He passed directly in front of me on his way to the right. He didn't look at me. He ran a hundred yards or so along the shore before turning in. His gait was clumsy and uncoordinated. He fell several times. At the edge of the jungle, he stopped. I was certain he would turn my way. He would look at me. He would flatten his ears. He would growl. In some such way, he would **conclude** our relationship. He did nothing of the sort. He only looked fixedly into the jungle. Then Richard Parker, companion of my torment, awful, fierce thing that kept me alive, moved forward and disappeared forever from my life.

I struggled to shore and fell upon the sand. I looked about. I was truly alone, orphaned not only of my family, but now of Richard Parker, and nearly, I thought, of God. Of course, I wasn't. This beach, so soft, firm and vast, was like the cheek of God, and somewhere two eyes were glittering with pleasure and a mouth was smiling at having me there.

After some hours a member of my own species found me. He left and returned with a group. They were six or seven. They came up to me with their hands covering their noses and mouths. I wondered what was wrong with them. They spoke to me in a strange tongue. They pulled the lifeboat onto the sand. They carried me away. *The one piece of turtle meat I had brought from the boat they wrenched from my hand and threw away.*

I wept like a child. It was not because I was overcome at having survived my ordeal, though I was. Nor was it the presence of my brothers and sisters, though that too was very moving. I was weeping because Richard Parker had left me so unceremoniously. What a terrible thing it is to botch a farewell. I am a person who believes in form, in the harmony of order. Where we can, we must give things a meaningful shape. For example, I wonder—could you tell my jumbled story in exactly one hundred chapters, not one more, not one less? I'll tell you, that's one thing I hate about my nickname, the way that number runs on forever. It's important in life to conclude things properly. Only then can you let go. Otherwise you are left with words you should have said but never did, and your heart is heavy with remorse. That bungled goodbye hurts me to this day. I wish so much that I'd had one last look at him in the lifeboat, that I had provoked him a little, so that I was on his mind. I wish I had said to him then — yes, I know, to a tiger, but still—I wish I had said, "Richard Parker, it's over. We have survived. Can you believe it? I owe you more gratitude than I can express. I couldn't have done it without you. I would like to say it formally: Richard Parker, thank you. Thank you for saving my life. And now go where you must. You have known the **confined** freedom of a zoo most of your life ; now you will know the free confinement of a jungle. I wish you all the best with it. Watch out for Man. He is not your friend. But I hope you will remember me as a friend. I will never forget you, that is certain. You will always be with me, in my heart. What is that hiss? Ah, our boat has touched sand. So farewell, Richard Parker, farewell. God be with you."

The people who found me took me to their village, and there some women gave me a bath and scrubbed me so hard that I wondered if they realized I was naturally brown skinned and not a very dirty white boy. I tried to explain. They nodded and smiled and kept on scrubbing me as if I were the deck of a ship. I thought they were going to skin me alive. But they gave me food. Delicious food. Once I started eating, I couldn't stop.

The next day a police car came and brought me to a hospital, and there my story ends.

I was overwhelmed by the generosity of those who rescued me. Poor people gave me clothes and food. *Doctors and nurses cared for me as if I were a premature baby*. Mexican and Canadian officials opened all doors for me so that from the beach in Mexico to the home of my **foster** mother to the classrooms of the University of Toronto, there was only one long, easy corridor I had to walk down. To all these people I would like to extend my heartfelt thanks.

我们到达陆地的时候，具体地说，是到达墨西哥的时候，我太虚弱了，简直连高兴的力气都没有了。靠岸非常困难。救生艇差点儿被海浪掀翻。我让海锚——剩下的那些——完全张开，让我们与海浪保持垂直，一开始往浪峰上冲，我就起锚。我们就这样不断地下锚和起锚，冲浪来到岸边。这很危险。但是我们正好抓住了一个浪头，这个浪头带了我们很远，带过了高高的、墙一般坍塌的海水。我最后一次起锚，剩下的路程是被海浪推着前进的。小船发出嘶嘶声，冲上海滩停了下来。

我从船舷上爬了下来。我害怕松手，害怕在就要被解救的时候淹死在这两英尺深的海里。我向前看要走多远。那一看在我心里留下了对理查德·帕克的最后几个印象之一，因为就在那一刻它朝我扑了过来。我看见它充满了无限活力，在我身体上方的空中伸展开来，仿佛一道飞逝的毛绒绒的彩虹。它落进了海里，后腿展开，尾巴翘得高高的，只跳了几下，就从那儿跳到了海滩上。它向左走去，爪子挖开了潮湿的沙滩，后来又改变了主意，转过身来。它向右走去时径直从我面前走过。它没有看我。它沿着海岸跑了大约一百码远，然后才调转过来。它步态笨拙又不协调，它摔倒了好几次。在丛林边上，它停了下来。我肯定它会转过身看着我，它会耷拉下耳朵，它会咆哮，它会以某种诸如此类的方式为我们之间的关系作一个总结。然而，它并没有这么做，只是目不转睛地看着丛林。然后，理查德·帕克——我忍受折磨时的伙伴；激起我求生意志的可怕的猛兽，向前走去，从我的生活中永远的消失了。

我挣扎着向岸边走去，倒在了海滩上。我四处张望。我真的是孤独一人，不仅被家人抛弃，现在理查德·帕克也抛弃了我，而且上帝也抛弃了我，但我并没有被遗弃。这座海滩如此柔软、坚实、广阔，就像上帝的胸膛。而且，在某个地方，有两只眼睛正闪烁着快乐的光芒，有一张嘴正因为有我在那儿而微笑着。

几个小时以后，我的一个同类发现了我。他找了一群人来。大约有六七个人。他们用手捂着鼻子和嘴，我怀疑他们是不是有什么问题啊。他们用一种奇怪的语言跟我说话。他们把救生艇拖到了沙滩上，把我抬走了。我手里拿着一块从船上带下来的海龟肉，他们把肉抠出来扔了。

我像个孩子一样哭了起来。不是因为我对自己历尽磨难最后生存下来而感到激动，尽管这也令我非常感动。我哭是因为理查德·帕克如此轻易地离开了我。不能好好的告别是件多么可怕的事啊。我是一个相信形式、相信秩序和谐的人。只要可能，我们就应该赋予事物一个有益的形式。比如说——我想知道——你能一章不多、一章不少，用正好一百章把我的杂乱的故事说出来吗？我告诉你，我讨厌自己外号的一个原因就是，那个数字会一直循环下去。事物应该恰当的结束，这在生活中很重要，只有在这时你才能放手。否则你的心里就会装满应该说却不曾说的话，你的心情就会因为悔恨而沉重。那个没有说出的再见直到今天仍让我伤心。我真希望自己在救生艇里看了它最后一眼，希望我稍稍激怒了它，这样它就会牵挂我。我希望自己当时就对它说——是的，我知道，对一只老虎，但是我还是要说——我希望自己说："理查德·帕克，一切都过去了。我们活了下来，你能相信吗？我对你的感激无法用语言来表达。如果没有你，我做不到这一点。我要郑重地对你说，理查德•帕克，谢谢你。谢谢你救了我的命。现在去你想去的地方吧。这大半辈子，你已经了解了什么是动物园里有限的自由；现在你将会了解什么是丛林里无限的自由。我祝你好运。小心人类。他们不是你的朋友。但我希望你记住我这个朋友。我不会忘记你的，这是肯定的。你会永远在我心里。那嘶嘶声是什么？啊，我们的小船触到沙滩了。那么，再见了，理查德•帕克，再见。上帝与你同在。”

发现我的人把我带到了他们村子里，在那里，几个女人给我洗了个澡。她们擦洗得好用力啊，我不知道她们是否意识到我的皮肤是天生的棕色，不是非常脏的白人小伙子。我试图解释。她们点了点头，笑了笑，然后继续擦洗，仿佛我是船甲板。我以为她们要把我活剥了。但是她们给了我食物，非常可口的食物。我一吃起来，就停不下来了。

第二天，来了一辆警车，把我送进了医院。我的故事到此结束了。

救我的人慷慨大方，让我深受感动。村民送给我衣服和食物。医生和护士照顾我，仿佛我是个早产的婴儿。墨西哥和加拿大的官员为我敞开了所有的大门，因此从墨西哥海滩到我养母家，再到多伦多大学的课堂，我只需走一道长长的、通行方便的走廊。我要对所有这些人表示衷心的感谢。

作者介绍

扬·马特尔，1963 年出生于西班牙，父母是加拿大人。他曾在哥斯达黎加、法国、墨西哥和加拿大生活。大学哲学系毕业后，他做过洗碗工、植树工和保安，之后开始写作。《少年 Pi 的奇幻漂流》是扬·马特尔的第三部作品。2002 年，这部小说获得了当代英语小说界的最重要奖项——布克奖。

____

单词注解

glance [glɑːns] *v.* 一瞥；扫视

conclude [kən'kluːd] *v.* 结束；推断出，断定

wrench [rentʃ] *v.* 猛拧；扭伤

confine ['kɔnfain] *v.* 限制；禁闭；幽禁；使卧床

foster ['fɔstə] *v.* 养育，领养；培养，促进

名句大搜索

我手里抓着一块从船上带下来的海龟肉，他们把肉抠出来扔了。

____

我像个孩子一样哭了起来。

____

医生和护士照顾我，仿佛我是个早产的婴儿。

____

Don Quixote
唐·吉诃德

［西班牙］米盖儿·塞万提斯（Miguel de Cervantes Saavedra）

《唐·吉诃德》是一部讽刺骑士小说。主人公唐·吉诃德因沉迷于骑士小说，决定外出历险，做一名行侠仗义的骑士。他找来同村的农民桑丘·潘沙作他的侍从，把邻村的一位农家女儿杜尔希尼亚作为他的意中人。他三次外出历险，做了好多可笑的事。最后他被化装成白月骑士的朋友打败，放弃行侠游历，回家不久后病倒。临死前，他终于醒悟了。

In a village of La Mancha, the name of which I have no desire to call to mind, there lived not long since one of those gentlemen that keep a lance in the lance-rack, an old buckler, a lean hack, and a greyhound for coursing. An olla of rather more beef than mutton, a salad on most night, scraps on Saturdays, lentils on Fridays, and a pigeon or so extra on Sundays, made away with three-quarters of his income. The rest of it went in a doublet of fine cloth and velvet breeches and shoes to match for holidays, while on week-days he made a brave figure in his best homespun. He had in his house a housekeeper past forty, a niece under twenty, and a lad for the field and market-place, who used to saddle the hack as well as handle the bill-hook. The age of this gentleman of ours was bordering of fifty ; he was of a hardy habit, spare, gauntfeatured, a very early riser and a great sportsman. They will have it his surname was Quixada or Quesada (for here there is some difference of opinion among the authors who write on the subject), although from reasonable conjectures it seems plain that he was called Quexana. This, however, is of but little importance to our tale ; it will be enough not to stray a hair's breadth from the truth in the telling of it.

You must know, then, that the above-named gentleman whenever he was at leisure (which was mostly all the year round) gave himself up to reading books of **chivalry** with such ardour and avidity that he almost entirely neglected the pursuit of his field-sports, and even the management of his property ; *and to such a pitch did his eagerness and infatuation go that he sold many an acre of tillageland to buy books of chivalry to read, and brought home as many of* *them as he could get.* But of all there were none he liked so well as those of the famous Feliciano de Silva's. composition, for their **lucidity** of style and complicated conceits were as pearls in his sight, particularly when in his reading he came upon courtships and cartels, where he often found passages like "the reason of the unreason with which my reason is afflicted so weakens my reason that with reason I murmur at your beauty;" or again, "the high heavens, that of your divinity divinely fortify you with the stars, render you deserving of the desert your greatness deserves." Over conceits of this sort the poor gentleman lost his wits, and used to lie awake striving to understand them and worm the meaning out of them; what Aristotle himself could not have made out or extracted had he come to life again for that special purpose. He was not at all easy about the wounds which Don Belianis gave and took, because it seemed to him that, great as were the surgeons who had cured him, he must have had his face and body covered all over with seams and scars. He commended, however, the author's way of ending his book with the promise of that interminable adventure, and many a time was he tempted to take up his pen and finish it properly as is there proposed, which no doubt he would have done, and made a successful piece of work of it too, had not greater and more absorbing thoughts prevented him.

Many an argument did he have with the curate of his village (a learned man, and a graduate of Siguenza) as to which had been the better knight, Palmerin of England or Amadis of Gaul. Master Nicholas, the village barber, however, used to say that neither of them came up to the Knight of Phoebus, and that if there was any that could compare with him it was Don Galaor, the brother of Amadis of Gaul, because he had a spirit that was equal to every occasion, and was no finikin knight, nor lachrymose like his brother, while in the matter of valour he was not a whit behind him. In short, he became so absorbed in his books that he spent his nights from sunset to sunrise, and his days from dawn to dark, poring over them; and what with little sleep and much reading his brains got so dry that he lost his wits.

His fancy grew full of what he used to read about in his books, enchantments, quarrels, battles, challenges, wounds, wooings, loves, agonies, and all sorts of impossible nonsense; *and it so possessed his mind that the whole fabric of invention and fancy he read of was true*, that to him no history in the world had more reality in it. He used to say the Cid Ruy Diaz was a very good knight, but that he was not to be compared with the Knight of the Burning Sword who with one backstroke cut in half two **fierce** and monstrous giants. He thought more of Bernardo del Carpio because at Roncesvalles he slew Roland in spite of enchantments, availing himself of the artifice of Hercules when he strangled Antaeus the son of Terra in his arms. *He approved highly of the giant Morgante, because, although of the giant breed which is always arrogant and ill-conditioned, he alone was affable and well-bred.* But above all he admired Reinaldos of Montalban, especially when he saw him sallying forth from his castle and robbing everyone he met, and when beyond the seas he stole that image of Mahomet which, as his history says, was entirely of gold. To have a bout of kicking at that traitor of a Ganelon he would have given his housekeeper, and his niece into the bargain.

曼查有个地方，地名就不提了，不久前住着一位贵族。他那类贵族，矛架上有一支长矛，还有一面皮盾、一匹瘦马和一只猎兔狗。锅里牛肉比羊肉多，晚餐常吃凉拌肉丁，星期六吃脂油煎鸡蛋，星期五吃扁豆，星期日加一只野雏鸽，这就用去了他四分之三的收入，其余的钱买了节日穿的黑呢外套、长毛绒袜子和平底鞋，而平时，他总是得意洋洋地穿着上好的棕色粗呢衣。家里有一个 40 多岁的女管家，一个不到 20 岁的外甥女，还有一个能种地、能采购的小伙子，为他备马、修剪树枝。我们的这位贵族年近五旬，体格健壮，肌肉干瘪，脸庞清瘦，每天起得很早，喜欢打猎。据说他还有一个别名，叫基哈达或克萨达（各种记载略有不同）。推论起来，他应该叫吉哈纳。不过，这对我们的故事并不重要，只要我们谈起他来不失真就行。

人家说这位贵族一年到头闲的时候居多，闲时常读骑士小说，而且读得津津有味，几乎忘记了习武和理财。他痴心不已，简直走火入魔，居然卖掉了好多田地去买骑士小说。他把所有能弄到的骑士小说都搬回了家。不过，所有这些小说，他都觉得不如闻名遐迩的费利西亚诺•德席尔瓦写得好，此人的平铺直叙和繁冗陈述被他视为明珠，特别在读到那些殷勤话和挑逗信时更是如此。许多地方这样写道：“以你无理对我有理之道理，使我自觉理亏，因此我埋怨你漂亮也有道理。”还有：“高空以星星使你的神圣更加神圣，使你受之无愧地接受你受之无愧的伟大称号而受之无愧。”这些话使得这位可怜的贵族惶惑不已。他夜不能寐，要理解这些即使亚里士多德再世也理解不了的句子。他对唐贝利亚尼斯打伤了别人而自己也受了伤略感不快，可以想象，即使是病被高明的外科医生治好了，但是在脸上和身上也不免会留下累累伤疤。然而，他很欣赏书的末尾说故事还没有完结，很多次，他甚至提笔续写。如果不是其他更重要的想法不断打扰他，他肯定会续写，而且是会写完的。

他常常和当地的神父（一位知识渊博的人，毕业于锡古恩萨）争论，谁是最优秀的骑士，是英格兰的帕尔梅林，还是高卢的阿马迪斯？可是同村的理发师尼古拉斯师傅却说，谁都比不上太阳神骑士。如果有人能够与之相比，那么，只能是高卢的阿马迪斯的兄弟加劳尔。他符合各方面的条件，不是矫揉造作的骑士，而且不像他兄弟那样爱哭，论勇敢也不比他兄弟差。

总之，他沉湎于书，每天晚上通宵达旦，白天也读得天昏地转。这样，睡得少，读得多，终于思维枯竭，精神失常，满脑袋都是书上虚构的那些东西，都是想入非非的魔术、打斗、战争、挑战、负伤、献殷勤、爱情、暴风雨、胡言乱语等。他确信他在书上读到的都是真的。对他来说，世界上只有那些故事才是实事。他说熙德·鲁伊·迪亚斯是一位杰出的骑士，可是无法与火剑骑士比。火剑骑士反手一击，就把两个巨大的恶魔劈成了两半。他最推崇卡皮奥的贝尔纳多。在龙塞斯瓦列斯，贝尔纳多借助赫拉克勒斯把地神之子安泰举起扼死的方法，杀死了会魔法的罗尔丹。他十分称赞巨人摩根达。其他巨人都傲慢无礼，唯有他文质彬彬。不过，他最赞赏的是蒙塔尔万的雷纳尔多斯，特别是看到故事中说，他走出城堡，逢物便偷，而且还到海外偷了穆罕默德渡金像的时候，更是赞叹不止。为了能狠狠地踢一顿叛徒加拉隆，他情愿献出他的女管家，甚至可以再加上他的外甥女。

Behavior is a mirror in which every one shows his image.

——Johann Wolfgang von Goethe

行为是一面镜子，每个人都把自己的形象显现于其中。

——德国诗人　歌德

作者介绍

米盖儿·塞万提斯（1547–1616）是文艺复兴时期西班牙小说家、剧作家、诗人。他被誉为是西班牙最伟大的作家。评论家们称他的小说《唐·吉诃德》是文学史上的第一部现代小说，同时也是世界文学的瑰宝之一。

____

单词注解

chivalry [ˈʃivəlri] *n.* 骑士精神；骑士制度

lucidity [luːˈsiditi] *n.* 清晰；清澈

fabric [ˈfæbrik] *n.* 织物；结构；组织

fierce [fiəs] *adj.* 凶猛的；残酷的；好斗的

名句大搜索

他痴心不已，简直走火入魔，居然卖掉了许多田地去买骑士小说。他把所有能弄到的骑士小说都搬回了家。

____

对他来说，世界上只有那些故事才是实事。

____

其他巨人都傲慢无礼，唯有他文质彬彬。

____

The Great Gatsby

了不起的盖茨比

[美] 费·司各特·菲茨杰拉德（F.Scott Fitzgerald）

《了不起的盖茨比》通过完美的艺术形式描写了20年代贩酒暴发户盖茨比所追求的“美国梦”的幻灭，揭示了美国社会的悲剧。盖茨比与黛西的恋爱和分手本来是个很普通的爱情故事。但作者出手不凡，把盖茨比热恋的姑娘当作青春、金钱和地位的象征，当作靠手段追求富裕物质生活的“美国梦”。盖茨比为了追求黛西耗尽了自己的感情和才智，最后葬送了自己的生命。他天真地以为：有了金钱就能重温旧梦，赎回失去的爱情。可惜，他错了。他看错了黛西这个粗俗浅薄的女人，他看错了表面上灯红酒绿而精神上空虚无聊的社会。他生活在梦幻之中，被黛西抛弃，被社会冷落，最终酿成了无法挽回的悲剧。

I spent my Saturday nights in New York because those gleaming, dazzling parties of his were with me so vividly that I could still hear the music and the laughter, faint and **incessant**, from his garden, and the cars going up and down his drive. One night I did hear a material car there, and saw its lights stop at his front steps. But I didn't investigate. *Probably it was some final guest who had been away at the ends of the earth and didn't know that the party was over.*

On the last night, with my trunk packed and my car sold to the grocer, I went over and looked at that huge incoherent failure of a house once more. On the white steps an obscene word, scrawled by some boy with a piece of brick, stood out clearly in the moonlight, and I erased it, drawing my shoe raspingly along the stone. Then I wandered down to the beach and sprawled out on the sand.

Most of the big shore places were closed now and there were hardly any lights except the shadowy, moving glow of a ferryboat across the Sound. And as the moon rose higher the inessential houses began to melt away until gradually I became aware of the old island here that flowered once for Dutch sailors' eyes—a fresh, green breast of the new world. Its vanished trees, the trees that had made way for Gatsby's house, had once pandered in whispers to the last and greatest of all human dreams; for a **transitory** enchanted moment man must have held his breath in the presence of this continent, compelled into an **aesthetic** contemplation he neither understood nor desired, face to face for the last time in history with something commensurate to his capacity for wonder.

And as I sat there brooding on the old, unknown world, I thought of Gatsby's wonder when he first picked out the green light at the end of Daisy's dock . He had come a long way to this blue lawn, and his dream must have seemed so close that he could hardly fail to grasp it. *He did not know that it was already behind him, somewhere back in that vast obscurity beyond the city, where the dark fields of the republic rolled on under the night.*

Gatsby believed in the green light, the orgiastic future that year by year recedes before us. It eluded us then, but that's no matter — tomorrow we will run faster, stretch out our arms farther... And one fine morning...

So we beat on, boats against the current, borne back ceaselessly into the past.

每星期六晚上我都是在纽约度过的，因为盖茨比举办的那些灯火辉煌、光彩炫目的宴会使我记忆犹新，所以我仍然可以听到微弱的音乐声和欢笑声不断地从他的园子里飘过来，还有一辆辆汽车在他的车道上开来开去。一天晚上我确实听见那儿有一辆汽车，也看见车灯照在他门前的台阶上。我没有去调查。那大概是最后一位客人，刚从天涯海角归来，还不知道宴会早已收场了。

在最后那个晚上，我的行李已经收拾好了，车子也卖给了杂货店老板，我走过去又看了一眼那座庞大而零乱的、意味着失败的房子。白色台阶不知被哪个男孩用砖头写了一个脏字儿，映在月光里分外醒目，于是我把它擦了，鞋子在石头上蹭出沙沙的响声。然后我又漫步到海边，仰天躺在沙滩上。

那些海滨大别墅现在大多已经关闭了，除了海湾上一只渡船的幽暗漂移的灯光，四周几乎没有灯火。当明月上升的时候，那些微不足道的房屋慢慢消逝，我逐渐看见了当年曾令荷兰水手眼睛大放异彩的这个古岛——一片清新碧绿的新世界。它那些消失了的树木，那些为盖茨比的别墅让路而被砍伐的树木，曾经一度迎风飘拂，在这里低声响应着人类最后的也是最伟大的梦想；在那个昙花一现的神妙的瞬间，人在面对这个新大陆时一定屏息惊异，不由自主地堕入他既不理解也不企求的一种美学的观赏中，在历史上最后一次面对着和他感到惊奇的能力相称的奇观。

当我坐在那里缅怀那个古老的、未知的世界时，我也想起了盖茨比第一次认出了黛西的那个码头的尽头的那盏绿灯时所感到的巨大惊奇。他经历了漫漫长路才来到这片草坪上，那时候他的梦一定就近在眼前，他几乎不可能抓不住的。他不知道那个梦已经丢在他背后了，丢在这个城市不知何处的一片无垠的混沌之中了，在那里，美利坚合众国的黑黝黝的田野在夜色中向前伸展。

盖茨比信奉这盏绿灯，这个逐年在我们眼前渐渐远去的极乐未来。它从前逃脱了我们的追求，不过没关系——明天我们跑得更快一点，把手臂伸得更远一点……总有一天……

于是我们奋力向前划，逆流向上的小舟，不停地倒退，进入过去。

作者介绍

费·司各特·菲茨杰拉德（1896-1940），美国小说家。1920 年出版了长篇小说《人间天堂》，从此出了名，小说出版后他与吉姗尔达结婚。婚后携妻寄居巴黎，结识了安德逊、海明威等多位美国作家。1925 年《了不起的盖茨比》问世，奠定了他在现代美国文学史上的地位，成了 20 年代“爵士时代”的发言人和“迷惘的一代”的代表作家之一。

单词注解

incessant [in'sesnt] *adj.* 不停的，连续的，持续不断的

transitory ['trænsitəri] *adj.* 短暂的；瞬息的

aesthetic [i:s'θetik] *adj.* 美学的；美的；艺术的

obscurity [əb'skjuəriti] *n.* 暗淡；晦涩，难解

ceaselessly ['si:slisli] *adv.* 不停地；持续地

名句大搜索

那大概是最后一位客人，刚从天涯海角归来，还不知道宴会早已收场了。

他不知道那个梦已经丢在他背后了，丢在这个城市不知何处的一片无垠的混沌之中了，在那里，美利坚合众国的黑黝黝的田野在夜色中向前伸展。

于是我们奋力向前划，逆流向上的小舟，不停地倒退，进入过去。

The Story of an Hour

一个小时的故事

[美] 凯特·肖邦（Kate Chopin）

《一个小时的故事》精炼地概述了在一个小时里，玛拉德夫人对一偶发事件的反应。故事的主人公玛拉德夫人患有心脏病，当她听到丈夫在一场车祸中丧生之后，先是痛不欲生，失声痛哭，但独自回到房间后，她竟很快从悲痛中恢复了过来，有了“自由”的喜悦。等她再从房间里走出来的时候，她感受到了新生。但此时，逃过一劫的玛拉德先生出现在门口，玛拉德夫人心脏病突发，倒地猝死。

Knowing that Mrs.Mallard was afflicted with a heart trouble, great care was taken to break to her as gently as possible the news of her husband's death.

It was her sister Josephine who told her, in broken sentences ; veiled hints that revealed in half concealing.

Her husband's friend Richards was there, too, near her. It was he who had been in the newspaper office when **intelligence** of the railroad disaster was received ; with Brently Maitard's name leading the list of "killed" . He had only taken the time to assure himself of its truth by a second telegram, and had hastened to forestall any less careful, less tender friend in bearing the sad message.

She did not hear the story as many women have heard the same, with a paralyzed inability to accept its significance. She wept at once, with sudden, wild abandonment, in her sister's arms. When the storm of grief had spent itself she went away to her room alone. She would have no one follow her.

There stood, facing the open window, a comfortable, roomy armchair. Into this she sank, pressed down by a physical exhaustion that haunted her body and seemed to reach into her soul.

She could see in the open square before her house the tops of trees that were all aquiver with the new spring life. The **delicious** breath of rain was in the air.

In the street below a peddler was crying his wares. The notes of a distant song which someone was singing reached her **faintly**, and countless sparrows were twittering in the eaves.

There were patches of blue sky showing here and there through the clouds that had met and piled one above the other in the west facing her window.

She sat with her head thrown back upon the cushion of the chair, quite motionless, except when a sob came up into her throat and shook her, as a child who has cried itself to sleep continues to sob in its dreams.

She was young, with a fair, calm face, whose lines bespoke repression and even a certain strength. But now there was a dull stare in her eyes, whose gaze was fixed away off yonder on one of those patches of blue sky. It was not a glance of reflection, but rather indicated a suspension of intelligent thought.

There was something coming to her and she was waiting for it, fearfully. What was it? She did not know ; *it was too subtle and elusive to name.* But she felt it, creeping out of the sky, reaching toward her through the sounds, the scents, the color that filled the air.

Now her bosom rose and fell tumultuously. She was beginning to recognize this thing that was approaching to possess her, and she was striving to beat it back with her will—as powerless as her two white slender hands would have been.

When she abandoned herself, a little whispered word escaped her slightly parted lips. *She said it over and over under her breath: "free, free, free!" The vacant stare and the look of terror that had followed it went from her eyes.* They stayed keen and bright. Her pulses beat fast, and the coursing blood warmed and relaxed every inch of her body.

She did not stop to ask if it were or were not a monstrous Joy that held her. A clear and exalted perception enabled her to dismiss the suggestion as trivial.

She knew that she would weep again when she saw the kind, tender hands folded in death ; the face that had never looked save with love upon her, fixed and gray and dead. But she saw beyond that bitter moment a long procession of years to come that would belong to her **absolutely**. And she opened and spread her arms out to them in welcome.

There would be no one to live for her during those coming years; she would live for herself. *There would be no powerful will bending hers in that blind persistence with which men and women believe they have a right to impose a private will upon a fellow creature.* A kind intention or a cruel intention made the act seem no less a crime as she looked upon it in that brief moment of illumination.

And yet she had loved him — sometimes. Often she had not. What did it matter! What could love, the unsolved mystery, count for in face of this possession of self-assertion which she suddenly recognized as the strongest impulse of her being! "Free! Body and soul free!" she kept whispering.

Josephine was kneeling before the closed door with her lips to the keyhole, imploring for admission. "Louise, open the door! I beg; open the door — you will make yourself. What are you doing, Louise? For heaven's sake open the door."

"Go away. I am not making myself." No; she was drinking in a very elixir of life through that open window.

Her fancy was running riot along those days ahead of her. Spring days, and summer days, and all sorts of days that would be her own. She breathed a quick prayer that life might be long. It was only yesterday she had thought with a shudder that life might be long.

She arose at length and opened the door to her sister's importunities. There was a feverish triumph in her eyes, and she carried herself **unwittingly** like a goddess of Victory. She clasped her sister's waist, and together they descended the stairs. Richards stood waiting for them at the bottom.

Someone was opening the front door with a latchkey. It was Brently Mallard who entered, a little travel-stained, composedly carrying his gripsack and umbrella. He had been far from the scene of accident, and did not know there had been one. He stood amazed at Josephine's piercing cry; at Richards's quick motion to screen him from the view of his wife.

But Richards was too late.

When the doctors came they said she had died of heart disease — of joy that kills.

因为知道玛拉德太太的心脏有毛病，所以人们尽可能婉转地告知她丈夫的死讯。

是她姐姐约瑟芬吞吞吐吐、半遮半掩地暗示了她。

她丈夫的朋友理查德也在场，就在她旁边。当火车事故的消息传来时，他正在报馆里，而布兰特里·玛拉德的名字就列在“死亡”名单的第一个。紧接其后的电报，使他在最短的时间里确认了消息的真实性，他急忙赶来，力图赶在那些朋友之前。

她没有像别的女人那样，带着麻木的神情接受这个消息。她立刻就哭了起来，近似绝望地扑到她姐姐的怀里。当这暴风雨般的悲伤过后，她独自回到自己的房间里，不让任何人跟着她。

窗户是开着的，对面放着一把舒服宽大的扶手椅。她筋疲力尽地坐了下来，这种疲惫不仅折磨着她的身体，似乎也侵入了她的灵魂。

透过窗户，她看到屋前广场上的树梢在新春的气息中随风摇摆。空气中弥漫着芬芳的雨的气息。一个小贩在下面的街道上叫卖着他的货物。远处传来缥缈的歌声，还有无数的麻雀在房檐上叽叽喳喳地叫个不停。

对着窗口的西边的天空上，朵朵白云层层叠叠地堆积着，间或露出一绺绺蔚蓝的天空。

她把头靠在椅背上，非常平静。偶尔也会呜咽一两声，就像小孩子哭着睡着了，但在梦中还会继续呜咽一样。

她还很年轻，有着一张姣好平静的脸，脸上的表情显示着一种压抑，甚至是一种力量。但是现在，她的目光有些阴郁，呆呆地凝望着远处白云间的绺绺蓝天。这并不是匆匆的一瞥，而是一种长久的深思熟虑。

有种东西正向她靠近，而她正恐惧地等待着。那是什么？她不知道。那东西太微妙太难以捉摸了，她说不清楚。但是她能感觉得到，它正在空中蔓延，穿过弥漫于空气中的声音、气味和颜色慢慢地向她靠近。

现在，她的内心骚动不安。她开始认识到那种向她步步逼近并渐渐控制她的感觉是什么了。她挣扎着想靠自己的意志把它击退——可这意志却和她那白皙纤弱的双手一样软弱无力。

她放弃了反抗，从她微微张开的双唇间喃喃地溢出了一个词，她屏住呼吸一遍又一遍地重复着："自由，自由，自由！"曾经茫然的目光和恐惧的眼神已经逐渐退去。现在，她的目光透着机敏，炯炯有神。她的心跳加快，沸腾的热血温暖了身体的每一个部位，使她感觉到身心完全地放松了。

她没有停下来问自己，是不是有一种邪恶的快感在控制着她。一种清清楚楚的、兴奋的感觉让她根本无暇顾及此事。

她知道，当她看到丈夫那双温柔亲切的双手变得僵硬，那张从不会对她吝啬爱意的脸变得毫无表情、灰白如纸的时候，她肯定还会哭的。但在这痛苦之外，她看到了长远的未来，那些只属于她自己的岁月。而她张开双臂迎接那些岁月的到来。

在未来的岁月里，她不再为别人而活着，而只为她自己。那时，她不必再盲目地屈从于任何专横的意志。人们总是认为他们有权把个人的意志强加于他人。无论其动机是善良的还是残酷的，她突然感到这种做法绝不亚于犯罪。

当然，她是爱过他的——有时候是爱他的。但更多的时候她不爱他。那又有什么关系呢！有了独立的意志——她突然意识到这是她身上最强烈的一种冲动。在这种自信面前，爱情，那未解的谜团，算得了什么！“自由了！身心都自由了！”她不停地低声说。

约瑟芬跪在紧闭的门外，嘴唇对着钥匙孔，苦苦地哀求着让她进去。“露易丝，开开门！求求你啦，开开门——你这样会得病的。你干什么呢，露易丝？看在上帝的份儿上，开开门吧！”

“走开。我不会让自己生病的。”不会的，她正陶醉在窗外那不息的生命里。

她的想象像脱缰的野马一样狂奔着。她想象着未来的日子，春天，夏天，那些所有属于她自己的日子。她飞快地轻声向上帝祈祷着让生命长一点。而就在昨天，她还觉得生命太长了。

最后，她终于在姐姐的一再请求下，打开了门。她眼神里充满了胜利的激情，她丝毫没有意识到自己表现得就像一位胜利女神。她紧搂着姐姐的腰，一起走下楼去。理查德正站在楼下等着她们。

有人用钥匙打开大门。进来的是布兰特里·玛拉德，虽略显旅途劳顿，但泰然自若地提着他的大旅行包和伞。事发当时他离现场很远，根本就不知道发生了车祸。他惊愕地站在那里，听着约瑟芬的尖叫，看着理查德飞快地移动着，想挡住他，不让他妻子看见他。

但是理查德还是太晚了。

医生来了，他们说她死于心脏病——说她是死于极度高兴。

For man is man and master of his fate.

——Alfred Tennyson

人就是人，是自己命运的主人。

——阿尔弗雷德·丁尼生

作者介绍

凯特·肖邦(1851–1904)出生于美国圣路易斯。她在快四十岁的时候出版了第一本小说。主要作品有《一双丝袜》、《觉醒》等。在十九世纪末，肖邦试图直白地描写女性与男性、儿童的关系及她们本身性欲中的感受和情绪。这一点被认为是冒犯了当时上流社会的读者。那些挑战传统社会行为的作品，如《一小时的故事》，常常遭到杂志编辑的拒绝。然而半个多世纪后，女权主义评论家却大力提倡。

单词注解

intelligence [in'telidʒəns] *n.* 智能；智慧；理解力

delicious [di'liʃəs] *adj.* 美味的；香喷喷的

faintly ['feintli] *adv.* 微弱地；黯淡地；模糊地

absolutely ['æbsəlu:tli] *adv.* 绝对地，完全地

unwittingly [ˌʌn'witiŋli] *adv.* 无意地；不经意地；不知不觉地

名句大搜索

那东西太微妙太难以捉摸了，她说不清楚。

她屏住呼吸一遍又一遍地重复着："自由，自由，自由！"曾经茫然的目光和恐惧的眼神已经逐渐退去。

那时，她不必再盲目地屈从于任何专横的意志。人们总是认为他们有权把个人的意志强加于他人。

Sister Carrie
嘉莉妹妹

［美］西奥多·德莱塞（Theodore Dreiser）

嘉莉是个俊俏的农村姑娘，她羡慕大都市的物质生活，便来到了芝加哥谋生。严酷的现实破碎了她的美梦，迎接她的是失业和疾病。在走投无路时，她做了推销员德鲁埃的情妇，后来由于更大的欲望又做了酒店经理赫斯渥的情妇。与赫斯渥私奔后，在纽约由于偶然的机会她成了走红一时的演员，挤上了上流社会，实现了她的幻想。然而，所谓的“上流社会生活”又给她带来了什么呢？她感到空虚，找不到生活的真正意义，在寂寞和凄凉中，她坐在摇椅里梦想着那终不可得的幸福。

In the light of the world's attitude toward woman and her duties,the nature of Carrie's mental state deserves consideration. Actions such as hers are measured by an arbitrary scale. *Society possesses a conventional standard whereby it judges all things.* All men should be good, all women virtuous. Wherefore, villain, hast thou failed?

For all the liberal analysis of Spencer and our modern **naturalistic** philosophers, we have but an infantile perception of morals. There is more in the subject than mere conformity to a law of evolution. It is yet deeper than conformity to things of earth alone. It is more involved than we, as yet, perceive. Answer, first, why the heart thrills ; explain wherefore some plaintive note goes wandering about the world, undying ; make clear the rose's subtle alchemy evolving its ruddy lamp in light and rain. In the **essence** of these facts lie the first principles of morals.

"Oh," thought Drouet, "how delicious is my conquest."

"Ah," thought Carrie, with mournful misgivings, "what is it I have lost?"

Before this world—old proposition we stand, serious, interested, confused ; endeavouring to evolve the true theory of morals— the true answer to what is right.

In the view of a certain stratum of society, Carrie was comfortably established—in the eyes of the starveling, beaten by every wind and gusty sheet of rain, she was safe in a halcyon harbour.

Drouet had taken three rooms, furnished, in Ogden Place, facing Union Park, on the West Side. That was a little, green-carpeted breathing spot, than which, today, there is nothing more Beautiful in Chicago. It afforded a vista pleasant to **contemplate**.

The best room looked out upon the lawn of the park, now sear and brown, where a little lake lay sheltered. Over the bare limbs of the trees, which now swayed in the wintry wind, rose the steeple of the Union Park Congregational Church, and far off the towers of several others.

The rooms were comfortably enough furnished. There was a good Brussels carpet on the floor, rich in dull red and lemon shades, and representing large jardinieres filled with gorgeous, impossible flowers. There was a large pier-glass mirror between the two windows. A large, soft, green, plush-covered couch occupied one corner, and several rocking-chairs were set about. Some pictures, several rugs, a few small pieces of bric-a-brac, and the tale of contents is told.

In the bedroom, off the front room, was Carrie's trunk, bought by Drouet, and in the wardrobe built into the wall quite an array of clothing — more than she had ever possessed before, and of very becoming designs. There was a third room for possible use as a kitchen, where Drouet had Carrie establish a little **portable** gas stove for the preparation of small lunches, oysters, Welsh rarebits, and the like, of which he was exceedingly fond; and, lastly, a bath. The whole place was cosey, in that it was lighted by gas and heated by furnace registers, possessing also a small grate, set with an asbestos back, a method of cheerful warming which was then first coming into use. By her industry and natural love of order, which now developed, the place maintained an air pleasing in the extreme.

Here, then, was Carrie, established in a pleasant fashion, free of certain difficulties which most ominously confronted her, laden with many new ones which were of a mental order, and altogether so turned about in all of her earthly relationships that she might well have been a new and different individual. She looked into her glass and saw a prettier Carrie than she had seen before ; she looked into her mind, a mirror prepared of her own and the world's opinions, and saw a worse. Between these two images she wavered, hesitating which to believe.

"My, but you're a little beauty," Drouet was wont to exclaim to her. She would look at him with large, pleased eyes.

"You know it, don't you?" he would continue.

"Oh, I don't know," she would reply, feeling delight in the fact that one should think so, hesitating to believe, though she really did, that she was vain enough to think so much of herself.

Her conscience, however, was not a Drouet, interested to praise. There she heard a different voice, with which she argued, pleaded, excused. *It was no just and sapient counsellor, in its last analysis.* It was only an average little conscience, a thing which represented the world, her past environment, habit, convention, in a confused way. With it, the voice of the people was truly the voice of God.

"Oh, thou failure! " said the voice.

"Why?" she questioned.

"Look at those about," came the whispered answer. "Look at those who are good. How would they scorn to do what you have done. Look at the good girls ; how will they draw away from such as you when they know you have been weak. You had not tried before you failed."

It was when Carrie was alone, looking out across the park, that she would be listening to this. It would come infrequently—when something else did not **interfere**, when the pleasant side was not too apparent, when Drouet was not there. It was somewhat clear in utterance at first, but never wholly convincing. There was always an answer, always the December days threatened. She was alone ; she was desireful ; she was fearful of the whistling wind. The voice of want made answer for her.

Once the bright days of summer pass by, a city takes on that sombre garb of grey, wrapt in which it goes about its labours during the long winter. Its endless buildings look grey, its sky and its streets assume a sombre hue ; the scattered, leafless trees and wind-blown dust and paper but add to the general solemnity of colour. There seems to be something in the chill breezes which scurry through the long, narrow thoroughfares productive of rueful thoughts. Not poets alone, nor artists, nor that superior order of mind which arrogates to itself all refinement, feel this, but dogs and all men. These feel as much as the poet, though they have not the same power of expression. The sparrow upon the wire, the cat in the doorway, the dray horse tugging his weary load, feel the long, keen breaths of winter. It strikes to the heart of all life, animate and inanimate. If it were not for the artificial fires of merriment, the rush of profit-seeking trade, and pleasure-selling amusements ; if the various merchants failed to make the customary display within and without their establishments ; if our streets were not strung with signs of **gorgeous** hues and thronged with hurrying purchasers, we would quickly discover how firmly the chill hand of winter lays upon the heart ; how dispiriting are the days during which the sun withholds a portion of our allowance of light and warmth. We are more dependent upon these things than is often thought. We are insects produced by heat, and pass without it.

In the drag of such a grey day the secret voice would reassert itself，feebly and more feebly.

Such mental conflict was not always uppermost. Carrie was not by any means a gloomy soul. More,she had not the mind to get firm hold upon a definite truth. When she could not find her way out of the labyrinth of ill-logic which thought upon the subject created,she would turn away entirely.

按照世俗对女人及其职责的看法，嘉莉的心态确实值得推敲。像她这种行为，人们总要用一种专断的尺度来加以衡量。本来判断一切行为，社会上就有一套传统标准。男人应该刚正不阿，女人应该玉洁冰清。恶人啊，你为什么所谋不遂呢！

根据斯宾塞和我们当代自然主义哲学家们的分析研究，我们对道德的认识还很少；其内涵除了它仅仅符合进化规律以外，还有很多。反正它比仅仅符合尘世间的事物这一标准更深刻，而且比我们已知的还要复杂。首先，请回答，心为什么会颤抖？请解释，为什么某些哀伤的曲子在世上广为流传且经久不衰？谁又能说清，玫瑰花为什么在日光和雨露微妙的魔力之下灼然盛开，有如一盏红灯？道德的首要原则，寓于所有这些现象的实质之中。

“啊，”德鲁埃暗自欣喜地想道，“我初战告捷，该有多美。”

“啊，”嘉莉忧心忡忡地暗自思忖道，“我，从个人来说，失去了什么呢？”

面对这个像世界一样古老的难题，我们态度严肃，满怀兴趣，却又感到困惑不解；努力找出道德的真谛，寻求正确行为的真正答案。

照某些社会阶层的标准看，如今嘉莉的境遇是够舒适的了——在那些饱受风吹雨打、忍饥挨饿的人的眼里，嘉莉正安身在风平浪静的海港里。德鲁埃在西区协和公园对过的奥格登公寓给她租下了一套三间带家具的房子。那里绿草成茵，空气新鲜。如今在芝加哥再也找不到比这更优美的地方了。从窗户看出去，景色美不胜收，令人心旷神怡。最好的那个房间俯瞰着公园里的大草坪，这时草木早已枯黄，可小湖上却依然树影婆娑。树梢后面耸立着联合公园公理会教堂的尖顶，再远处，还有好几个教堂的塔楼耸立着。

房间布置得舒舒服服。地上铺着漂亮的布鲁塞尔地毯，暗红配淡黄的鲜艳底色上织着插满奇花异卉的大花瓶图案。两扇窗子之间有一个大穿衣镜。房间的一个角落里摆着一张大而柔软的长沙发，上面盖着绿厚绒布，还散放着几把摇椅。几张画，几块小地毯，还有几件小古玩，这些就是屋里的全部摆设了。

在前屋后面的卧室里，有嘉莉的一个大箱子，是德鲁埃给她买的。壁橱里挂着一大排漂亮衣服——嘉莉穿着不仅非常合身——而且数量之多是嘉莉一辈子都没有过的。第三个房间用作厨房，德鲁埃在那里装了一个可以移动的煤气灶，让嘉莉做一些简单的便餐和德鲁埃最爱吃的牡蛎、烤奶酪面包之类的食品。最后还有一个浴室。整个房子很舒适，因为室内使用煤气照明，还有调温取暖设备，那种设备还带有一个衬着石棉的炉栅。这是当时最新潮的、最舒适的取暖设备。由于嘉莉的勤劳和整洁，这套房间始终保持着一种格外宜人的气氛。

嘉莉就在这种惬意的地方安顿了下来，摆脱了那些一直在生活上威胁着她的困顿，可是同时又添了许多心理负担。她的人际关系发生了如此大的改变，真可以把她看成是一个与旧日告别的新人。她从镜子里看到一个比以前漂亮的嘉莉，但是从她脑子里的那面镜子里，她看到了一个比以前丑陋的嘉莉，那面镜子代表了她自己的看法和世俗的见解。她在这两个影像之间摇摆不定。不知道该相信哪一个。

“哎呀，你——好一个小美人儿！”德鲁埃常常喜欢这样大声嚷嚷。于是，她就睁大眼睛高兴地望着他。

“你知道你有多美，是不是？”他会继续说。

“哦，我不知道。”嘉莉这么回答，有人认为她美，她心里不禁感到欣喜，尽管她相信自己很美，她还是不敢肯定，生怕自己太虚荣，自视过高。

不过，凭良心说，她不像德鲁埃那样喜欢一味恭维。她的良心听到了另一种声音，她在这种声音面前争辩，并且还试图替自己开脱。归根到底，她的良心也不是公正贤明的顾问。这只是世俗庸人那种渺小的良心，其中混杂着世人的见解，还有嘉莉在过去的环境、习惯和世风流俗中曾亲身经历过的。有了它，人们的声音真的就无异于上帝的声音了。

“嘿，你堕落了。”那个声音低声对她说。

“为什么？”嘉莉问。

“看看你周围的那些人吧，”那个声音低声说，“看看那些正派人吧，他们不屑于做你所做的事。看看那些好姑娘，要是让她们知道你那么经不住诱惑，她们会躲开你。你还没有真正试图反抗，就认输了。”

嘉莉一个人在家，凭窗眺望公园的时候，她就会听到这个声音。每当百无聊赖的时候，生活中的安适和逸乐赫然在目的时候，或者德鲁埃不在她身边的时候，这个声音就会出现。这个声音起初很清晰，不过嘉莉从来没有完全信服过，因为她总是有话可说。12 月严冬的威胁啦，她很孤单啦，她渴望着太多的东西，她害怕呼啸的寒风。穷困的声音替她做了回答。

明媚的夏天一过去，城市就变得灰蒙蒙的，在这个漫长的冬天，一望无际的楼宇都显得灰不溜秋，天空和街道也都蒙上了一层灰暗的色调。光秃秃的树木以及在风中飞舞的灰尘和废纸，更增添了阴沉严峻的气氛。席卷大街小巷的阵阵寒风，仿佛带有悔恨的意思。并非只有诗人、艺术家、或者感情细腻的上流人物才能感受到这种愁思。连狗和普通人都受了感染。他们的感受并不亚于诗人，只是他们没有诗人那样的表达能力而已。站在电线上的麻雀，躲在门洞里的猫，还有负重跋涉的辕马，全都感受到了漫长严冬刺骨的寒风。世上万物，一切有生命的和没有生命的东西，都深切感受到这气息刺心入肺。要是没有那些欢乐的炉火，没有以营利为目的的商业活动，没有出售欢乐的游乐场所，要是没有那些在店堂内外照常展出的货物，没有街上那些花花绿绿的招牌，没有熙熙攘攘的顾客，我们会迅速感受到冰冷的冬之手沉重地压在我们心上。碰到阴雨天，太阳不肯赐予我们那一份应得的光和热，这种日子是多么让人沮丧。我们对光和热的依赖，远远超出了常人的想象。我们只是一群由光和热孕育的昆虫，离开了光和热，我们就不复存在了。

在这种灰蒙蒙的漫漫寒冬，这个神秘莫测的声音就会越来越弱，越来越无力了。

这种思想斗争并非时时浮上心头。嘉莉并不是一个郁郁寡欢的人，她也没有不达真理誓不罢休的决心。她在这个问题上左思右想，陷入了逻辑混乱的迷宫，实在找不到一条出路，于是就干脆不想了。

One thorn of experience is worth a whole wilderness of warning.

——James Russell Lowell

一次痛苦的经验抵得上千百次的告诫。

——英国诗人　洛威尔

实战提升
Practising & Exercise

作者介绍

西奥多•德莱塞（1871–1945），美国小说家了，出生于印第安纳州特雷霍特镇。他的第一部小说《嘉莉妹妹》，因被指控“有破坏性”而长期禁止发行，但一些散发出去的赠阅本却引起了许多作家的注意。德莱塞以他的代表作《美国的悲剧》、《珍妮姑娘》和《欲望三部曲》，奠定了在美国文学界的地位。1944 年，德莱塞被美国文学艺术学会授予荣誉奖。

单词注解

naturalistic [ˌnætʃərəˈlistik] *adj.* 博物学的；自然主义的

essence [ˈesns] *n.* 本质，实质；要素；

contemplate [ˈkɔntempleit] *vt.* 思忖，思量

portable [ˈpɔːtəbl] *adj.* 便于携带的，手提式的；轻便的

interfere [ˌintəˈfiə] *v.* 妨碍；冲突；抵触

gorgeous [ˈgɔːdʒəs] *adj.* 灿烂的，华丽的，豪华的

名句大搜索

本来判断一切行为，社会上就有一套传统标准。

归根到底，她的良心也不是公正贤明的顾问。

在这种灰蒙蒙的漫漫寒冬，这个神秘莫测的声音就越来越弱，越来越无力了。

Ulysses
尤利西斯

［爱尔兰］詹姆斯·乔伊斯（James Joyce）

小说以时间为顺序，描述了苦闷彷徨的都柏林小市民、广告推销员利奥波德·布卢姆于 1904 年 6 月 16 日一昼夜之内在都柏林的日常经历。乔伊斯将布卢姆在都柏林街头的一日游荡比作奥德修斯海外十年的漂泊，同时刻画了他不忠诚的妻子摩莉以及斯蒂芬寻找精神上的父亲的心理。

Stately, plump Buck Mullingan came from the stainhead, bearing a bowl of lather on which a mirror and a razor lay crossed. A yellow dressing gown, ungirdled, was sustained gently–behind him by the mild morning air. He held the bowl aloft and intoned:

Introibo ad altare Dei.

Halted, he peered down the dark winding stairs and called up coarsely:

"Come up, Kinch. Come up, you fearful jesuit."

Solemnly he came forward and mounted the round gunrest. He faced about and **blessed** gravely thrice the tower, the surrounding country and the awaking mountains. Then, catching sight of Stephen Dedalus, he bent towards him and made rapid crosses in the air, gurgling in his throat and shaking his head. Stephen Dedalus, displeased and sleepy, leaned his arms on the top of the staircase and looked coldly at the shaking gurgling face that blessed him, equine in its length, and at the light untonsured hair, grained and hued like pale oak.

Buck Mulligan peeped an instant under the mirror and then covered the bowl smartly.

"Back to barracks." he said sternly.

He added in a preacher's tone:

"For this, O dearly beloved, is the genuine Christine: body and soul and blood and ouns. Slow music, please. Shut your eyes, gents. One moment. A little trouble about those white corpuscles. Silence, all."

He peered sideways up and gave a long low whistle of call, then paused a while in rapt attention, his even white teeth glistening here and there with gold points. Chrysostomos. Two strong shrill whistles answered through the calm.

"Thanks, old chap," he cried briskly. "That will do nicely. Switch off the current, will you? "

He skipped off the gunrest and looked gravely at his watcher, gathering about his legs the loose folds of his gown. *The plump shadowed face and sullen oval jowl recalled a prelate, patron of arts in the middle ages.* A pleasant smile broke quietly over his lips.

"The mockery of it." he said gaily. "Your absurd name, an ancient Greek. "

He pointed his finger in friendly jest and went over to the parapet, laughing to himself. Stephen Dedalus stepped up, followed him **wearily** half way and sat down on the edge of the gunrest, watching him still as he propped his mirror on the parapet, dipped the brush in the bowl and lathered cheeks and neck.

Buck Mulligan's gay voice went on.

"My name is absurd too Malachi Mulligan, two dactyls. But it has a Hellenic ring, hasn't it? Tripping and sunny like the buck himself. We must go to Athens. Will you come if I can get the aunt to fork out twenty quid? "

He laid the brush aside and, laughing with delight, cried:

"Will he come? The jejune jesuit. "

Ceasing, he began to shave with care.

"Tell me, Mulligan." Stephen said quietly.

"Yes, my love? "

"How long is Haines going to stay in this tower? "

Buck Mulligan showed a shaven cheek over his right shoulder.

"God, isn't he dreadful? " he said **frankly**. "A ponderous Saxon. He thinks you're not a gentleman God, these bloody

English. Bursting with money and indigestion. Because he comes from Oxford You know, Dedalus ; you have the real Oxford manner. He can't make you out. O, my name for you is the best. Kinch, the knife-blade."

He shaved warily over his chin.

"He was raving all night about a black panther," Stephen said. "Where is his guncase? "

"A woful lunatic! " Mulligan said. "Were you in a funk? "

"I was", Stephen said with energy and growing fear. "Out here in the dark with a man I don't know raving and moaning to himself about shooting a black panther. You saved men from drowning. I'm not a hero, however. If he stays on here I am off."

Buck Mulligan frowned at the lather on his razorblade. He hopped down from his perch and began to search his trouser pockets **hastily**.

"Scutter," he cried thickly.

He came over to the gunrest and, thrusting a hand into Stephen's upper pocket, said:

" Lend us a loan of your noserag to wipe my razor. "

Stephen suffered him to pull out and hold up on show by its corner a dirty crumpled handkerchief. Buck Mulligan wiped the razorblade neatly. Then, gazing over the handkerchief, he said:

"The bard's noserag. A new art colour for our Irish poets: snotgreen. You can almost taste it, can't you? "

He mounted to the parapet again and gazed out over Dublin bay, his fair oak-pale hair stirring slightly.

"God," he said quietly. "Isn't the sea what Algy calls it: a grey sweet mother? The snotgreen sea. The scrotumtightening sea. Epi oinopa ponton. Ah, Dedalus, the Greeks. I must teach you. You must read them in the **original**. Thalatta! Thalatta! She is our great sweet mother. Come and look. "

Stephen stood up and went over to the parapet. Leaning on it he looked down on the water and on the mailboat clearing the harbour mouth of Kingstown.

"Our mighty mother." Buck Mulligan said.

He turned abruptly his great searching eyes from the sea to Stephen's face.

"The aunt thinks you killed your mother, he said. That's why she won't let me have anything to do with you. "

"Someone killed her," Stephen said **gloomily**.

"You could have knelt down, damn it, Kinch, when your dying mother asked you," Buck Mulligan said. "I'm hyperborean as much as you. But to think of your mother begging you with her last breath to kneel down and pray for her. And you refused. There is something sinister in you. "

He broke off and lathered again lightly his farther cheek. A tolerant smile curled his lips.

"But a lovely mummer," he murmured to himself. "Kinch, the loveliest mummer of them all. "

He shaved evenly and with care, in silence, seriously.

Stephen, an elbow rested on the jagged granite, leaned his palm against his brow and gazed at the fraying edge of his shiny black coat-sleeve. Pain, that was not yet the pain of love, **fretted** his heart. Silently, in a dream she had come to him after her death, her wasted body within its loose brown grave-clothes giving off an odour of wax and rosewood, her breath, that had bent upon him, mute, reproachful, a faint odour of wetted ashes. Across the threadbare cuffedge he saw the sea hailed as a great sweet mother by the well-fed voice beside him. *The ring of bay and skyline held a dull green mass of liquid*. A bowl of white china had stood beside her deathbed holding the green sluggish bile which she had torn up from her rotting liver by fits of loud groaning vomiting.

体态丰满而有风度的勃克•穆利根在楼梯口出现。他手里托着一钵肥皂沫，上面交叉放了一面镜子和一把剃胡刀。他没系腰带，淡黄色浴衣被习习晨风吹得稍微向后蓬着。他把那只钵高高举起，吟诵道：

我要走上主的祭台。

他停下脚步，朝那昏暗的螺旋状楼梯下边瞥了一眼，粗声粗气地喊道：

“上来，金赤。上来，你这敬畏天主的耶稣会士。”

他庄严地向前走去，登上圆形的炮座。他朝四下里望望，肃穆地对这座塔和周围的田野以及逐渐苏醒着的群山祝福了三遍。他一瞧见斯蒂芬•迪达勒斯就朝他弯下身去，在空中迅速地画了好几个十字，喉咙里还发出咯咯声，摇着头。斯蒂芬•迪达勒斯气恼而昏昏欲睡，双臂倚在楼梯栏杆上，冷冰冰地瞅着一边摇头一边发出咯咯声向他祝福的那张马脸，以及那顶并未剃光、色泽和纹理都像是浅色橡木的淡黄色头发。

勃克•穆利根朝镜下瞅了一眼，赶快合上钵。

“回到营房去。”他厉声说。

接着又用布道人的腔调说：

“啊，亲爱的人们，这是真正的克里斯廷：肉体和灵魂，血和伤痕。请把音乐放慢一点儿。闭上眼睛，先生们。等一下。这些白血球有点儿不消停。请大家肃静。”

他朝上方斜睨，悠长地低声吹了下呼唤的口哨，随后停下来，全神贯注地倾听着。他那口洁白齐整的牙齿有些地方闪射着金光。克里索斯托两声尖锐有力的口哨划破寂静回应了他。

“谢谢啦，老伙计，”他精神抖擞地大声说。“蛮好，请你关上电门，好吗？”

他从炮座上跳下来，神色庄重地望着那个观看他的人，并将浴衣那宽松的下摆拢在小腿上。他那郁郁寡欢的胖脸和阴沉的椭圆形下颚令人联想到中世纪作为艺术保护者的高僧。他的唇边徐徐地绽出了愉快的笑意。

“多可笑。”他快活地说。“你这姓名太荒唐了，一个古希腊人。”

他友善而打趣地指了一下，暗自笑着走到炮座那儿。斯蒂芬·迪达勒斯爬上塔顶，无精打采地跟着他走了几步，就在炮座边上坐了下来，静静地望着他怎样把镜子靠在炮座上，将刷子在钵里浸了浸，往面颊和脖颈上涂起皂沫。

勃克·穆利根用愉快的声调继续讲下去。

“我的姓名也荒唐，玛拉基·穆利根，两个扬抑抑格。可它带些古希腊味道，对不？轻盈快活得像只公鹿。咱们总得去趟雅典。要是姑妈肯给我们 20 镑，你要一道去吗？”

他把刷子撂在一边，开心地大声笑着说：

“他去吗，那位枯燥乏味的耶稣会士？”

他闭上嘴，仔细地刮起脸来。

“告诉我，穆利根。”斯蒂芬轻声说。

“嗯？乖乖。”

“海恩斯还要在这座塔里住多久？”

勃克·穆利根从右肩侧过他那半边刮好的脸。

“老天啊，那小子真是讨人嫌！”他坦率地说，“这种笨头笨脑的撒克逊人，他就没把你看作一位有身份的人。天哪，那帮混账的英国人。腰缠万贯，脑满肠肥。因为他是牛津出身呗。喏，迪达勒斯，你才真正有牛津派头呢。他捉摸不透你。哦，我给你起的名字再好不过啦：利刃金赤。”

他小心翼翼地刮着下巴。

“他整夜都在说着关于一只什么黑豹的梦话，”斯蒂芬说，“他的猎枪套在哪儿？”

“一个可悯可悲的疯子！”穆利根说。“你害怕了吧？”

“是啊，”斯蒂芬越来越感到恐怖，热切地说，“黑咕隆咚的在郊外，跟一个满口胡话、哼哼唧唧要射杀一只黑豹的陌生人呆在一块儿。你曾救过快要淹死的人。可我不是英雄。要是他继续呆在这儿，那我就走。”

勃克·穆利根朝着剃胡刀上的肥皂沫皱了皱眉，从坐着的地方跳了下来，慌忙地在裤兜里摸索。

“糟啦！”他瓮声瓮气地嚷道。

他来到炮座跟前，把手伸进斯蒂芬的胸兜，说：

“把你那块鼻涕布借咱使一下，擦擦剃胡刀。”

斯蒂芬听任他拽出那条皱巴巴的脏手绢，捏着一角，把它抖落开来。勃克·穆利根干净利索地擦完剃胡刀，望着手绢说：

“‘大诗人’的鼻涕布。属于咱们爱尔兰诗人的一种新的艺术色彩，鼻涕。简直可以尝得出它的滋味，对吗？”

他又跨上炮座，眺望着都柏林湾。他那浅橡木色的黄头发微微飘动着。

“喏！”他安详地说。“这海不就是阿尔杰所说的吗：一位伟大可爱的母亲！鼻涕的海，使人睾丸紧缩的海。到葡萄紫的大海上去。喂，迪达勒斯，那些希腊人啊。我得教给你。你非用原文来读不可。海！海！她是我们伟大可爱的母亲。过来瞧瞧。”

斯蒂芬站起来，走到炮座跟前。他倚着炮座，俯瞰水面和正在驶出国王镇港口的邮轮。

“我们强有力的母亲”。勃克·穆利根说。

他那双目光锐利的灰色眼睛猛地从海洋移到斯蒂芬的脸上。

“姑妈认为你母亲死在你手里，”他说，“所以她不让我跟你有任何往来”。

“是有人害的她。”斯蒂芬神色阴郁地说。

“该死，金赤，当你那位奄奄一息的母亲央求你跪下来的时候，你总应该照办呀，”勃克·穆利根说，“我跟你一样是个冷血动物。可你想想看，你那位快咽气的母亲恳求你跪下来为她祷告。而你拒绝了。你身上有股邪气……”

他忽然打住，又往另一边面颊上轻轻涂起肥皂沫来。一抹宽厚的笑容使他撇起了嘴唇。

“然而却是个可爱的哑剧演员，”他自言自语着。“金赤是所有的哑剧演员当中最可爱的一个。”

他仔细地刮着脸，默默地，专心致志地。

斯蒂芬一只肘支在坑洼不平的花岗石上，手心扶额头，凝视着自己发亮的黑上衣袖子那磨破了的袖口。痛苦——还说不上是爱的痛苦——煎熬着他的心。她去世之后，曾在梦中悄悄地来找过他，她那枯槁的身躯裹在宽松的褐色衣袋里，散发出蜡和黄檀的气味；当她带着微嗔一声不响地朝他俯下身来时，依稀能闻到一股淡淡的湿灰气味。隔着褴褛的袖口，他瞥见被身旁那个吃得很好的人称作伟大可爱的母亲的海洋。海湾与天际构成环形，盛着大量的暗绿色液体。母亲弥留之际，床头曾放着一只白瓷钵，里边盛着粘糊糊的绿色胆汁，那是伴着她一阵阵的高声呻吟，撕裂她那腐烂了的肝脏吐出来的。

All I am, or can be, I owe to my angel mother.

——Abraham Lincoln

我之所有，我之所能，都归功于我天使般的母亲。

——美国前总统　林肯

作者介绍

詹姆斯·乔伊斯（1882-1941），生于都柏林信奉天主教的家庭。他的作品有长篇小说《青年艺术家画像》、《尤利西斯》、《芬尼根守夜人》，还有诗集《室内乐集》和剧本《流亡者》等。詹姆斯·乔伊斯是二十世纪最伟大的作家之一，他的作品及“意识流”手法对全世界产生了巨大的影响。

单词注解

blessed ['blesid] *adj.* 神圣的；受祝福的

glisten [glisn] *v.* 闪耀，反光

wearily ['wirili] *adv.* 疲倦地，困乏地；消沉地

frankly ['fræŋkli] *adv.* 率直地；坦白地

hastily ['heistili] *adv.* 匆忙地，仓促地

original [ə'ridʒənəl] *adj.* 最初的，本来的；原始的

gloomily ['glu:mili] *adv.* 阴暗地；阴沉地

fretted ['fretid] *adj.* 焦躁的；腐蚀的

名句大搜索

他朝上方斜睨，悠长地低声吹了下呼唤的口哨，随后停下来，全神贯注地倾听着。他那口洁白齐整的牙齿有些地方闪射着金光。

他那郁郁寡欢的胖脸和阴沉的椭圆形下颚，令人联想到中世纪作为艺术保护者的高僧。

海湾与天际构成环形，盛着大量的暗绿色液体。

Life on the Mississippi

密西西比河上的生活

[美] 马克·吐温（Mark Twain）

《密西西比河上的生活》是美国作家马克·吐温的代表之作。在这篇小说中，作者描述了他在美国南北战争前在密西西比河上的轮船上面当水手和领航员的经历。这篇小说真实而生动地描写了密西西比河上的生活。

The Boys' Ambition

When I was a boy, there was but one **permanent** ambition among my comrades in our village on the west bank of the Mississippi River. That was, to be a steamboatman. *We had transient ambitions of other sorts, but they were only transient.*

When a circus came and went, it left us all burning to become clowns; the first Negro minstrel show that came to our section left us all suffering to try that kind of life; now and then we had a hope that if we lived and were good, God would permit us to be pirates. These ambitions faded out, each in its turn; but the ambition to be a steamboatman always remained.

Once a day a cheap, gaudy packet arrived upward from St. Louis, and another downward from Keokuk. Before these events, the day was glorious with **expectancy**; after them, the day was a dead and empty thing. Not only the boys, but the whole village, felt this. After all these years I can picture that old time to myself now, just as it was then: the white town drowsing in the sunshine of a summer's morning; the streets empty, or pretty nearly so; one or two clerks sitting in front of the Water Street stores, with their splintbottomed chairs tilted back against the wall, chins on breasts, hats slouched over their faces, asleep—with **shingle** shavings enough around to show what broke them down; a sow and a litter of pigs loafing along the sidewalk, doing a good business in watermelon rinds and seeds; two or three lonely little freight piles scattered about the levee; a pile of skids on the slope of the stonepaved wharf, and the fragrant town drunkard asleep in the shadow of them; two or three wood flats at the head of the wharf, but nobody to listen to the peaceful lapping of the wavelets against them; the great Mississippi, the majestic, the magnificent Mississippi, rolling its mile-wide tide along, shining in the sun ;the dense forest away on the other side ;the point above the town, and the point below, bounding the river-glimpse and turning it into a sort of sea. and withal a very still and brilliant and lonely one. Presently a film of dark smoke appears above one of those remote points ;instantly a Negro drayman, famous for his quick eye and prodigious voice,lifts up the cry "S-t-e-a-m-boat acomin!" and the scene changes! The town drunkard stirs, the clerks wake up, a **furious** clatter of drays follows , every house and store pours out a human contribution, and all in a twinkling the dead town is alive and moving. Drays, carts, men, boys, all go hurrying from many quarters to a common center, the wharf. Assembled there, the people fasten their eyes upon the coming boat as upon a wonder they are seeing for the first time. And the boat is rather a handsome sight, too. She is long and sharp and trim and pretty ;she has two tall, fancy-topped chimneys, with a gilded device of some kind swung between them ;a fanciful pilothouse, all glass and gingerbread, perched on top of the texas deck behind them ;the paddleboxes are gorgeous with a picture or with gilded rays above the boat's name ;the boiler deck, the hurricane deck, and the texas deck are fenced and ornamented with clean white railings ;there is a flag gallantly flying from the jackstaff ;the furnace doors are open and the fires glaring bravely ; the upper decks are black with passengers ;the captain stands by the big bell, calm, imposing, the envy of all ;great volumes of the blackest smoke are rolling and tumbling out of the chimneys — a husbanded grandeur created with a bit of pitch pine just before arriving at a town ; the crew are grouped on the forecastle ; the broad stage is run far out over the port bow, and an envied deckhand stands picturesquely on the end of it with a coil of rope in his hand ;the pent steam is screaming through the gauge cocks ;the captain lifts his hand, a bell rings, the wheels stop ; then they turn back, churning the water to foam, and the steamer is at rest. Then such a scramble there is to get aboard, and to get ashore, and to take in **freight** and to discharge freight, all at one and the same time ;and such a yelling and cursing as the mates facilitate it all with! Ten minutes later the steamer is under way again, with no flag on the jack staff and no black smoke issuing from the chimneys. After ten more minutes the town is dead again, and the town drunkard asleep by the skids once more.

My father was a justice of the peace, and I supposed he possessed the power of life and death over all men and could hang anybody that **offended** him. *This was distinction enough for me as a general thing ; but the desire to be a steam-boatman kept intruding, nevertheless.* I first wanted to be a cabin boy, so that I could come out with a white apron on and shake a tablecloth over the side, where all my old comrades could see me ;later I thought I would rather be the deckhand who stood on the end of the stage plank with the coil of rope in his hand, because he was particularly conspicuous. But these were only daydreams — they were too heavenly to be contemplated as real possibilities. By and by one of our boys went away. He was not heard of for a long time. At last he turned up as apprentice engineer or striker on a steamboat. This thing shook the bottom out of all my Sunday-school teachings. That boy had been notoriously worldly, and I just the reverse ;yet he was exalted to this eminence, and I left in obscurity and misery. There was nothing generous about this fellow in his greatness. He would always manage to have a rusty bolt to scrub while his boat tarried at our town, and he would sit on the inside guard and scrub it, where we could all see him and envy him and loathe him. And whenever his boat was laid up he would come home and swell around the town in his blackest and greasiest clothes, so that nobody could help remembering that he was a steamboatman; and he used all sorts of steamboat technicalities in his talk, as if he were so used to them that he forgot common people could not understand them. He would speak of the labboard side of a horse in an easy, natural way that would make one wish he was dead. And he was always talking about "St. Looey" like an old citizen; he would refer casually to occasions when he "was coming down Fourth Street", or when he was "passing by the Planter's House", or when there was a fire and he took a turn on the brakes of "the old Big Missouri"; and then he would go on and lie about how many towns the size of ours were burned down there that day. Two or three of the boys had long been persons of consideration among us because they had been to St. Louis once and had a vague general knowledge of its wonders, but the day of their glory was over now. They lapsed into a humble silence, and learned to disappear when the ruthless cub engineer approached. This fellow had money, too, and hair oil. Also an ignorant silver watch and a showy brass watch chain. He wore a leather belt and used no suspenders. If ever a youth was **cordially** admired and hated by his comrades, this one was. No girl could withstand his charms. He cut out every boy in the village. When his boat blew up at last, it diffused a tranquil contentment among us such as we had not known for months. But when he came home the next week, alive, renowned, and appeared in church all battered up and bandaged, a shining hero, stared at and wondered over by everybody, it seemed to us that the partiality of Providence for an undeserving reptile had reached a point where it was open to criticism.

This creature's career could produce but one result, and it speedily followed. Boy after boy managed to get on the river. The minister's son became an engineer. The doctor's and the postmaster's sons became mud clerks; the wholesale liquor dealer's son became a barkeeper on a boat; four sons of the chief merchant, and two sons of the county judge, became pilots. Pilot was the grandest position of all. The pilot, even in those days of trivial wages, had a princely salary — from a hundred and fifty to two hundred and fifty dollars a month, and no board pay. Two months of his wages would pay a preacher's salary for a year. Now some of us were left disconsolate. We could not get on the river — at least our parents would not let us.

So by and by I ran away. *I said I never would come home again till I was a pilot and could come in glory*. But somehow I could not manage it. I went meekly aboard a few of the boats that lay packed together like sardines at the long St. Louis wharf, and very humbly inquired for the pilots, but got only a cold shoulder and short words from mates and clerks. I had to make the best of this sort of treatment for the time being, but I had comforting daydreams of a future when I should be a great and honored pilot, with plenty of money, and could kill some of these mates and clerks and pay for them.

男孩们的志向

我的童年是在密西西比河西岸的村庄里度过的。我和伙伴们有一个永恒的志向，那就是，做一个蒸汽船员。我们也有其他短暂的志向，但那些都转瞬即逝了。

当一个马戏团来了又去的时候，我们都狂热地希望能成为小丑；而第一次来我们那个地区表演的黑人吟游诗人，又使我们都被想尝试那种生活的愿望煎熬着；我们时而还会想，如果我们活着并且表现不错，也许上帝会允许我们去当海盗。这些志向，一个个都消逝了，但是成为蒸汽船员的志向却总是能留下来。

一艘从圣路易斯向上游航行的廉价俗艳的轮船，每天都要来我们这里，还有另一艘从齐奥库克向下游去的。在这两件事以前，这一天因为期待而美好，而在那以后，这一天就变成死气沉沉、空虚无聊的日子了。不只是男孩们，而是整个村庄的人，都有这样的感觉。经过这些年以后，那段旧日时光，一切都历历在目：白色的城镇在夏日清晨的阳光中昏昏欲睡；街上空无一人，或是差不多那样；一两个职员坐在水街商店前面，他们坐着薄木板镶底的椅子向后斜靠在墙上，下巴垂在胸前，帽子耷拉在脸上，睡着觉——周围有足够多的墙板刨花说明他们为什么那么疲倦；一只母猪和一窝小猪顺着人行道溜溜达达，在西瓜皮和西瓜子中胡闹一番；几小堆孤零零的货物散布在大堤上；石头铺成的码头斜坡上有一堆垫木，镇上那些身上散发着酒气的醉鬼就睡在那木头堆的阴影中；两三艘木头平底船停在码头的顶端，没人去倾听那小小的浪头平和地轻拍它们的声音；那伟大的密西西比，那宏伟的、壮丽的密西西比，一路翻滚着几英里宽的大浪，在阳光下闪耀着光芒；对岸远处茂密的森林；城镇中上部映照于河流之中，使它像个海洋似的，而且是一个非常沉静、绚丽和孤寂的海洋。不久，一道黑色的烟幕就出现在远方的上空；马上就传来那个以敏锐视力和惊人声音而出名的黑人马车车夫的喊声："蒸——汽——船——来——啦——！"整幅景象变化了！镇里的醉鬼开始挪动身子，职员醒来了，紧跟着传来一阵运货马车的喧嚣，每所房子和每间店铺里都涌出一股人流，转瞬之间那死气沉沉的城镇活了过来，动了起来。运货车、马车、男人、孩子，都急急忙忙地从各个地方来到了一个共同的中心——码头。人们聚集在那里，眼光盯着慢慢驶来的船，仿佛看着一个他们第一次见到的奇迹。那船也确实相当壮观。它又长又尖，整齐漂亮；它有两个高高的、顶部精美的烟囱，它们之间摇晃着一条镀金的链子；一个不同寻常的驾驶室，全部由玻璃和鲜艳的装饰组成，位于烟囱后面的主甲板上；桨格上用图画或镀金线装饰得非常华丽；汽炉甲板、防风甲板和主甲板都用干净的白色栏杆围起来作为修饰；国旗杆上飞扬着一面漂亮的旗子；火炉门敞开着，里面的火焰熊熊闪耀；上层甲板上站着黑压压的乘客；船长站在大钟旁边，镇静威风，是所有人羡慕的焦点；浓烈的黑烟从烟囱中翻卷着冲了出来——那是到达城镇之前用一点儿多脂松木制造出来的庄严景象；船员们集中在前甲板上；一块宽阔的木板从左弦弓上方远远地伸出来，一个令人嫉妒的甲板水手像一幅图画般地站在木板顶端，手里拿着一卷绳子；高压蒸汽在计量塞中尖叫着；船长举起一只手，铃响了，轮子停下了；然后它们向后面转着，把河水搅成泡沫，接着蒸汽机停止工作了。然后就是人们全都在同一时间上船、下船、把货物装上船和运下船的一片混乱：还有水手们催促的喊叫和咒骂声！十分钟，蒸汽船又上路了，没有旗子在旗杆上飘扬，也没有黑烟从烟囱里冒出。再过十分钟以后，整个城镇又变得死气沉沉，那镇上的醉汉又在垫木旁睡着了。

我父亲是一位治安法官，我以为他拥有决定所有人生死的权利，可以绞死任何侵犯了他的人。一般来说，我觉得这是足够有地位的了，但是成为一个蒸汽船员的渴望却不断地侵入我的脑海。我起初希望成为一个船上的侍者，那样我就可以围着一条白色的围裙走出来，把一块桌布向一边抖开，让我的旧日伙伴都能看到我；后来我又觉得我宁愿当那个站在木板顶端、手里拿着那卷绳子的甲板水手，因为他特别引人注目。但是那都只是白日梦罢了——它们都太神圣了，不能当成真正有可能的事情来考虑。渐渐地，我们中间的一个男孩离开了，很长时间他都杳无音讯。最后他出现了，成为一艘蒸汽船上的实习轮机手或水手。这件事把我从周日学校学到的所有道理都颠覆了。那个男孩的世俗众人皆知，而我却恰恰相反；然而，他居然高升到了那么显赫的地位，而我却还在身份卑微、心灵悲惨的境地里。这个家伙虽然地位显赫，但他一点也不大方。当他的船在我们镇上靠岸时，他总会想办法搞到一个生锈的螺钉，然后他就会坐在护栏里擦螺钉，让我们都能看见他，羡慕他，憎恨他。而只要他的船进坞停留时，他就会回家来，穿着他最黑最油腻的衣服在镇子里四处炫耀，那样所有人就都不能不记得他是一个蒸汽船员了；他在说话的时候使用各种蒸汽船上的技术用语，仿佛他那么习惯使用那些术语，以至于忘了普通人根本不明白词的意思。他会用一种轻松自然的方式谈到一匹马的“左舷”，让人希望他马上去死。而且他总是像一个老居民那样谈到“圣路易”；他会随随便便地说到他“顺着第四街走”或是“经过种植主店”的情况，或是那次着火的时候，他在“老大密苏里”那儿停了车；然后他就会接着谎称说那天有多少个像我们镇这么大的镇都烧掉了。我们中有两三个男孩一直都是重要人物，就因为他们去过圣路易斯一次，对那儿的奇妙景象有一个模模糊糊的大概印象，但是现在他们神气的日子到头了。他们陷入了谦卑的沉默，学会了在那无情的年轻轮机手走近的时候迅速消失。这个家伙也有钱，还有发油。他还有一块银怀表和一条炫耀的铜表链。他系着一条皮带，根本不用吊裤带。如果曾经有哪个年轻人受到他的伙伴们十足的崇拜和憎恨，那就是这个家伙了。没有一个女孩能抵挡他的魅力。他让镇里的所有男孩都出了局。当他的船最后终于起锚出发的时候，一种我们仿佛几个月都不曾拥有过的宁静的满足感慢慢散播开来。但是他下星期又回来了，活着，还出了名，满身伤痕、绑着绷带出现在教堂里，他成了一个闪光的英雄、所有人凝视和惊叹的焦点。这时候在我们看来，命运对于一个根本不配的卑鄙的人的偏心，已经到了可以公开批评的程度了。

这家伙的经历只能引起一个后果，而实际上这后果很快就出现了。男孩们一个接一个地想办法到河上去了。牧师的儿子成了一个轮机手；医生和邮政局长的儿子成了船上的清洁工；批发酒的商人的儿子在一艘船上开了个酒吧；大商人的四个儿子和郡法官的两个儿子成了领航员。领航员是所有这些职业中最高级的。在那个工资微薄的时候，领航员也能得到一笔丰厚的薪水——每个月 150 到 250 美元，还不用付伙食费。他两个月的工资就相当于一个牧师一年的工资了。现在我们中的一些人都郁郁寡欢，因为我们不能到河上去——至少是我们的父母不允许我们去。

所以，我不久以后就逃走了。我说直到我成了一个领航员、能衣锦还乡的时候我才会回来。但是不知为什么我一直没能做到。我怯懦地上了几艘在圣路易斯长长的码头边像沙丁鱼一样紧挨在一起的船，非常谦恭地要求和领航员说话，然而我得到的却只是副手和职员们冷冰冰的几句话。我不得不暂时用最好的态度来接受这种待遇，但是在我那抚慰心灵的、关于未来的白日梦中，我却成了一个伟大的、受人尊敬的领航员，有很多钱，可以杀死这些副手和职员中的一些人，然后再用钱把事情摆平。

Life is just a series of trying to make up your mind.

——T. Fuller

生活是由一系列下决心的努力所构成的。

——富　勒

作者介绍

马克·吐温（1835–1910）本名塞缪尔·朗赫恩·克莱门斯，马克·吐温是其笔名。出生于密西西比河畔汉尼拔的一个乡村律师家庭，从小在外拜师学艺。当过排字工人，密西西比河水手，南军士兵，还经营过木材业、矿业和出版业，还当过记者，写过幽默文学。马克·吐温是美国批判现实主义文学的奠基人，世界著名的短篇小说大师。马克·吐温被誉为“美国文学界的林肯”。

单词注解

permanent ['pə:mənənt] *adj.* 永久的，永恒的；永远的

expectancy [ik'spektənsi] *n.* 期望；预期

shingle ['ʃiŋgl] *n.* 屋顶板，木瓦

furious ['fjuəriəs] *adj.* 狂怒的；狂暴的，猛烈

freight [freit] *n.*(船运的)货物；运费

offend [ə'fend] *v.* 冒犯；触怒；伤害……的感情

cordially ['kɔ:djəli] *adv.* 热诚地，诚挚地，友善地

名句大搜索

我们也有其他短暂的志向，但那些都转瞬即逝了。

一般来说，我觉得这是足够有地位的了，但是成为一个蒸汽船员的渴望却不断地侵入我的脑海。

我说直到我成了一个领航员、能衣锦还乡的时候我才会回来。

你们必须努力寻找自己的声音
You must strive to find your own voice

The Catcher in the Rye
麦田里的守望者

[美] 杰罗姆·大卫·塞林格（J.D.Salinger）

本书以主人公霍尔顿自叙的语气讲述自己被学校开除后在纽约城游荡将近两昼夜的经历和感受。霍尔顿是个个性复杂而又矛盾的青少年的典型。他有一颗纯洁善良、追求美好生活和崇高理想的童心。他对那些热衷于女人和酒的人十分反感，对校长的虚伪势利非常厌恶，看到墙上的下流字眼便愤愤擦去，遇到修女为受难者募捐就慷慨解囊。他对妹妹菲碧真诚爱护，百般照顾。可是，愤世嫉俗思想引起的消极反抗，他抽烟、酗酒、打架、调情，甚至找妓女玩。他认为成人社会里没有一个人可信，全是“假仁假义的伪君子”。他看不惯现实社会中的那种世态人情，他渴望的是朴实和真诚，但遇到的全是虚伪和欺骗，而他又无力改变这种现状，只好苦闷、彷徨、放纵，最后甚至想逃离这个现实世界。

Old Phoebe said something then, but I couldn't hear her. She had the side of her mouth right smack on the pillow, and I couldn't hear her.

"What?" I said. "Take your mouth away. I can't hear you with your mouth that way."

"You don't like anything that's happening."

It made me even more depressed when she said that.

"Yes I do. Yes I do. Sure I do. Don't say that. Why the hell do you say that?"

"Because you don't. You don't like any schools. You don't like a million things. You don't."

"I do! That's where you're wrong—that's exactly where you're wrong! Why the hell do you have to say that?" I said. Boy, was she depressing me.

"Because you don't," she said. "Name one thing."

"One thing? One thing I like?" I said. "Okay."

The trouble was, I couldn't **concentrate** too hot. Sometimes it's hard to concentrate.

"One thing I like a lot you mean?" I asked her.

She didn't answer me, though. She was in a cock-eyed position way the hell over the other side of the bed. She was about a thousand miles away. "C'mon, answer me," I said. "One thing I like a lot, or one thing I just like?"

"You like a lot."

...

"Anyway, I like it now," I said. "I mean right now. Sitting here with you and just chewing the fat and horsing —"

"That isn't anything really!"

"It is so something really! Certainly it is! Why the hell isn't it? People never think anything is anything really. I'm getting goddam sick of it."

"Stop swearing. All right, name something else. Name something you'd like to be. Like a scientist. Or a lawyer or something."

"I couldn't be a scientist. I'm no good in science."

"Well, a lawyer — like Daddy and all."

"Lawyers are all right, I guess — but it doesn't appel to me," I said. "I mean they're all right if they go around saving innocent guy's lives all the time, and like that, but you don't do that kind of stuff if you're a lawyer. All you do is make a lot of dough and play golf and play bridge and buy cars and drink Martinis and look like a hot-shot. And besides. Even if you did go around saving guys' lives and all, how would you know if you did it because you really wanted to save guys' lives, or because you did it because what you really wanted to do was be a **terrific** lawyer, with everybody slapping you on the back and congratulating you in court when the goddam trial was over, the reporters and everybody, the way it is in the dirty movies? How would you know you weren't being a phony? The trouble is, you wouldn't."

I'm not too sure old Phoebe knew what the hell I was talking about. I mean she's only a little child and all. But she was listening, at least. If somebody at least listens, it's not too bad.

"Daddy's going to kill you. He's going to kill you," she said.

I wasn't listening, though. I was thinking about something else — something crazy. "You know what Id like to be?" I said. "You know what I'd like to be? I mean if I had my goddam choice?"

"What? Stop swearing."

"You know that song 'If a body catch a body comin'

through the rye'? I'd like —"

"It's 'If a body meet a body coming through the rye'!" old Phoebe said. "It's a poem. By Robert Burns."

"I know it's a poem by Robert Burns."

She was right, though. It is "If a body meet a body coming through the rye." I didn't know it then, though.

"I thought it was 'If a body catch a body'," I said. "Anyway, I keep picturing all these little kids playing some game in this big field of rye and all. Thousands of little kids, and nobody's around — nobody big, I mean, except me. And I'm standing on the edge of some crazy cliff. What I have to do, I have to catch everybody if they start to go over the cliff — I mean if they're running and they don't look where they're going I have to come out from somewhere and catch them. That's all I'd do all day. *I'd just be the catcher in the rye and all. I know it's crazy, but that's the only thing I'd really like to be. I know it's crazy."*

Old Phoebe didn't say anything for a long time. Then, when she said something, all she said was, "Daddy's going to kill you."

老菲碧这时说了句什么话，我没听清。她把一个嘴角整个儿压在枕头上，所以我听不清她说的话。

"什么？"我说，"把你的头拿开。你这样把嘴压着，我根本听不清你在说什么。"

"你不喜欢正在发生的事情，所有的。"

她这么一说，我心里不由得更烦了。

“我喜欢，我喜欢，我当然喜欢。别说这种话。你干吗要说这种见鬼的话呢？”

“因为你不喜欢。你讨厌上学。你讨厌好多东西。你不喜欢。”

“我喜欢！你错就错在这里——你完完全全错在这里！你为什么非要说这种见鬼的话呢？”我说。天哪，她真让我烦透了。

“因为你不喜欢，”她说。“说一样东西让我听听。”

“说一样东西？一样我喜欢的东西？”我说，“好吧。”

问题是，我没法集中思想。思想有时候是很难集中的。

“你是说，一样我非常喜欢的东西？”我问她。

她没作声。她躺在床的另一边，斜着眼看我。感觉好像离得很远。“喂，回答我，”我说。“是一样我非常喜欢的东西呢，还是我喜欢的东西就行？”

“你非常喜欢的。”

……

“不管怎样，我喜欢现在这样，”我说。“我是说就像现在这样，跟你一起坐着，聊聊天，逗逗乐……”

“这可不是什么真正的东西！”

“这是真正的东西！当然是的！他妈的为什么不是？人们就是不把真正的东西当东西看待。我他妈的都腻烦透这个了。”

“别骂啦。好吧，说些别的吧，说说你的理想吧。你是想当个科学家呢，还是想当个律师什么的。”

“我当不了科学家，我不懂科学。”

“那，当个律师，像爸爸一样。”

“律师倒是不错，我想——可是不适合我，”我说。“我是说他们要是老出去搭救受冤枉的人的性命，那倒是不错，可你一旦当了律师，就不干那样的事了。你只知道挣大钱，打高尔夫球，打桥牌，买汽车，喝马提尼酒，摆臭架子。再说，即便你真的出去救人了，你怎么知道这样做到底是因为你真的想要救人性命呢，还是因为你真正的动机是想当一个大律师，等审判一结束，那些记者什么的就会向你涌来，向你道贺，就像那些下流电影里演的那样？你怎么知道自己不是个伪君子？问题是，你根本就不知道。"

我不知道我说的那些话老菲碧到底听懂了多少，我是说她毕竟还是个小孩子。不过她至少在好好听着。只要对方在听，那就不错了。

"爸爸会要了你的命。他会要了你的命，"她说。

可我没在听，我在想一些别的事——一些异想天开的事。"你知道我将来想做什么吗？"我说。"你知道我将来想做什么吗？我是说将来要是能他妈的让我自由选择的话。"

"什么？别骂啦。"

"你知道《你要是在麦田里捉到了我》这首歌吗？我将来想——"

"是《你要是在麦田里遇到了我》！"老菲碧说。"这是一首诗，罗伯特·彭斯写的。"

"我知道那是罗伯特·彭斯写的诗！"

她说得对。那的确是《你要是在麦田里遇到了我》。可我当时并不知道。

"我还以为是《你要是在麦田里捉到了我》呢，"我说。"不管怎样，我老是在幻想着有那么一群小孩子在一大块麦田里做游戏，很多个小孩子，附近没有一个人，我是说，除了我以外，没有一个大人。我呢，就站在悬崖边。我做的就是在那儿守望，要是有哪个孩子往悬崖边奔来，我就把他拉住——我是说孩子们都在狂奔，也不知道自己是在往哪儿跑，我得从什么地方出来，把他们拉住。我整天就干这样的事。我只想当个麦田里的守望者。我知道这有点异想天开，可我真正喜欢干的就是这个。我知道这不像话。”

老菲碧有好一会儿没吭声。后来她开口了，可她只说了句：“爸爸会要了你的命。”

Nothing is more terrible than ignorance in action.

——Desiderius Eramus

最可怕的事莫过于行动中的无知。

——荷兰人文主义者　伊拉莫斯

作者介绍

杰罗姆·大卫·塞林格（1919– ），美国作家，他的《麦田里的守望者》被认为是二十世纪美国文学的经典作品之一。塞林格在 1942 年从军，1944 年他前往欧洲战场从事反间谍工作。1946 年塞林格退伍，回到纽约开始专心创作。他的第一本长篇小说《麦田里的守望者》一经出版就大获成功。他的作品还有《弗兰尼与卓埃》、《木匠们，把屋梁升高》和《西摩：一个介绍》和收录了他的短篇故事的《九故事》。

单词注解

concentrate ['kɔnsentreit] *v.* 集中；聚集，集结

innocent ['inəsnt] *adj.* 无罪的，清白的

terrific [tə'rifik] *adj.* 可怕的，吓人的

catcher ['kætʃə] *n.* 捕手

名句大搜索

你不喜欢正在发生的事情，所有的。

我当不了科学家，我不懂科学。

我只想当个麦田里的守望者。我知道这有点异想天开，可我真正喜欢干的就是这个。

On the Road

在路上

[美] 杰克·凯鲁亚克（Jack Kerouac）

《在路上》的主人公萨尔为了追求刺激，与几个年轻男女沿途搭便车或自己开车，几次横越美国大陆，最终到达墨西哥。一路上他们狂喝烂饮，吸大麻，玩女人，高谈东方禅宗，走累了就挡道拦车，夜宿村落，从纽约游荡到旧金山，最后作鸟兽散。

That night I found Carlo and to my amazement he told me he'd been in Central City with Dean.

"What did you do?"

"Oh, we ran around the bars and then Dean stole a car and we drove back down the mountain curves ninety miles an hour."

"I didn't see you."

"We didn't know you were there."

"Well, man, I'm going to San Francisco."

"Dean has Rita lined up for you tonight."

"Well, then, I'll put it off." I had no money. *I sent my aunt an airmail letter asking her for fifty dollars and said it would be the last money I'd ask*; after that she would be getting money back from me, as soon as I got that ship.

Then I went to meet Rita Bettencourt and took her back to the apartment. I got her in my bedroom after a long talk in the dark of the front room. She was a nice little girl, simple and true, and **tremendously** frightened of sex. I told her it was beautiful. I wanted to prove this to her. She let me prove it, but I was too **impatient** and proved nothing. She sighed in the dark. "What do you want out of life?" I asked, and I used to ask that all the time of girls.

"I don't know," she said. "Just wait on tables and try to get along." She yawned. I put my hand over her mouth and told her not to yawn. I tried to tell her how excited I was about life and the things we could do together; saying that, and planning to leave Denver in two days. She turned away wearily. *We lay on our backs, looking at the ceiling and wondering what God had wrought when He made life so sad.* We made **vague** plans to meet in Frisco.

My moments in Denver were coming to an end, I could feel it when I walked her home, on the way back I stretched out on the grass of an old church with a bunch of hobos, and their talk made me want to get back on that road. Every now and then one would get up and hit a passer-by for a dime. They talked of harvests moving north. It was warm and soft. I wanted to go and get Rita again and tell her a lot more things, and really make love to her this time, and calm her fears about men. Boys and girls in America have such a sad time together ; sophistication demands that they submit to sex immediately without proper **preliminary** talk. Not courting talk — real straight talk about souls, *for life is holy and every moment is precious.* I heard the Denver and Rio Grande locomotive howling off to the mountains. I wanted to pursue my star further.

那天晚上我见到了卡罗，使我吃惊的是他告诉我，他和狄恩去了中央城。

“你们去那儿干什么？”

“噢，我们到那儿的酒吧里转了转，后来狄恩偷了一辆汽车，我们以每小时 90 英里的速度从山上歪歪扭扭把它开了下来。”

“我没见到你们。”

“我们不知道你也在。”

“噢，老兄，我要去旧金山了。”

“狄恩让莉塔今晚等你。”

"好的，那么我就推迟几天走。"我一分钱也没有了。我已发了一封航空信给姨妈，跟她要50美元，并且告诉她这是我最后一次向她要钱。以后等我在船上找到工作了，就把钱都还给她。

然后我去找莉塔·贝特科特，带她到我的公寓。我们在前面漆黑的房间里聊了很长时间，然后进了卧室。她是一个好姑娘，纯真、朴实，对性生活极其恐惧。我告诉她这是件很美的事。我想向她证明这一点，她也允许我向她证明，但我太不耐烦了，以致什么也没做。她在黑暗中叹了口气。"你想从生活中得到什么呢？"我问她，我总是对女孩子提这样的问题。

"我不知道，"她说，"我只想在饭店好好干，别出乱子就行。"她哀叹着。我用手捂住了她的嘴，告诉她不要叹息。我想告诉她我的生活是多么激动人心，告诉她我们可以在一起做许多事。我对她说两天后我就要离开丹佛了。她伤心地转过身去。我们躺在一起，凝望着天花板。为什么上帝要让人类如此痛苦，对此，我们都感到迷惑不解。我们初步计划在旧金山再见。

当我送她回家的时候，我感到自己在丹佛的生活快要结束了。回来的路上，我伸开四肢躺在教堂前的草坪上，这儿还躺着许多流浪汉，他们的谈话令我更想上路了。他们随时都可能爬起来向过路的人要上几个子儿，他们谈论着自己的收获。空气是温柔而又舒适的。我真想返回去找莉塔，给她讲更多的东西，这次要真的与她做爱，安慰她，让她不再害怕任何男人。美国的男孩和女孩总是这样伤心地呆在一起，老于世故使他们立即屈服于性欲，在这之前没有任何温柔和爱抚，甚至没有任何交谈——那种心灵与心灵的交流。然而生活是神圣的，生命的每一刻都是珍贵的。我听到丹佛和里奥格兰河正咆哮着离我而去，我要去追求我远方的星星了。

作者介绍

杰克·凯鲁亚克（1922—1969）美国小说家。出生于马萨诸塞州洛厄尔城的一个信奉天主教的工人家庭。凯鲁亚克是美国五十年代中期崛起的“垮掉的一代”的重要代表人物之一，他一生共创作了18部小说，大多带有自传性质。他的作品有《乡村与城市》、《地下室居民》、《达摩流浪者》、《萨克斯医生》和《麦琪·卡西迪》，凯鲁亚克的作品对社会现实有独到的认识。

单词注解

tremendously [tri'mendəsli] *adv.* 极大地；极其；非常

impatient [im'peiʃ ənt] *adj.* 不耐烦的；无法忍受的

vague [veig] *adj.*（形状等）模糊不清的，朦胧的

preliminary [pri'liminəri] *adj.* 预备的；初步的；开端的

名句大搜索

我已发了一封航空信给姨妈，向她要50美元，并且告诉她这是我最后一次向她要钱。

我们都感到迷惑不解，为什么上帝要让人类如此痛苦。

然而生活是神圣的，生命的每一刻都是珍贵的。

The House on Mango Street

芒果街上的小屋

[美] 桑德拉·希斯内罗丝（S. Cisneros）

《芒果街上的小屋》由几十个短篇组成，一个短篇讲述了一个人、一件事、一个梦想、几朵云，几棵树、几种感觉，语言清澈如流水，点缀着零落的韵脚和新奇的譬喻。所有的讲述都归于一个叙述中心：居住在芝加哥拉美移民社区芒果街上的女孩埃斯佩朗莎（埃斯佩朗莎，是西班牙语里的希望）。生就对弱的同情心和对美的感觉力，她用清澈的双眼打量周围的世界，用美丽稚嫩的语言讲述成长，讲述沧桑，讲述生命的美好与不易。

Hairs

Everybody in our family has different hair. *My Papa' s hair is like a broom, all up in the air.* And me, my hair is lazy. It never **obeys** barrettes or bands. Carlos'hair is thick and straight. He doesn't need to comb it. Nenny's hair is slippery—slides out of your hand. And Kiki, who is the youngest, has hair like fur.

But my mother's hair, my mother's hair, like little rosettes, like little candy circles all curly and **pretty** because she pinned it in pincurls all day, sweet to put your nose into when she is holding you, holding you and you feel safe, is the warm smell of bread before you bake it, is the smell when she makes room for you on her side of the bed still warm with her skin, and you sleep near her, the rain outside falling and Papa snoring. The snoring, the rain, and Mama's hair that smells like bread.

Darius & the Clouds

You can never have too much sky. You can fall asleep and wake up drunk on sky, and sky can keep you safe when you are sad. Here there is too much **sadness** and not enough sky. Butterflies too are few and so are flowers and most things that are beautiful. Still, we take what we can get and make the best of it.

Darius, who doesn't like school, who is sometimes stupid and mostly a fool, said something wise today, though most days he says nothing. Darius, who chases girls with firecrackers or a stick that touched a rat and thinks he's tough, today pointed up because the world was full of clouds, the kind like pillows.

You all see that cloud, that fat one there? Darius said, See that? Where? That one next to the one that look like popcorn. That one there. See that. That's God, Darius said. God? somebody little asked. God, he said, and made it simple.

Four Skinny Trees

They are the only ones who understand me. I am the only one who understands them. Four **skinny** trees with skinny necks and pointy elbows like mine. Four who do not belong here but are here. Four raggedy excuses planted by the city. From our room we can hear them, but Nenny just sleeps and doesn't appreciate these things.

Their strength is secret. They send ferocious roots beneath the ground. They grow up and they grow down and grab the earth between their hairy toes and bite the sky with violent teeth and never quit their anger. This is how they keep. Let one forget his reason for being, they'd all droop like tulips in a glass, each with their arms around the other. Keep, keep, keep, trees say when I sleep. They teach.

When I am too sad and too skinny to keep keeping, when I am a tiny thing against so many bricks, then it is I look at trees. When there is nothing left to look at on this street. Four who grew despite **concrete**. Four who reach and do not forget to reach. Four whose only reason is to be and be.

头发

我们家里每个人的头发都不一样。爸爸的头发像扫把，根根直立往上插。而我，我的头发挺懒惰。它从来不听发夹和发带的话。卡洛斯的头发又直又厚。他不用梳头。蕾妮的头发滑滑的——会从你手里溜走。还有奇奇，他最小，茸茸的头发像毛皮。

只有妈妈的头发，妈妈的头发，好像一朵朵小小的玫瑰花结，一枚枚小小的糖果圈儿，全都那么卷曲，那么漂亮，因为她成天给它们上发卷。当她搂你时，把鼻子伸进去闻一闻吧，这时，你觉得是那么的安全，闻到的气味又那么香甜。是那种待烤的面包暖暖的香味，是那种她给你让出一角被窝时，和着体温散发的芬芳。你睡在她身旁，外面下着雨，爸爸打着鼾。哦，鼾声、雨声，还有妈妈那闻起来像面包的头发。

大流士和云

你永远不能拥有太多的天空。你可以在天空下睡去，醒来又沉醉。在你忧伤的时候，天空会给你安慰。可是忧伤太多，天空不够，蝴蝶也不够，花儿也不够，大多数美的东西都不够。于是，我们取我们所能取，好好地享用。

大流士，不喜欢上学的他，有时很傻，几乎是个笨人，今天却说了一句聪明的话，虽然大多数日子他什么都不说。大流士，喜欢用爆竹，用碰过老鼠的小棍子去追逐女孩，自以为很了不起的他，今天却指着天空，因为那里有满天的云朵，样子像枕头的云朵。

你们都看到那朵云了吗，那朵胖乎乎的云？大流士说，看到了吗？哪里？那朵看起来像爆米花的旁边的那朵。那边那朵。看，那是上帝。大流士说。上帝？有个小点的问道。上帝。他说。简洁地说。

四棵细瘦的树

它们是唯一能够懂我的。我是唯一懂得它们的人。四棵跟我一样有着细手肘的树。不属于这里但到了这里的四棵树。市政栽下这四棵残次树，只是用来充数的。从我的房间里我们可以听到它们的声音，可蕾妮只是睡觉，不能领略这些。

它们的力量是个秘密，它们在地底下猛烈地生根，它们往下往上长，用头发一样的脚趾紧攥泥土，用牙齿粗暴地嘶哑天空，怒气从不懈怠。这就是它们坚持的方式。假如有一棵忘记了它存在的理由，它们就全都会像玻璃瓶里的郁金香一样耷拉下来，手挽着手。坚持，坚持，坚持。树儿在我睡着的时候说，它们教会我。

当我太悲伤、太瘦弱，无法坚持再坚持的时候，当我如此渺小却要对抗这么多砖块的时候，当街上没有别的东西可看的时候，我就会看着树儿。这四棵不畏混凝土而生长的树，从不忘记伸展的四棵树。唯一的理由是存在的四棵树。

What makes life dreary is the want of motive.

——George Eliot

没有目的，人生就黯淡无光。

——艾略特

作者介绍

桑德拉·希斯内罗丝，1954 年生，当代美国著名女诗人，30 岁时凭借《芒果街上的小屋》一书成名。另著有短篇故事集《喊女溪及其他》和诗集若干。

单词注解

obey [ə'bei] *v.* 服从；听从

pretty ['priti] *adj.* 漂亮的；秀丽的；可爱的

sadness ['sædnis] *n.* 悲哀，悲伤

skinny ['skini] *adj.* 皮的；似皮的；薄膜状的

concrete ['kɔnkri:t] *adj.* 有形的，实在的；

名句大搜索

爸爸的头发像扫把，根根直立往上插。

你永远不能拥有太多的天空。你可以在天空下睡去，醒来又沉醉。

它们的力量是个秘密，它们在地底下猛烈地生根，它们往下往上长，用头发一样的脚趾紧攥泥土，用牙齿粗暴地嘶哑天空，怒气从不懈怠。

Araby
阿拉比

[爱尔兰] 詹姆斯·乔伊斯(James Joyce)

《阿拉比》是詹姆斯·乔伊斯小说集《都柏林人》中一篇反映少年心理变化的短篇小说。小说讲述了一个都柏林少年对同伴的姐姐产生了朦胧的爱情，在经过漫长而又焦急的等待之后，最终爱情幻想以破灭而告终。

Every morning I lay on the floor in the front parlor watching her door. The blind was pulled down to within an inch of the sash so that I could not be seen. When she came out on the doorstep my heart leaped. I ran to the hall, seized my books and followed her. I kept her brown **figure** always in my eye and, when we came near the point at which our ways diverged, I quickened my pace and passed her. This happened morning after morning. I had never spoken to her, except for a few casual words, and yet her name was like a summons to all my foolish blood.

Her image accompanied me even in places the most hostile to romance. On Saturday evenings when my aunt went marketing I had to go to carry some of the parcels. We walked through the flaring streets, jostled by drunken men and bargaining women, amid the curses of laborers, the shrill litanies of shop boys who stood on guard by the barrels of pigs'cheeks, the nasal chanting of street singers, who sang a come-all-you about O' Donovan Rossa, or a ballad about the troubles in our native land. These noises **converged** in a single sensation of life for me:I imagined that I bore my chalice safely through a throng of foes. Her name sprang to my lips at moments in strange prayers and praises which I myself did not understand. My eyes were often full of tears (I could not tell why) and at times a flood from my heart seemed to pour itself out into my bosom. I thought little of the future. I did not know whether I would ever speak to her or not or, if I spoke to her, how I could tell her of my confused adoration. But my body was like a harp and her words and gestures were like fingers running upon the wires.

One evening I went into the back drawing room in which the priest had died. It was a dark rainy evening and there was no sound in the house. Through one of the broken panes I heard the rain impinge upon the earth, the fine **incessant** needles of water playing in the sodden beds. Some distant lamp or lighted window gleamed below me. I was thankful that I could see so little. All my senses seemed to desire to veil themselves and, feeling that I was about to slip from them, I pressed the palms of my hands together until they **trembled**, murmuring: "O love! O love !" many times.

At last she spoke to me. When she addressed the first words to me I was so confused that I did not know what to answer. She asked me was I going to Araby. I forgot whether I answered yes or no. It would be a splendid bazaar, she said ; *she would love to go.*

"And why can't you?" I asked.

While she spoke she turned a silver bracelet round and round her wrist. She could not go, she said, because there would be a retreat that week in her **convent**. Her brother and two other boys were fighting for their caps and I was alone at the railings. She held one of the spikes, bowing her head towards me. The light from the lamp opposite our door caught the white curve of her neck, lit up her hair that rested there and, falling, lit up the hand upon the railing. It fell over one side of her dress and caught the white border of a petticoat, just visible as she stood at ease.

"It's well for you," she said.

"If I go," I said, "I will bring you something."

What innumerable follies laid waste my waking and sleeping thoughts after that evening! I wished to annihilate the tedious intervening days. I chafed against the work of school. At night in my bedroom and by day in the classroom her image came between me and the page I strove to read. The syllables of the word Araby were called to me through the silence in which my soul luxuriated and cast an Eastern **enchantment** over me. I asked for leave to go to the bazaar on Saturday night. My aunt was surprised and hoped it was not some Freemason affair. I answered few questions in class. I watched my master's face pass from amiability to sternness; he hoped I was not beginning to idle. I could not call my wandering thoughts together. I had hardly any patience with the serious work of life which, now that it stood between me and my desire, seemed to me child's play, ugly monotonous child's play.

On Saturday morning I reminded my uncle that I wished to go to the bazaar in the evening. He was fussing at the hall stand, looking for the hat brush, and answered me curtly: "Yes, boy, I know."

As he was in the hall I could not go into the front parlor and lie at the window. I left the house in bad humor and walked slowly towards the school. The air was pitilessly raw and already my heart misgave me.

When I came home to dinner my uncle had not yet been home. Still it was early. I sat staring at the clock for some time and, when its ticking began to irritate me, I left the room. I mounted the staircase and gained the upper part of the house. The high cold empty gloomy rooms liberated me and I went from room to room singing. From the front window I saw my companions playing below in the street. Their cries reached me weakened and indistinct and, leaning my forehead against the cool glass, I looked over at the dark house where she lived. I may have stood there for an hour, seeing nothing but the brown-clad figure cast by my imagination, touched discreetly by the lamplight at the curved neck, at the hand upon the railings and at the border below the dress.

When I came downstairs again I found Mrs. Mercer sitting at the fire. She was an old garrulous woman, a pawnbroker's widow, who collected used stamps for some pious purpose. I had to **endure** the gossip of the tea table. The meal was prolonged beyond an hour and still my uncle did not come. Mrs. Mercer stood up to go:she was sorry she couldn't wait any longer, but it was after eight o'clock and she did not like to be out late, as the night air was bad for her. When she had gone I began to walk up and down the room, clenching my fists. My aunt said:

"I'm afraid you may put off your bazaar for this night of Our Lord."

At nine o'clock I heard my uncle's latchkey in the hall door. I heard him talking to himself and heard the hall stand rocking when it had received the weight of his overcoat. I could **interpret** these signs. When he was midway through his dinner I asked him to give me the money to go to the bazaar. He had forgotten.

"The people are in bed and after their first sleep now," he said.

I did not smile. My aunt said to him energetically:

"Can't you give him the money and let him go? You've kept him late enough as it is."

My uncle said he was very sorry he had forgotten. *He said he believed in the old saying: "All work and no play makes Jack a dull boy."* He asked me where I was going and, when I had told him a second time he asked me did I know The Arab's Farewell to His Steed. When I left the kitchen he was about to **recite** the opening lines of the piece to my aunt.

I held a florin tightly in my hand as I strode down Buckingham Street towards the station. The sight of the streets thronged with buyers and glaring with gas recalled to me the purpose of my journey. I took my seat in a third–class carriage of a deserted train. After an intolerable delay the train moved out of the station slowly. It crept onward among ruinous houses and over the twinkling river. *At Westland Row Station a crowd of people pressed to the carriage doors*；but the porters moved them back, saying that it was a special train for the bazaar. I remained alone in the bare carriage. In a few minutes the train drew up beside an improvised wooden platform. I passed out on to the road and saw by the lighted dial of a clock that it was ten minutes to ten. In front of me was a large building which displayed the **magical** name.

每天早晨，我躺在前客厅的地板上，望着她家的门，百叶窗拉下来，只留不到一英寸的缝隙，那样别人就看不见我了。当她出现在台阶上时，我的心就怦怦跳。我冲到过道里，抓起书就跑，跟在她后面。我紧盯着她穿着棕色衣服的身影。快到岔路口时，我便加快步伐超过她。每天早晨都是如此。除了随便招呼一下之外，我从没跟她讲过话。可是，她的名字总能让我情绪激动。

她的样子甚至在最不浪漫的场合也陪伴着我。每逢周末傍晚，我都要跟姑姑上街买东西，替她拎包儿，我们穿行在五光十色的大街上，被醉鬼和讨价还价的婆娘们挤来挤去，周围一片喧嚣：劳工们的诅咒，站在一桶桶猪头肉旁守望的伙计的尖声叫嚷，街头卖唱的用浓重的鼻音哼着的关于奥唐纳万•罗沙的《大伙儿都来》，或一支关于爱尔兰动乱的歌谣。在我看来，这些噪声汇合成一片熙熙攘攘的众生相。我仿佛感到自己正端着圣餐杯，在一群对头中间穿过。有时，在莫名其妙地做祷告或唱赞美诗时，她的名字几乎从我嘴里脱口而出，我时常热泪盈眶(自己也说不清为什么)。有时，一股沸腾的激情从心底涌起，流入胸中。我很少想到前途。我不知道自己究竟会不会同她说话，要是说了，怎么向她倾诉我那迷茫的爱慕。这时，我的身子好似一架竖琴，她的音容笑貌宛如拨弄琴弦的纤指。

有一天，薄暮时分，我踅到教士死亡的画室。那是一个漆黑的雨夜，屋子里一片沉寂。透过破碎的玻璃窗，我听到雨密密麻麻地泻在土地上，如针般的细雨在湿透了的泥地上不断跳跃。远处，有路灯的光或是哪一家窗口透出来的光在下面闪烁。我庆幸自己的视线模糊。我的全部感官似乎都想隐蔽起来，我觉得自己快要失去知觉了，于是把双手紧紧地合在一起，以致手都颤抖了，同时嘴里还喃喃自语："啊，爱！啊，爱！"

她终于跟我说话了。她一开口，我就慌乱不堪，呆在那儿，不知道说什么好。她问我去不去阿拉比。我记不得是怎么回答的。她说那儿的集市一定很热闹，她很想去呐。

"为啥不去呢？"我问。

她不断地转动着手腕上的银镯子说，她不能去，因为这星期女修道院里要做静修。这时，她的弟弟正在和两个男孩抢帽子。我独自站在栏杆旁。她手中握着一支熏衣草，低着头，凑近我。门对面，街灯的光照着她白嫩的脖子，照亮了披垂的头发，也照亮了扶在栏杆上的手。她从容地站在那里，灯光使她衣服的一边清晰可见，显出了裙子的白色镶边。

“你真该去看看。”她说。

“要是我去的话，”我说，“一定会给你捎点什么的。”

从那时起，数不清的愚蠢的怪念头充塞在我白天的幻想和夜半的梦中！但愿出发之前那段乏味的日子快点过去。学校里的功课使我烦躁。每当夜晚在寝室里或白天在教室中读书时，她的形象便闪现在书页之间。阿拉比的音节在静谧中向我召唤，我的心灵沉溺在寂静中，四周弥漫着迷人的东方气息。我要求星期六晚上要到阿拉比的集市去。我姑姑听了后大吃一惊，怀疑我跟共济会有什么勾搭。在课堂上，我很少能回答得出问题。我看着老师的脸从和蔼到严峻。他说，希望你不要变懒。我成天神思恍惚。生活中的正经事使我厌烦，它们使我的愿望不能尽快实现，所以在我看来，这些正经事就像小孩子的游戏，单调乏味的小孩子游戏。

星期六早晨，我对姑父说晚上我要到集市去。他正在前厅的衣帽架那里手忙脚乱地找帽刷子，漫不经心地说：“行，孩子，我知道了。”

他待在过道里，我没法去前客厅，就躺在窗边了。我悻悻地走出家门，去上学。那刺骨的阴冷，使我心里一阵阵忐忑不安。

当我放学回家时，姑父还没回来。时间还早呢。我呆呆地坐着，滴答滴答的钟声让我心烦意乱，我便走出房间，登上楼梯，走到楼上。那些高敞的空房间，寒冷而阴沉，却使我无拘无束。我唱起歌来，从一个房间跑到另一个房间。透过正面的玻璃窗，我看见伙伴们在街上玩。他们的喊声隐隐约约传到我耳边。我把前额贴在冰冷的玻璃窗上，望着她家。大约一个小时过去了，我还站在那儿，什么都没看见，脑海中全是她那穿着棕色衣服的身影，街灯的光朦胧地照亮呈曲线的脖子、扶在栏杆上的手以及裙子下摆的镶边。

我再下楼时，看见当铺老板的遗孀莫塞太太坐在火炉边。她为了某种虔诚的目的在收集用过的邮票。我陪着吃茶点，耐着性子听她嚼舌。开饭的时间早已过了一个小时，姑父还没回来。莫塞太太站起身来说对不起，不能久等，8点多了，她不愿在外面待得太晚，夜里的风她受不了。她走后，我在屋里踱来踱去，紧攥着拳头。姑姑说：

“兴许你今晚去不成了，改天再去集市吧。”

9点，我忽然听见姑父用钥匙开过道门的声音。接着听见他在自言自语，听到挂衣服时衣架的晃荡声。我很明白这些举动的含义。晚饭吃到一半，我跟他要钱到集市去。他已把这件事忘得一干二净了。

“人们早已睡了一觉了。”他说。

我没笑。姑姑大声地说：

“还不给钱让他去？他等的时间已经够长啦！”

他说非常抱歉，忘了这件事。然后又说他很欣赏的那句老话：“只工作不玩，聪明孩子也变傻。”他又问我去哪儿，于是我又说了一遍。他问我知不知道《阿拉伯人向骏马告别》。我走出厨房时，他正要给姑姑背诵那故事的开场白。

我紧紧攥着一枚两先令硬币，沿着白金汉大街大步走向火车站。街上熙熙攘攘，尽是买东西的人，煤气灯的照耀如同白昼，这景象提醒我快到集市去。我在一列空荡荡的火车的三等车厢找了个座位。火车迟迟不开，叫人等得恼火，过了好久才缓慢地驶出车站，爬行在沿途倾圮的房屋中间，驶过一条闪闪发亮的河流。在威斯特兰罗车站，来了一大群乘客，直拥向车厢门。列车员说，这是直达集市的专车，这才把他们挡回去。我独自坐在空荡荡的车厢里。几分钟后，火车停在一个临时用木头搭起的月台旁。我下车走到街上。有一只钟被亮光照着，我瞅了一眼：9:50。我的面前矗立着一座高大的建筑物，上面是那魅人的名字。

First love is only a little foolishness and a lot of curiosity.

——George Bernard Shaw

初恋就是一点点笨拙外加许许多多好奇。

——英国剧作家　萧伯纳

作者介绍

詹姆斯·乔伊斯 (1882–1941)，他自小就显露出在音乐、宗教哲学及语言文学方面的才能，并开始诗歌、散文习作。他谙熟欧洲大陆作家作品，受易卜生影响尤深，并渐渐表现出对人类精神世界特殊的感悟及对家庭笃信的宗教和自己生活环境中的习俗、传统的叛逆。詹姆斯·乔伊斯是二十世纪最伟大的作家之一，他的作品及“意识流”思想对全世界产生了巨大的影响。

单词注解

figure ['figə] *n.* 外形；数量；金额
converge [kən'və:dʒ] *v.* 会合；趋于会合
tremble ['trembl] *v.* 发抖；震颤
convent ['kɔnvənt] *n.* 修女团；女修道院
enchantment [in'tʃɑ:ntmənt] *n.* 魅力，迷人之处
endure [in'djuə] *v.* 忍耐，忍受
interpret [in'tə:prit] *v.* 解释，说明，诠释
recite [ri'sait] *v.* 背诵；朗诵，当众吟诵
magical ['mædʒikəl] *adj.* 魔术的，魔法的

名句大搜索

她说那儿的集市一定丰富多彩，她很想去呐。

然后又说他很欣赏那句老话：“只工作不去玩，任何孩子都变傻。”

在威斯特兰罗车站，来了一大群乘客，直拥向车厢门。

The Little Prince

小王子

[法] 安东尼·圣埃克苏佩里 (Antoine de saint–Exupery)

小说的叙述者飞行员讲了 6 年前他因飞机故障迫降在撒哈拉沙漠遇见小王子的故事。神秘的小王子来自另一个星球。飞行员讲了小王子和他的玫瑰的故事；小王子离开自己星球的原因；以及他访问过的星球。他转述了小王子对六个星球的历险，他遇见了国王、爱虚荣的人、酒鬼、商人、点灯人、地理学家、蛇、三枚花瓣的沙漠花、玫瑰园、扳道工、商贩、狐狸以及叙述者飞行员本人。飞行员和小王子在沙漠中共同拥有过一段极为珍贵的友谊。当小王子无法回到他的玫瑰身边时，他选择了死亡。飞行员非常难过。

Once when I was six years old I saw a magnificent picture in a book, called True Stories from Nature, about the **primeval** forest. It was a picture of a boa constrictor in the act of swallowing an animal. Here is a copy of the drawing.

In the book it said, "Boa constrictors swallow their prey whole, without chewing it. After that they are not able to move, and they sleep through the six months that they need for digestion." I pondered deeply, then, over the adventures of the jungle. And after some work with a colored pencil I succeeded in making my first drawing. My Drawing Number One. It looked like this.

I showed my masterpiece to the grown-ups, and asked them whether the drawing frightened them. But they answered, "Frighten? Why should any one be frightened by a hat?" My drawing was not a picture of a hat. It was a picture of a boa constrictor digesting an elephant. But since the grown-ups were not able to understand it, I made another drawing, I drew the inside of the boa constrictor, so that the grown-ups could see it clearly. They always need to have things explained. My Drawing Number Two looked like this:

The grown-ups' response, this time, was to **advise** me to lay aside my drawings of boa constrictors, whether from the inside or the outside, and devote myself instead to geography, history, arithmetic and grammar. That is why, at the age of six, I gave up what might have been a magnificent career as a painter. I had been disheartened by the failure of my Drawing Number One and my Drawing Number Two. *Grown-ups never understand anything by themselves, and it is tiresome for children to be always and forever explaining things to them.*

So then I chose another profession, and learned to pilot

airplanes. I have flown a little over all parts of the world ; and it is true that geography has been very useful to me. At a glance I can distinguish China from Arizona. *If one gets lost in the night, such knowledge is valuable*. In the course of this life I have had a great many **encounters** with a great many people who have been concerned with matters of consequence. I have lived a great deal among grown-ups. I have seen them intimately, close at hand. And that hasn't much improved my opinion of them.

Whenever I met one of them who seemed to me at all clear-sighted, I tried the experiment of showing him my Drawing Number One, which I have always kept. I would try to find out, so, if this was a person of true understanding. But, whoever it was, he, or she, would always say: "That is a hat." Then I would never talk to that person about boa constrictors, or primeval forests, or stars. I would bring myself down to his level. I would talk to him about bridge, and golf, and politics, and neckties. And the grown-up would be greatly pleased to have met such a **sensible** man.

我6岁的时候，在一本描写原始森林的名叫《真实的故事》的书中，看到了一副精彩的插画，画的是一条蟒蛇正在吞食一只大野兽。页面上就是那幅画的摹本。

这本书中写道："这些蟒蛇把它们的猎物不加咀嚼地囫囵吞下，尔后就不能再动弹了；然后在长达六个月的睡眠中消化这些食物。”当时，我对丛林中的奇遇想得很多，于是，我也用彩色铅笔画出了我的第一幅图画，也是我的第一号作品。

我把这幅杰作拿给大人们看，我问他们，我的画是不是很可怕。他们说："一顶帽子有什么可怕的？"我画的不是帽子，是一条巨蟒在消化着一头大象。于是我又把巨蟒肚子里的情况画了出来，以便让大人们能够看懂。这些大人总是需要解释。这是我的第二号作品。

大人们劝我把这些画着开着肚皮的，或合上肚皮的蟒蛇的图画放在一边，还是把兴趣放在地理、历史、算术、语法上。就这样，在6岁那年，我就放弃了当画家这一美好的理想。第一号、第二号作品的不成功，使我泄了气。这些大人们，靠他们自己什么也弄不懂，还得不断地给他们做解释。这真叫孩子们腻味。

后来，我只好选择了另外一个职业，我学会了开飞机，世界各地差不多都飞到过。的确，地理学帮了我很大的忙。我一眼就能分辨出中国和亚里桑那。要是夜里迷失了航向，这是很有用的。这样，在我的生活中、我跟许多严肃的人有过很多的接触。我在大人们中间生活过很长时间。我仔细地观察过他们，但这并没有让我对他们的看法有多大改变。

当我遇到一个看起来头脑稍微清楚的大人时，我就拿出一直保存着的我那第一号作品来测试他。我想知道他是否真的有理解能力。可是，得到的回答总是“这是顶帽子”。要是这样，我就不和他谈巨蟒呀，原始森林呀，或者星星之类的事了。我只得迁就他们的水平，和他们谈些桥牌呀，高尔夫球呀，政治呀，领带呀这些。于是大人们就很高兴能认识我这样一个通情达理的人。

实战提升
Practising & Exercise

作者介绍

安东尼·德·圣埃克苏佩里（1900–1944）他的家庭属于古高卢人榆树勇士部族的后裔。他的母亲是普罗旺斯人，因此他具有普罗旺斯人的血统。他的大部分作品都取材于他个人的经历。他的一部脍炙人口的儿童文学作品《小王子》深受全世界儿童的喜爱。在第二次世界大战期间的一次飞行任务中，他驾驶着飞机失踪，就再也没有回来。

单词注解

primeval [prai'mi:vəl] *adj.* 初期的；太古的；原始的

advise [əd'vaiz] *v.* 劝告，忠告

tiresome ['taiəsəm] *adj.* 使人疲劳的；令人厌倦的

encounter [in'kauntə] *v.* 遭遇；遇到

sensible ['sensəbl] *adj.* 明智的；合情理的

名句大搜索

这些大人们，靠他们自己什么也弄不懂，还得老是不断地给他们作解释。这真叫孩子们腻味。

要是夜里迷失了航向，这是很有用的。

我遇到一个看起来头脑稍微清楚的大人时，我就拿出一直保存着的我那第一号作品来测试他。

Dead Poets Society

春风化雨

[法] N.H. 克雷鲍牧（N.H.Kleinbaum）

1959 年，威尔顿预备学院以它凝重的风格受到了人们的尊敬。在那里，教育的模式是固定的，不仅单调而且束缚了思想。然而这一切在一个新教师的手中发生了改变。老师反传统的教育方法给学院带来了一丝生气：在他的课堂上，他鼓励学生站在课桌上，用一个崭新的视角去观察周围的世界；他向学生介绍了许多有思想的诗歌；他所提倡的自由发散式的思维哲学在学生中引起了巨大的反响。

Keating: "Oh Captain, My Captain" who knows where that comes from? Anybody? Not a clue? It's from a poem by Walt Whitman about Mr. Abraham Lincoln. Now in this class you can either call me Mr. Keating. Or, if you're slightly more daring, Oh Captain, My Captain. *Now let me dispel a few rumors so they don't fester into facts.* Yes, I too attended Welton and survived. And no, at that time I was not the mental giant you see before you. I was the intellectual **equivalent** of a ninety-eight pound weakling. I would go to the beach and people would kick copies of Byron in my face. Now, Mr. Pitts? That's a rather unfortunate name. Mr. Pitts, where are you? Mr. Pitts? Would you open your hymnal to page 542 and read the first stanza of the poem you find there?

Pitts: To the virgins, to make much of time?

Keating: Yes, that's the one. Somewhat appropriate, isn't it.

Pitts: Gather ye rosebuds while ye may, old time is still a flying, and this same flower that smiles today, tomorrow will be dying.

Keating: Thank you Mr. Pitts. "Gather ye rosebuds while ye may." The Latin term for that **sentiment** is Carpe Diem. Now who knows what that means?

Meeks: Carpe Diem. That's "seize the day" .

Keating: Very good, Mr.–

Meeks: Meeks.

Keating: Meeks. Another unusual name. Seize the day. Gather ye rosebuds while ye may. Why does the writer use these lines?

Charlie: Because he's in a hurry.

Keating: No, ding! Thank you for playing anyway. Because we are food for worms, lads. Because, believe it or not, each and every one of us in this room is one day going to stop breathing, turn cold, and die. Now I would like you to step forward over here and peruse some of the faces from the past. You've walked past them many times. I don't think you've really looked at them. They're not that different from you, are they? Same haircuts, full of hormones, just like you. **Invincible**, just like you feel. The world is their oyster. *They believe they're destined for great things, just like many of you.* Their eyes are full of hope, just like you. Did they wait until it was too late to make from their lives even one iota of what they were capable? Because you see, gentlemen, these boys are now fertilizing daffodils. But if you listen real close, you can hear them whisper their **legacy** to you. Go on, lean in. Carpe. Hear it? Carpe. Carpe. Carpe Diem. *Seize the day boys, make your lives extraordinary.*

基　丁：“哦，船长！我的船长”这句话，有谁知道出自哪儿吗？有吗？没人知道？它出自沃尔特·惠特曼为亚伯拉罕·林肯写的一首诗。听好啦，在班上你们可以叫我基丁老师，或者有胆量的话就叫“哦，船长！我的船长”。我首先要澄清一些谣言，免得误人子弟。没错，我也上过这所地狱学校并活了下来。不过，那时候我可不是你们现在看到的这个思想巨人。我的智慧跟一个 98 磅重的弱智差不多，我到海滩念诗，人们会把拜伦诗集往我脸上砸。好了，哪位是皮茨先生？这名字太不幸了。皮茨，哪位是皮茨？皮茨，把诗集翻到第 542 页，念一下那首诗的第一节。

皮　茨：“劝少女们珍惜时光”？

基　丁：是，就是那首。对你们很合适，对吧？

皮　茨：及时采撷你的花蕾
旧时光一去不回
今天尚在微笑的花朵
明日便在风中枯萎

基　丁：谢谢，皮茨。“及时采撷你的花蕾”这种感慨用拉丁语说就叫“卡匹迪恩”。有谁知道是什么意思吗？

米克斯：“卡匹迪恩”就是抓紧时间的意思。

基　丁：很好，你叫？

米克斯：米克斯

基　丁：好，米克斯。又一个不寻常的名字。抓紧时间，“及时采撷你的花蕾”。为什么作者要写这几句话？

查　理：因为他很着急。

基　丁：不！不！不过还是要感谢你的幽默。小伙子们，因为我们是蛆虫的食物，因为不管你们信不信，在这儿的每一个人，有一天都会停止呼吸，变冷，死亡。你们到前面来，好好看看他们——过去的这些面孔。你们从这儿经过多少次了，但肯定没有仔细看过。他们和你们差别不大，对吧？他们和你们一样，同样的发型，充满活力，认为自己所向披靡，就像你们现在这样。世界在他们手中。他们相信自己一定能成就伟大的事业，就像你们中的很多人一样。他们眼中充满希望，就像你们一样。但他们是不是曾经蹉跎而错过他们本可能成就的任何事业？因为，你瞧，各位，当年的年轻人已变成了花下之尘。但如果仔细听，你们还能听见他们给你们留下的忠告。来吧，靠近一点。听见了吗？卡匹………听见了吗？卡匹………卡匹迪恩。抓紧时间，孩子们，让你的生命不同寻常。

A man, like a watch, is to be valued by this manner of going.

——William Penn

一个人，正如一个时钟，是以他的行动来定其价值的。

——英国海军上将　佩恩

作者介绍

N.H. 克莱鲍姆毕业于美国西北大学麦迪尔新闻学院，曾经做过报纸记者和编辑。她和丈夫及三个孩子现居住在纽约附近的克斯科山。

单词注解

equivalent [i'kwivələnt] *adj.* 相等的，相同的

sentiment ['sentimənt] *n.* 感情，心情；情操

invincible [in'vinsəbl] *adj.* 无敌的；无法征服的；不屈不挠的

legacy ['legəsi] *n.* 遗产；遗赠

名句大搜索

我首先要澄清一些谣言，免得误人子弟。

他们相信自己一定能成就伟大的事业，就像你们中的很多人一样。

抓紧时间，孩子们，让你的生命不同寻常。

Vive La Paris

我是女生，我叫巴黎

[美] 爱斯米•科德尔(Esmé Raji Codell)

巴黎，是一个很普通的小女孩。和其他小女孩一样，她善良、无知、任性、虚荣，想要快点长大，对世界充满好奇。她在学钢琴的时候，遇到了诺森太太。诺森太太为她打开了一扇真实世界的窗户，让她意识到什么是真正的勇气，应该怎样用自己的眼睛来看待这个真实的世界，怎样学会相处，学会宽容。

When I came to school the next day, I no longer cared about being a polite person. It' s just like Django and Debergerac say:

1. If you're likely to get in trouble for doing nothing you might as well get in trouble for doing something.
2. When a fight's coming, throw the first punch because then no matter what happens at least you'll know you got a good one in, and
3. Don't put your thumb inside your fist when you fight, because you can break it that way.

So when there were only a couple of minutes until recess, I said to Tanaeja, "Guess what, I hope you got some nice ones in on my brother yesterday, because that's the last day you're going to get to do that."

"You and your brother," hissed Tanaeja. "You always flaunting him, walking with all your brothers around town. You think you all that."

What she is saying to me doesn't make sense, but I am wise now, I know things don't have to make sense, just that I have to take her down because This Cannot Continue. "Why do you beat on my brother?"

"What's it to you? He can defend hisself," she said. "Why he gotta be like that? It's wrong."

"Like what? He never did anything to anybody. He wouldn't even know your name if you weren't up in his face." I felt myself winding up, like one of Debergerac's toy cars that has a little coil that twists tighter and tighter before it spins so fast it smells like metal melting. "That's not right, Tanaeja, he can't hit you back because you're a girl."

"So is he," said Tanaeja. "He keep acting like that, he going to die."

I didn't even feel myself leave my seat. All I hear is the screech of desks sliding and girls screaming. I feel my fingernails digging into the braids against her head. I feel her teeth wet against my cheek, trying to bite down. I feel people pulling us apart, but we're like Velcro, little barbs of a long, long anger **hooked** into each other. "Stop it, stop it!" Miss Pointy was shouting. Luz ran to the intercom button, chest heaving and big worried eyes, looking for Miss Pointy to tell her to buzz the office. But the recess bell had rung.

"You want to tell me what's going on?" Miss Pointy demanded, checking my cheek for cuts, checking Tanaeja's scalp for blood.

"Not really." Tanaeja crossed her arms.

"I'll tell you," said Darrell. "Tanaeja's been pushing Paris's brother around at recess."

"Be quiet," warned Tanaeja. "You–all better mind your business."

"Oh, yeah? What you gone do about it?" asked Darrell. "Bring it, Miss Dark and Lovely, just don't expect me to stand here and take it. I'm the man."

"Oh, don't start up, Darrell." Miss Pointy rolled her eyes.

"It's true! My brother has bruises all over his back, Miss Pointy? I told. I told!"

"No he doesn't!" Tanaeja exploded.

"How would you know?" *I felt my head reel around on my neck in a nasty way*. "You think it's not gone come around, well I got news for you."

"I'll take you right here, Minnie Mouse." Tanaeja faced me.

"Ooo," said the class.

"What are you people still doing here?" Miss Pointy's voice rose. "Usually you can't get to **recess** fast enough. Trust me, nobody's bringing anything or taking anybody" The class gave us a wide berth as they filed out.

Miss Pointy looked back and forth between Tanaeja and me. "*I'm very disappointed in you both. How do you expect there to be peace in the world if we can' t even have peace in this classroom?*"

"I don't expect it," I blurted.

For the second time, Miss Pointy looked at me and didn't seem to recognize who I was. It took her a beat or two before she could speak. "You think your mother needs this right now?" Miss Pointy asked Tanaeja.

"No, ma'am" said Tanaeja, rubbing her head with her forearm. I tried to hide my wondering about what Momma would do if she were called in a second time, but Miss Pointy didn't seem to wonder if my mother needed this. Tanaeja started looking that same miserable way she uses in church. You're kid-ding, right? Girl, you have got to be kidding.

Then Miss Pointy told Tanaeja to go and cool off in the art teacher's room, and Tanaeja didn't need to be asked twice. Not fair, not fair!

"How come she gets to go?" I **demanded**, but then politeness set in. "I mean, you don't have to work on me first."

"I think I do." Miss Pointy pulled up a chair so I would sit right beside her. Then there was a long minute with just me and Miss Pointy. "This has been going on a while, huh? A lot going on," she said, finally.

My mouth was doing a crazy twitchy thing, turning down at the corners, and I could not look at her at all for what seemed like forever, but when I looked up, there she was, looking at me with the most concerned, sad expression I have ever seen. I burst out crying so hard that I put my head down on her desk. I could feel her patting me on the place where if I had wings, they would sprout.

"I'm trying to be brave," I finally said. I wanted her to say,

1. Poor Paris,
2. You are brave,
3. I know you are a polite person and that you would never behave this way if you weren't pushed.

Instead, she said, "So is Tanaeja."

"Who cares about Tanaeja?" I snorted

"I want to tell you something," said Miss Pointy, "and even though you are angry, I hope you will hear me. Sometimes people become our enemies not because they are so different, but because there is something in them that is so much the same, it hurts us to look at it."

"There's nothing about me that is the same as Tanaeja," I insisted.

"Maybe there's something about Tanaeja that is the same as you. Maybe you have something that she also has. Maybe you have something she is about to lose."

"What?" I asked.

Miss Pointy looked a little torn, like there was something she wanted to tell me but she couldn't. "Let's just say maybe there's something that you share that you don't know you share. That's not to say she can beat on your brother." Miss Pointy straightened. "That's going to stop."

"Miss Pointy, it can't seem like I was the one to stop it." It was so hard to explain. "He's got to stand up for himself."

"It's hard to stand up when someone is beating you down," said Miss Pointy. "Sometimes a person needs a little help. I'd even say usually, Paris. There's no shame in that."

"There isn't?" I asked, because

1.I felt ashamed so there must be some shame in it, and

2. Louis says some teachers were never kids and maybe she is one of them.

"But don't worry. It will look like I'm stopping it, because I'm the one who is. Got that?" I nodded. "Paris, I'll tell you something else. My best friend when I was a little girl started out as my enemy."

Luz is already my best friend, I thought, I don't need Goliath for a friend. But I just said, "Really?"

"It's true. She used to try to copy from my math test in class. I thought, She's sneaky, she's a cheat, she's going to get me in trouble, and I didn't want to have anything to do with her. In time, though, I saw that she wanted to do well in school, just like me, and I started helping her with her math before the test. *She still calls me, Paris, we're still friends, twenty years later.* But I haven't really learned my lesson. Even now, there are women I meet, and I'm still so quick to think, Oh, we don't have anything in common, but it always turns out we have something in common, or they have something about them that is interesting. Maybe not enough to be the best of friends, but it's enough to have a really good time together. But I wouldn't know that if I didn't push the doubts and **prejudices** aside so there is a little space in my heart for them."

The bell rang. Miss Pointy looked at the clock and sighed. "That space is where peace lives, Paris. That little spot in our hearts that has room for other people, that place where we try to find our common ground. Maybe it's all the peace we can expect, Paris. But let's try to keep expecting that much."

"Yes ma'am." I gulped. "I'll try."

I felt like I needed to wash my face. But I didn't want to go into the bathroom by myself. I still wasn't prepared to expect that much peace.

第二天去学校的时候，我再也不关心自己是不是一个有教养的人了。就像迪金格和德贝拉克说的那样：

1. 如果你什么都没做也会惹来麻烦的话，那么最好还是做点什么吧。

2. 打架的时候，一定要先出第一拳，不管怎么样，你至少知道自己还是打出了一拳的。

3. 打架的时候千万不要把大拇指缩在拳头里，那样很容易受伤。

离课间休息还有几分钟的时候，我对塔娜佳说："你昨天打我哥哥的时候打得很痛快吧，不过你以后再也没机会这么做了。"

"你和你哥哥，"塔娜佳不屑地说，"你就只会拉着他到处炫耀，你就只会拉着你所有的哥哥们到处走来走去。"

我弄不明白她到底在说什么，不过我现在变聪明了，我知道有些事情没必要搞明白，我只知道我必须打倒她，因为我不会允许这样的事情再发生了。“你为什么要打我哥哥？”

“这跟你有什么关系？他自己可以还手，”她说，“他为什么要那么做？是他不对。”

“他做什么了？他从来没有对任何人做过任何不好的事。你要是不欺负他的话，他甚至连你叫什么都不知道。”我感到自己气得快爆炸了，就像德贝拉克的玩具车上的小转盘转得越来越紧，几乎都能闻到金属融化的味道了。“这不公平，塔娜佳，就因为你是女孩他才不还手的。”

“他才是女孩，”塔娜佳说，“他如果还是这样的话，死了活该。”

我觉得自己好像并没有离开座位，但是我听到课桌倒地的声音、女孩子们尖叫的声音；我感觉到我的指甲嵌进她的辫子里；我感觉到她的牙齿抵着我的脸颊，很显然她想咬我；我感觉到其他人在把我们拉开，可是我们像维可牢尼龙搭扣一样，这么长时间以来的愤怒像鱼钩一样咬得紧紧的，谁也没法拉开。“住手，住手！”波迪小姐大叫道。露兹跑到内部电话机旁，胸部一起一伏的，焦急地等待波迪小姐示意她给办公室打电话。这时下课铃响了。

“你们想告诉我到底出了什么事吗？”波迪小姐边问边察看我脸上有没有伤口，塔娜佳头上有没有出血。

“没事。”塔娜佳双手抱在胸前说道。

“让我告诉你吧，”德里说，“塔娜佳在课间休息的时候老是欺负巴黎的哥哥。”

“安静一点。”塔娜佳警告他。“你最好别管闲事。”

“哦，是吗？你想怎么样？”德里问道。“出手吧，塔娜佳小姐，不过你可别指望我一动不动地站在这儿。我可不是那么好欺负的。”

“噢，德里，你就别挑事了。”波迪小姐瞪着他说。

“他说的是实话！波迪小姐，我哥的背上被撞得青一块紫一块的。”我终于说出来了！我说出来了！

“不，他没有受伤！”塔娜佳大叫道。

“你怎么知道？”我感觉我的脑袋用一种想要恐吓人的方式转了转。“你以为你能一直这么下去吗？我会给你点颜色瞧瞧的。”

“我现在就可以把你打趴下，米妮鼠。”塔娜佳对着我嚷道。

“Ooooooo。”同学们炸开了锅。

“你们还待在这儿做什么？”波迪小姐抬高声音说，“课间休息的时候，你们不是希望跑得越远越好吗？相信我，谁也不会给谁颜色看，谁也不会把谁打趴下的。”他们离开以后，教室里空出了一大块。

波迪小姐看看塔娜佳，又看看我。“我对你们两个感到很失望。如果连教室里都找不到和平的话，你们还指望在这个世界的哪个地方能找到和平？”

“我一点都不指望世界上能有和平。”我大声说。

这是第二次，波迪小姐用一种好像根本就不认识我的表情看着我了。她半天说不出一句话来。“你认为你妈妈现在需要知道这件事吗？”波迪小姐问塔娜佳。

“不，波迪小姐。”塔娜佳边说边揉着她的额头。我不想让她们看出我的担忧，我很担心要是我妈第二次被叫到学校来她会怎么样，可是波迪小姐并没有问我。塔娜佳又开始表现出在教堂里的那副悲惨样子来。你在开玩笑，是吗？你一定是在开玩笑。

波迪小姐要塔娜佳去美术老师的办公室冷静一下，老师只问了她一次要不要请家长。这太不公平啦！

“她怎么能先走呢？”我追问道，我感到自己有点太不礼貌了。“我的意思是，你不一定先要从我开始问起。”

“我想先和你谈谈。”波迪小姐拉过一张椅子让我坐在她的对面。接下来是一段长时间的沉默。“这件事有一段时间了，是吗？发生了很多事是吗？”她最后开口道。

我低下头看着角落，不想回答。可是当我抬起头，看到她用最关注最悲伤的眼神看着我时，我忍不住趴在桌子上放声大哭起来。我感觉到她在轻轻拍着我的肩膀，如果我有翅膀的话，那里就是长出翅膀的地方。

“我一直想勇敢一些的。”我最后开口说。我希望她能这么回答我：

1. 可怜的巴黎，

2. 你很勇敢，

3. 我知道你是个有教养的孩子，如果不是忍无可忍的话，你是绝对不会动手的。

可是，她却说：“塔娜佳也是这样。”

“我才不管塔娜佳呢！”我不屑地说。

“我想告诉你一些事，”波迪小姐说，“虽然你现在很生气，我还是希望你能听我说下去。有时候有些人成为我们的敌人，并不是因为他们和我们不同，而是因为他们有些地方和我们太一样了，只是我们不想看到这些罢了。”

“我和塔娜佳没有任何相同的地方。”我坚持道。

“也许塔娜佳身上有些东西和你一样。也许你也有些东西和她一样。也许你有一些她就要失去的东西。”

“什么？”我问。

波迪小姐看起来欲言又止的样子。“这么说吧，也许你拥有一些连你自己都没有意识到的东西。不过，那并不代表她就可以欺负你哥哥。”波迪小姐坚定地说，“这件事不会再发生了。”

“波迪小姐，这件事不应该由我来插手的。”这件事解释起来实在太困难了。“我哥哥应该靠他自己来解决。”

“一个人被别人打倒时，很难靠自己的力量站起来。”波迪小姐说，“有时候，人们需要其他人的帮助才能站起来，其实我想说的是，大多数情况下人们都需要其他人的帮助才能站起来。人们不应该为此感到羞耻。”

“不会感到羞耻吗？”我这么问的原因是：

1. 我感到很羞耻，所以这里一定有让人感到羞耻的地方。

2. 路易斯说有些老师永远都是小孩，也许她就是那些老师中的一个。

“不过别担心，看起来我已经解决这件事了。这是我应该做的，你明白吗？”我点点头。“巴黎，我想告诉你一些别的事情。当我还是个小女孩的时候，我最好的朋友一开始却是我的敌人。”

我心想，露兹已经是我最好的朋友了，我可不想再有一个魔鬼做我的好朋友。可我嘴上只说了句“真的吗？”

“是真的，她经常在班上抄我的数学试卷。我当时想，她太卑鄙了，她是个骗子，她想把我拖下水，我不想和她有任何关系。后来我看到她其实只是想做个好学生，就像我一样，所以我开始在考试之前教她数学。她现在经常给我打电话，巴黎，我们仍然是好朋友，二十多年的好朋友了。但是我并没有吸取经验，直到现在，当我遇到一些女人的时候，我第一感觉还是不好，我想我们不会有任何相同的地方，可是后来我发现其实我们也有相同的地方，她们也有很多优点。我们之间可能不一定成为最好的

朋友，但彼此之间相处得很愉快就已经足够了。我不知道，如果我不把疑问和偏见扔掉的话，我心里是否还有地方能接受和容纳她们。”

上课铃响了。波迪小姐看了眼钟表，叹了口气说：“巴黎，那个地方就是和平居住的地方。我们心里那个小小的空间可以包容很多人，在那里我们将尽力找到与其他人的相同之处。巴黎，也许这就是我们能够期待的和平，让我们期待这样的和平尽快出现好吗？

“好的，波迪小姐。”我抽噎着说。“我会试试看的。”

我觉得自己该去洗洗脸，但是我不想一个人去卫生间。我还没准备好去迎接和平的到来。

作者介绍

爱斯米·科德尔，曾做过老师、图书管理员、小说家，现正在经营一个点击率极高的儿童网站 www.planetesme.com。她狂爱收集闪亮的贴纸，还有，她是个滑旱冰的好手！她住在美国芝加哥，在那里写了很多有意思的故事：《特别的女生萨哈拉》获 2004 年国际读者协会儿童图书奖；《新老师的新日记》赢得“美国最佳青少年读物”奖；《我是女生，我叫巴黎》获 2007 年希得妮·泰勒书奖。

单词注解

hook [huk] *n.* 钩，挂钩；(衣服的)钩扣

recess [ri'ses] *n.* 休息；休会；休庭

demand [di'mɑːnd] *n.* 要求，请求

shame [ʃeim] *n.* 羞耻(心)，羞愧(感)

prejudice ['predʒudis] *n.* 偏见，歧视

名句大搜索

我感觉我的脑袋用一种想要恐吓人的方式转了转。

我对你们两个感到很失望。连教室里都找不到和平的话，你们还指望在这个世界的哪个地方能找到和平？

她现在经常给我电话，巴黎，我们仍然是好朋友，二十多年的好朋友了。

为你，千千万万遍
For you, a thousand times over

Gone with the Wind

飘

[美] 玛格丽特·米切尔(Margaret Mitchell)

故事开始于美国南北关系非常紧张的1861年。原来任性的思嘉随着战事的吃紧经历着人生的转折。苦难的生活磨炼着思嘉，但也使她变得冷酷无情，不择手段。当她明白她的真爱就在她身边时，为时已晚。瑞德已经决定弃家出走，永远地离开她。而此刻，对于思嘉来说，生活中的一切光亮都消失了。她只有回到塔拉庄园这一条出路。她太累了，再也承受不了这些压力了。

She sat down, the **harsh** gas light falling on her white bewildered face. She looked into the eyes she knew so well — and knew so little — listened to his quiet voice saying words which at first meant nothing. This was the first time he had ever talked to her in this manner, as one human being to another, talked as other people talked, without **flippancy**, mockery or riddles.

"Did it ever occur to you that I loved you as much as a man can love a woman? Loved you for years before I finally got you? During the war I'd go away and try to forget you, but I couldn't and I always had to come back. After the war I risked arrest, just to come back and find you. I cared so much I believe I would have killed Frank Kennedy if he hadn't died when he did. I loved you but I couldn't let you know it. You're so brutal to those who love you, Scarlett. You take their love and hold it over their heads like a whip."

Out of it all only the fact that he loved her meant anything. At the faint echo of passion in his voice, pleasure and excitement crept back into her. She sat, hardly breathing, listening, waiting.

"I knew you didn't love me when 1 married you. I knew about Ashley, you see. But, fool that I was, I thought I could make you care. Laugh, if you like, but I wanted to take care of you, to pet you, to give you everything you wanted. I wanted to marry you and protect you and give you a free rein in anything that would make you happy. — just as I did Bonnie. You'd had such a struggle, Scarlett. No one knew better than I what you'd gone through and I wanted you to stop fighting and let me fight for you. I wanted you to play, like a child — for you were a child, a brave, frightened, bull-headed child. I think you are still a child. No one but a child could be so headstrong and so insensitive." His voice was calm and tired but there was something in the quality of it that raised a ghost of memory in Scarlett.

She had heard a voice like this once before and at some other crisis of her life. Where had it been? The voice of a man facing himself and his world without feeling, without flinching, without hope.

Why — why — it had been Ashley in the wintry, windswept orchard at Tara, talking of life and shadow shows with a tired **calmness** that had more finality in its timbre than any desperate bitterness could have revealed. Even as Ashley's voice then had turned her cold with dread of things he could not understand, so now Rhett's voice made her heart sink. His voice, his manner, more than the content of his words, disturbed her, made her realize that her pleasurable excitement of a few moments ago had been **untimely**. Something was wrong, badly wrong.

What it was she did not know but she listened desperately, her eyes on his brown face, hoping to hear words that would dissipate her fears.

"It was so obvious that we were meant for each other. *So obvious that I was the only man of your acquaintance who could love you after knowing you as you really are* — hard and greedy and unscrupulous, like me. I loved you and I took the chance. I thought Ashley would fade out of your mind. But," he shrugged, "I tried everything I knew and nothing worked. And I loved you so, Scarlett. If you had only let me, I could have loved you as gently and as tenderly as ever a man loved a woman. But I couldn't let you know, for I knew you'd think me weak and try to use my love against me. And always — always there was Ashley. It drove me crazy. I couldn't sit across the table from you every night, knowing you wished Ashley was sitting there in my place. And I couldn't hold you in my arms at night and know that — well, it doesn't matter now. I wonder, now, why it hurt. That's what drove me to Belle.There is a certain swinish comfort in being with a woman who loves you utterly and respects you for being a fine gentleman — even if she is an **illiterate** whore. It soothed my vanity. You've never been very soothing, my dear."

"Oh, Rhett..." she began, miserable at the very mention of Belle's name, but he waved her to silence and went on.

"And then, that night when I carried you upstairs — I thought — I hoped — I hoped so much I was afraid to face you the next morning, for fear I'd been mistaken and you didn't love me. I was so afraid you'd laugh at me I went off and got drunk. And when I came back, I was shaking in my boots and if you had come even halfway to meet me, had given me some sign, I think I'd have kissed your feet. But you didn't."

"Oh, but Rhett, I did want you then but you were so nasty! I did want you! I think — yes, that must have been when I first knew I cared about you. Ashley — I never was happy about Ashley after that, but you were so **nasty** that I —"

"Oh, well," he said. "It seems we've been at cross purposes, doesn't it? But it doesn't matter now. I'm only telling you, so you won't ever wonder about it all. When you were sick and it was all my fault, I stood outside your door, hoping you'd call for me, but you didn't, and then I knew what a fool I'd been and that it was all over."

He stopped and looked through her and beyond her, even as Ashley had often done, seeing something he could not see. And she could only stare speechless at his brooding face.

"But then, there was Bonnie and I saw that everything

wasn't over, after all. I liked to think that Bonnie was you, a little girl again, before the war and poverty had done things to you. She was so like you, so willful, so brave and gay and full of high spirits, and I could pet her and spoil her — just as I wanted to pet you. But she wasn't like you — she loved me. It was a blessing that I could take the love you didn't want and give it to her... When she went, she took everything."

Suddenly she was sorry for him, sorry with a completeness that wiped out her own grief and her fear of what his words might mean. It was the first time in her life she had been sorry for anyone without feeling **contemptuous** as well, because it was the first time she had ever approached understanding any other human being. And she could understand his shrewd caginess, so like her own, his obstinate pride that kept him from admitting his love for fear of a rebuff.

"Ah, darling," she said coming forward, hoping he would put out his arms and draw her to his knees. "Darling, I'm so sorry but I'll make it all up to you! We can be so happy, now that we know the truth and — Rhett — look at me, Rhett! There — there can be other babies — not like Bonnie but —"

"Thank you, no," said Rhett, as if he were refusing a piece of bread.

她坐下来，刺眼的灯光打在她那苍白困惑的脸上。她望着他的眼睛，熟悉但却读不懂，她听着他平静地说着一些起初让

她听不懂的话。这是他第一次用这种方式和她谈话，就像旁人一样的谈话，没有了尖刻，没有了嘲弄，也没有了晦涩费解的话。

"你有没有想过，我是怀着一个男人对一个女人的爱所能达到的最高境界在爱你，爱了那么多年才拥有你。在战争期间，我曾想要离开，忘了你，但我做不到，只好常常回来。战争结束后，我冒着被捕的危险跑回来，只是为了看看你。我非常嫉恨弗兰克·肯尼迪，要不是他后来死了，我想我很可能已经把他杀了。我爱你，但又不能让你知道。思嘉，你对那些爱你的人总是那么残酷。你得到了他们的爱，却把它像鞭子一样举在他们头上。"

然而所有的这些话，只有他爱她这一点对她是有意义的。她从他的话语中隐隐约约嗅到了一丝热情，这让她既开心又兴奋。她坐在那里，倾听着，等待着，几乎不能呼吸了。

"在我们结婚的时候我就知道你并不爱我。我知道艾希礼的事，这点你也明白。但我那时很傻，满以为能让你爱上我。你就笑吧，但那时，如果你愿意，我是真想照顾你，宠爱你的，给你任何你想要的东西。我想跟你结婚，保护你，让你可以随心所欲地做事……就像我对邦妮那样。思嘉，你确实经历了一段艰难的日子，我比谁都清楚。所以，我要你好好休息一下，让我为你奋斗。我要你去玩，像个孩子似的——何况你本来就是个孩子，一个勇敢、时常担惊受怕、刚强的孩子。我想你至今仍然是个孩子，因为只有孩子才会这般任性，这么迟钝。"他的声音疲惫而平静，但其中有些东西却勾起了思嘉模模糊糊的回忆。

她觉得这种声音好像在哪里听过，是在她面临某个危机的时候。是哪里呢？这是一个男子面对自己，面对世界，毫无感情，没有畏缩，没有希望的声音。

为什么……为什么……是艾希礼，在塔拉农场寒风凛冽的果园里，用一种疲惫而平静的声音谈论人生和影子戏，那最后决判般的口气比绝望还让人痛苦。那时艾希礼的声音曾使她对一些无法理解的事物惧怕得不寒而栗，而现在瑞德的声音使她的心沉了下来。他的声音，他的态度，比他说话的内容更令她不安，让她明白她刚才那开心兴奋的心情是为时过早了。她觉得事情有些不妙，非常不妙。

这到底是怎么回事，她还不清楚，只能绝望地听着，凝望着他黝黑的面孔，但愿能听到使这担忧最终消释的下文。

“很明显，我们俩真可谓是天生的一对。我是唯一一个既了解你的底细还可以爱你的人。我知道你残酷、贪婪、无耻，这跟我一样。我爱你，所以决定冒这个险。我想艾希礼会从你心中慢慢消失的。但，”他耸了耸肩，“我用尽了所有我知道的办法，但都毫无结果，而我依然那么爱你，思嘉。如果我有这个机会，我就会像一个男人爱一个女人那样竭尽所能，亲切而温柔地爱着你。但我不能让你知道，因为你知道了便会轻看我，会用我的爱来对付我。而且，一直……艾希礼一直都在那里。这逼得我快发疯了。我不能每天晚上和你面对面坐着吃饭，因为知道你心里希望坐在我位置上的是艾希礼。同样，在晚上我也无法抱着你睡觉，因为我知道……算了，没什么意义了。现在我在想，为什么要自讨苦吃呢。这样一来，我就只好到贝尔那儿去了。在那里可以得到某种低贱的慰藉，因为总归是跟一个女人在一起，而她又那样死心塌地爱着我，尊敬我，把我当做一位高贵的绅士……尽管她只是个没有文化的妓女，可她大大满足了我的虚荣心。而你却从不会安慰人，亲爱的。”

"哦，瑞德……"思嘉一听到贝尔的名字就恼怒了，忍不住插嘴，但瑞德摆摆手制止了她，自己继续说。

"然后，那天晚上，我把你抱上楼的时候……我想……我希望……我多么希望，但我害怕第二天早晨不敢面对你，害怕其实只是我自己弄错了，你并不爱我。我十分担心你会笑话我，就跑到外面，喝醉了。我回来的时候，浑身都在颤抖，但那时如果你出来迎接一下，哪怕给我一点表示，我想我是会去吻你的脚的，但你没有。"

"哦，但是，瑞德，我那时确实是需要你的，但你却那么别扭！我真需要你！我想……是的，当我第一次知道自己爱你的时候，这就是自然而然的事啊。至于艾希礼——从那以后我就再也不在意、不牵挂他了。可你真的很别扭，所以我……"

"哦，好了，"瑞德说，"看来我们的看法是完全相反的，不是吗？不过现在已经不重要了。我只想告诉你，免得你胡思乱想。你生病的那次，我站在你的房门口，希望你可以叫我，但你没有，这倒完全是我的错了，我觉得自己真像个傻瓜，但还好，现在一切都结束了。"

他停了停，眼神越过她，看着远方，就像艾希礼时常做的那样，仿佛远处有他看不见的东西。而她只是望着他那忧郁沉默的脸，默不作声。

"不过，那时，邦妮还在，我觉得事情毕竟还是有希望的。我喜欢把邦妮当作你，好像你又成了那个没有受过战争和贫困折磨的小姑娘。她很像你，任性，勇敢，快乐，对什么都兴致盎然的样子，我宠爱她，娇惯她——就像我想宠你的那样。但她跟你有一点不同——她爱我，所以我满怀欣慰地把你不稀罕的爱都拿来给她……现在她走了，把我们的一切都带走了。"

思嘉突然很难过，难过得连她自己的悲伤，和因不明白他这席话的用意而产生的恐惧全都忘了。这是她生平第一次为别人感到难过，而不是轻视这个人，因为这是她第一次尝试着去理解别人。她能够看懂他的精明狡诈，这和她自己很像，还有他那因为生怕碰壁而不肯承认自己的爱的一种顽固的自尊心。

“哦，亲爱的，”她边说边走向前去。此刻，她多么希望他能伸出双臂，把她拉过去抱在膝上。“亲爱的，真的对不起，我一定会加倍爱你的！我们会很幸福的，因为我们已经彼此了解，而且，瑞德……看着我，瑞德！我们一定还会有其他孩子的……不像邦妮，而是……

“不必了，谢谢。”瑞德说着，像是拒绝一片面包一般。

A man is called selfish, not pursuing his own good, but neglecting his neighbour's.

——Richard Whately

追求自身的利益，不是自私；只有忽视他人的利益，才是自私。

——美国牧师　惠特利

实战提升
Practising & Exercise

作者介绍

玛格丽特·米切尔（1900–1949）出生于美国佐治亚州亚特兰大市的一个律师家庭。米切尔一生只发表了《飘》这一部长篇巨著。《飘》从1926年开始创作，历经十年终在1936年出版。该书在1937年获普利策奖；1938年拍成电影《乱世佳人》又获奥斯卡奖，电影和小说都成为经典作品，并传遍全球。1949年8月11日，玛格丽特·米切尔死于车祸。

单词注解

harsh [hɑːʃ] *adj.* 粗糙的；刺耳的

flippancy ['flipənsi] *n.* 轻率，无礼

calmness ['kaːmnis] *n.* 平静；安宁

untimely [ʌn'taimli] *adj.* 过早的；不适时的；

illiterate [i'litərit] *adj.* 未受教育的

nasty ['næsti] *adj.* 龌龊的；卑鄙的，恶意的

contemptuous [kən'temptjuəs] *adj.* 轻蔑的；藐视的

名句大搜索

然而所有的这些话，只有他爱她这一点是对她有意义的。

我是唯一一个在你相识的人中，既了解你的底细还可以爱你的人。

“不必了，谢谢。”瑞德说着，像是拒绝一片面包一般。

Romeo and Juliet
罗密欧与朱丽叶

[英] 威廉·莎士比亚 (William Shakespeare)

凯普莱特和蒙太古是一座城市的两大家族，这两大家族有宿仇，甚至连仆人一碰面也会剑拔弩张。然而，这一切并不能阻挡罗密欧与朱丽叶的爱情狂潮。他们在劳伦斯神父的见证下，私结连理。但是，由于罗密欧误杀泰鲍，被逐出城外。而朱丽叶也被迫嫁人，最后，在神父的帮助下得以搪塞。但罗密欧一时万念俱灰，喝毒自尽，随后朱丽叶也幸福地相随而去。

Romeo: *He jests at scars that never felt a wound.*

(Juliet appears above at a window.)

But, soft! what light through yonder window breaks?
It is the east, and Juliet is the sun!
Arise, fair sun, and kill the envious moon,
Who is already sick and pale with **grief**,
That thou her maid art far more fair than she.
Be not her maid, since she is envious;
Her vestal livery is but sick and green,
And none but fools do wear it; cast it off.
It is my lady; O, it is my love. O, that she knew she were!
She speaks, yet she says nothing: what of that?
Her eye discourses, I will answer it.
I am too bold,'tis not to me she speaks.
Two of the fairest stars in all the heaven,
Having some business, do entreat her eyes
To twinkle in their spheres till they return.
What if her eyes were there, they in her head?
The brightness of her cheek would shame those stars,
As daylight doth a lamp; her eyes in heaven
Would through the airy **region** stream so bright
That birds would sing and think it were not night.
See, how she leans her cheek upon her hand! O, that
I were a glove upon that hand,
That I might touch that cheek!

Juliet: Ah me!

Romeo: She speaks!
O, speak again, bright angel! for thou art
As glorious to this night, being o'er my head

As is a winged messenger of heaven. Unto the white–upturned wondering eyes
Of mortals that fall back to gaze on him. When he bestrides the lazy–pacing clouds
And sails upon the bosom of the air.

Juliet: O Romeo, Romeo! wherefore art thou Romeo?
Deny thy father and refuse thy name ;
Or, if thou wilt not, be but sworn my love,
And I'll no longer be a Capulet.

Romeo: (Aside.) Shall I hear more, or shall I speak at this?

Juliet: Tis but thy name that is my enemy ;
Thou art thyself, though not a Montague.
What's Montague? It is nor hand, nor foot,
Nor arm, nor face, nor any other part
Belonging to a man. O, be some other name!
What's in a name? That which we call a rose
By any other name would smell as sweet ;
So Romeo would, were he not Romeo call'd,
Retain that dear perfection which he owes
Without that title. Romeo, doff thy name,
And for that name, which is no part of thee
Take all myself.

Romeo: I take thee at thy word.
Call me but love, and I'll be new baptiz'd ;
Henceforth I never will be Romeo.

Juliet: What man art thou that thus bescreen'd in night
So stumblest on my **counsel**?

Romeo: By a name
I know not how to tell thee who I am:

My name, dear saint, is hateful to myself,
Because it is an enemy to thee.
Had I it written, I would tear the word.

Juliet: My ears have yet not drunk a hundred words
Of that tongue's utterance, yet I know the sound ;
Art thou not Romeo, and a Montague?

Romeo: Neither, fair maid, if either thee dislike.

Juliet: How cam'st thou hither, tell me, and wherefore?
The orchard walls are high and hard to climb,
And the place death, considering who thou art,
If any of my kinsmen find thee here.

Romeo: With love's light wings did I o'erperch these walls ;
For stony limits cannot hold love out. And what love can do, that dares love attempt ;
Therefore thy kinsmen are no stop to me.

Juliet: If they do see thee, they will murder thee.

Romeo: Alack, there lies more peril in thine eye
Than twenty of their swords! look thou but sweet,
And I am **proof** against their enmity.

Juliet: I would not for the world they saw thee here.

Romeo: I have night's cloak to hide me from their sight ;
And, but thou love me, let them find me here.
My life were better ended by their hate,
an death prorogued, wanting of thy love.

罗密欧：没有受过伤的人才会嘲笑别人身上的伤痕。

(朱丽叶的身影出现在窗口)

轻声！那边窗子里亮起来的是什么光？

那就是东方，朱丽叶便是那朝阳！

起来吧，美丽的太阳！赶走那嫉妒的月亮。

它的侍女比它美丽，它因此气得面色惨白。

既然它这样对你，你何苦还要忠于它？

脱下它赏给你的那些惨绿色的道服吧。

那是做给愚人的衣服。

那是我的意中人，啊！那是我的爱！

啊，但愿她知道我在爱着她！

她欲言又止，她要说什么？

她的眼睛透露了她的心事。让我来回答她吧。

不，我太鲁莽了，她并不是在跟我说话。

天空中有两颗最灿烂的星星。

因为有事离开了，

恳求让她的眼睛代替它们在天空中闪耀，直到归来之时。

如果她的双眼真挂在天上，而把星星变成了她的眼睛，

那会是怎样呢？

她脸庞的光辉，将使那些星星黯然失色，

如同白昼掩盖了灯光一般。

在天庭中，她的眼睛将大放光芒，

让鸟儿误认为黑夜已经过去，而开始歌唱。

看，她用纤手托起自己的脸，真是太美了！
啊，我真愿是那纤手上的一只手套，
好一亲芳泽。
朱丽叶：唉。
罗密欧：她说话了！
啊，说下去吧，光明的天使！
我在黑夜中仰望你，像尘世的凡人一样，惊呆了，瞻仰着长着翅膀的天使，驾着白云缓缓地滑行，划破了天际。
朱丽叶：噢，罗密欧，罗密欧！你为什么偏偏叫罗密欧呢？
否认你的父亲，抛弃你的名字吧，
如果你不愿意，只要你发誓爱我，
我就不再是凯普莱特了。

罗密欧：（自语）我是继续听下去，还是现在就和她说话？

朱丽叶：只有你的名字是我的仇敌。
你即使不姓蒙太古，你仍然还是你。
名字是什么？它不是手臂不是脚，
不是胳膊也不是脸，更不是身体的其他任何部分。
啊，换个名字吧！
名字算什么？人们叫做玫瑰的那种花，
换个名字也同样芬芳！
罗密欧也一样，如果换个名字，
他那种可爱的完美，也不会有丝毫的改变。
罗密欧啊，改掉你的名字吧，
请接受我的一切来补偿你那空名。

罗密欧：那么我便听你的话。

只要你肯做我的情人，我便立刻去重新受洗，

从此以后不再叫罗密欧了。

朱丽叶：你是谁，竟敢在黑夜里躲躲闪闪偷听人家讲话？

罗密欧：无法告诉你，我的名字。亲爱的圣女，我自己都痛恨我的名字，因为它是你的仇敌。如果我把它写在纸上，一定把它撕个粉碎。

朱丽叶：虽然你没有多说话，可是我已分辨出了你的声音，你不是罗密欧吗，一个蒙太古家的人？

罗密欧：不是，美人，如果你不喜欢。

朱丽叶：你是怎么进来的，告诉我，从哪里来的？

这花园的墙又高又难爬，如果被我的家人发现你在这儿，他们决不会让你活命的。

罗密欧：我乘着爱的轻翼飞过高墙，因为土石的界限决不能禁阻爱情。凡是爱情的力量所能做到的，它都可以做到，所以你的家人绝不是我的阻碍。

朱丽叶：如果他们看见你，会杀了你的。

罗密欧：哦，你的眼神比他们的 20 把利剑还要厉害！只要你满怀柔情地望着我，他们就不能伤害到我。

朱丽叶：我不愿意让他们看见你在这里。

罗密欧：浓浓的夜色把我包围在这里，只要你爱我，就让他们发现我在这儿吧。与其在爱你的痛苦中活命，还不如死在他们仇恨的刀剑下。

作者介绍

威廉·莎士比亚（1564–1616）英国文艺复兴时期伟大的剧作家、诗人。公元 1564 年 4 月 23 日生于英格兰沃里克郡斯特拉福镇，代表作有四大悲剧《哈姆雷特》、《奥赛罗》、《李尔王》和《麦克白》。四大喜剧《第十二夜》、《仲夏夜之梦》、《威尼斯商人》、《无事生非》和历史剧《亨利四世》、《亨利六世》、《理查二世》等。他还写过 154 首十四行诗，三四首长诗。他是“英国戏剧之父”，本·琼斯称他为“时代的灵魂”，马克思称他为“人类最伟大的天才之一”。被称为“人类文学奥林匹斯山上的宙斯”。

单词注解

grief [gri:f] *n.* 悲痛，悲伤

region ['ri:dʒən] *n.* 地区，地带；行政区域

counsel ['kaunsəl] *n.* 商议，审议

proof [pru:f] *n.* 证据；物证

名句大搜索

没有受过伤的人才会嘲笑别人身上的伤痕。

啊，我真愿是那纤手上的一只手套，好一亲芳泽。

与其在爱你的痛苦中活命，还不如死在他们仇恨的刀剑下。

Letter from an Unknown Woman

一个陌生女人的来信

[奥地利] 斯蒂芬·茨威格 (Stephan Iweig)

《一个陌生女人的来信》是一个对爱情忠贞不贰的痴情少女的绝笔。一个十三岁的少女喜欢上了她的邻居——一个青年作家，而她由于母亲的再婚不得不离开这里。五年后她重返维也纳，每天到他窗下等候，一心只想委身于他。直到他俩的爱情结晶得病夭折，她自己也身患重病即将辞世，才写下这封没有具名的长信。

You took me in your arms. Again I stayed with you for the whole of one **glorious** night. But even then you did not recognise me. While I thrilled to your caresses, it was plain to me that your passion knew no difference between a loving mistress and a meretrix, that your spendthrift affections were wholly concentrated in their own expression. To me, the stranger picked up at a dancing-hall, you were at once affectionate and courteous. You would not treat me lightly, and yet you were full of an enthralling ardour. Dizzy with the old happiness, I was again aware of the two-sidedness of your nature, of that strange mingling of **intellectual** passion with sensual, which had already enslaved me to you in my childhood. In no other man have I ever known such complete surrender to the sweetness of the moment. No other has for the time being given himself so utterly as did you who, when the hour was past, were to relapse into an interminable and almost inhuman forgetfulness. But I, too, forgot myself. Who was I, lying in the darkness beside you? Was I the impassioned child of former days ; was I the mother of your son ; was I a stranger? Everything in this wonderful night was at one and the same time entrancingly familiar and entrancingly new. I prayed that the joy might last forever.

But morning came. It was late when we rose, and you asked me to stay to breakfast. Over the tea, which an unseen hand had discreetly served in the dining-room, we talked quietly. As of old, you displayed a cordial frankness ; and, as of old, there were no tactless questions, there was no curiosity about myself. You did not ask my name, nor where I lived. To you I was, as before, a **casual** adventure, a nameless woman, an ardent hour which leaves no trace when it is over. You told me that you were about to start on a long journey, that you were going to spend two or three months in Northern Africa. The words broke in upon my happiness like a knell: "Past, past, past and forgotten!" I longed to throw myself at your feet, crying, "Take me with you, that you may at length came to know me, at length after all these years!" But I was timid,cowardly,slavish,weak. All I could say was,"What a pity." You looked at me with a smile, "Are you really sorry?"

For a moment I was as if frenzied. I stood up and looked at you fixedly. Then I said, "The man I love has always gone on a journey." I looked you straight in the eyes. "Now, now," I thought, "now he will recognise me!" You only smiled, and said consolingly, "One comes back after a time." I answered, "Yes, one comes back, but one has forgotten by then."

I must have spoken with strong feeling, for my tone moved you. You, too, rose, and looked at me wonderingly and tenderly. You put your hands on my shoulders, "Good things are not forgotten, and I shall not forget you." Your eyes studied me attentively, as if you wished to form an enduring image of me in your mind. When I felt this penetrating glance, this exploration of my whole being, I could not but fancy that the spell of your blindness would at last be broken. "He will recognise me! He will recognise me!" My soul trembled with expectation.

But you did not recognise me. No, you did not recognise me. Never had I been more of a stranger to you than I was at that moment, for had it been otherwise you could not possibly have done what you did a few minutes later. You had kissed me again, had kissed me **passionately**. My hair had been ruffled, and I had to tidy it once more. Standing at the glass, I saw in it — and as I saw, I was overcome with shame and horror — that you were surreptitiously slipping a couple of banknotes into my muff. I could hardly refrain from crying out ; I could hardly refrain from slapping your face. You were paying me for the night I had spent with you, me who had loved you since childhood, me the mother of your son. To you I was only a prostitute picked up at a dancing-hall. It was not enough that you should forget me ; you had to pay me, and to **debase** me by doing so.

I hastily gathered up my belongings, that I might escape as quickly as possible ; the pain was too great. I looked round for my hat. There it was, on the writing-table, beside the vase with the white roses, my roses. I had an irresistible desire to make a last effort to awaken your memory. "Will you give me one of your white roses?" "Of course," you answered, lifting them all out of the vase. "But perhaps they were given you by a woman, a woman who loves you?" "Maybe," you replied, "I don't know. They were a present, but I don't know who sent them ; that's why I'm so fond of them." I looked at you intently: "Perhaps they were sent you by a woman whom you have forgotten!" You were surprised. I looked at you yet more intently. "Recognise me, only recognise me at last!" was the clamour of my eyes. *But your smile, though cordial, had no recognition in it.* You kissed me yet again, but you did not recognise me.

I hurried away, for my eyes were filling with tears, and I did not want you to see. In the entry, as I **precipitated** myself from the room, I almost cannoned into John, your servant. Embarrassed but zealous, he got out of my way, and opened the front door for me. Then, in this fugitive instant, as I looked at him through my tears, a light suddenly flooded the old man's face. In this fugitive instant, I tell you, he recognised me, the man who had never seen me since my childhood. I was so grateful, that I could have kneeled before him and kissed his hands. I tore from my muff the banknotes with which you had scourged me, and thrust them upon him. He glanced at me in alarm — *for in this instant I think he understood more of me than you have understood in your whole life.* Everyone, everyone, has been eager to spoil me ; everyone has loaded me with kindness. But you, only you, forgot me. You, only you, never recognised me.

你把我搂在怀里。我又在你那儿过了一个销魂之夜。可是在我赤身露体的时候，你仍没认出我来。我幸福地接受你那娴熟的温情和爱抚，我发现，你的激情对情人和对妓女都是一样的，没有区别。你恣意放纵自己的情欲，不加节制，不假思索地挥霍你的元气。你对我这个从交际场里带回来的女人是那么的温柔，那么优雅亲切而充满敬意；同时，你在享受女人方面又是如此的激情四溢；我陶醉在过去的幸福之中，又一次感觉到你本性上那独特的两重性，肉欲的沸腾中含着智慧与精神的激情，而这激情在当年就已使我这个小姑娘成了你的奴隶，对你百依百顺。我从来没有见过一个男人在温情爱抚之际这样贪图享受片刻的欢愉，这样纵情，将自己的内心深处展露无遗——而事后，一切都似如烟往事般散去了，全都飘到了遗忘的角落，忘得那么无影、那么彻底，无情得令人心痛。可在当时我也忘乎所以了：黑暗中躺在你身旁的这个我究竟是谁啊？是从前那个急切而炽烈的小姑娘吗？是你孩子的母亲或只是一个陌生的女人？啊，在这个激情之夜，一切是如此的亲切，如此的熟悉，而又是如此异乎寻常的新鲜。我祷告上苍，但愿这一夜能永远延续下去。

可惜黎明终于还是到来了，我们起得很晚，你请我与你共进早餐。不知道是哪位侍者早已谨慎地摆好了餐室里的茶点，我们一起喝着茶，闲聊。你又用你那诚挚坦率、亲呢和善的态度跟我说话，绝不会提任何不适宜的问题，也绝不探问关于我个人的任何情况。你没有问我姓谁名谁，也没有问我家住何处：对你来说，我不过只是又一次艳遇罢了，一个无名的女人，一段热情的燃烧，最后在遗忘的烟雾中消失得无影无踪。你告诉我说，你现在又要出远门，到北非呆两三个月；我在幸福之中又战栗起来，因为我的耳边又轰轰地响起这样的声音：完了，完了，他忘记了！我恨不得扑倒在你的脚下，大喊道："带我一起走吧，这样你最终会认出我来的，过了这么多年，你终于会认出我是谁！"可我在你面前是如此羞怯、胆小，奴性十足，性格十分懦弱。我只能说一句："多遗憾啊！"你微笑地望着我说："你真的觉得遗憾吗？"

此时一股突发的力量怂恿了我。我站起身来，久久地、聚精会神地盯着你看。然后我说道："我曾爱的那个男人也跟你一样，总是去旅行。"我凝视着你。"现在，现在他就要认出我来了！"可是你微笑着，安慰我说："他会回来的。""是的，"我回答道，"会回来的，可是回来就什么都忘了。"

我说话的腔调一定有一些特殊，一定有些激烈的东西蕴藏其中。因为你也站了起来，盯着我，那神情不胜惊讶，但又满怀关切。你抓住我的双肩，说道："美好的东西是不会被遗忘的，我永远不会忘记你。”说着，你的目光直穿入我的内心深处，仿佛是想把我的样子牢牢地印在脑海中似的。我感到这道目光一直穿透我的身体，在里面探索、感觉、吮吸着我整个生命，这时我相信，盲人重见光明。他就要认出我来了，他就要认出我来了！这个念头撼动了我的整个灵魂。

可是，你没有认出我来。没有，你根本没有认出我来。对你来说，我从来也没有像此刻这么陌生，要不然——你绝不会做出几分钟之后做的事情。你吻了我，又一次热情的狂吻。头发都给弄乱了，我只好再梳理一下，我刚好站在镜子前面，从镜子里我看到——我简直又惊讶又羞愧，几乎要跌倒在地上——我看到你正在非常小心地将几张大钞票塞进我的暖手筒。此时此刻，在这种境况下，我怎么会没有惊叫起来呢，怎么会没有扇你一个耳光呢！我从小就爱你，并且是你儿子的母亲，可你却为我们的这一夜付钱！对你来说，我只不过是交际场上的一个妓女，仅此而已。你竟然付钱给我！被你遗忘还不够，居然还受到这样的侮辱。

我急忙收拾好东西，我要走，马上离开。我的心都伤透了。我抓起搁在书桌上的帽子，它旁边就是那只插着白玫瑰、插着我的玫瑰的花瓶。突然我心里又产生一个强烈而无法抗拒的愿望，我想再次尝试来唤醒你的记忆：“你愿意送我一朵你的白玫瑰吗？”“非常乐意。”你说着马上就抽出一朵。“可这些花也许是一个女人、一个爱你的女人送给你的吧？”我说道。“也许吧，”你说，“我也不知道，是别人送我的，我不清楚是谁送的；正因为如此我才这么喜欢这些花儿。”我盯着你看。“没准儿也是一个被你遗忘的女人送来的！”当时你脸上露出一副惊愕的神情。我仍目不转睛地盯着你：“认出我来，快认出我来吧！”我的目光在呐喊着。可是你的眼睛微笑着，亲切但却一无所知。你又吻了我一下，可是你仍旧没认出我来。

我疾步走向门口，因为我的眼泪马上就要夺眶而出，可我不能让你看见。我急忙冲了出去，很急。在前屋我几乎和你的仆人约翰撞了个满怀。他胆怯地，连忙躲到一边，一把拉开了走廊门，让我出去。就在这一秒钟里，你听见了吗？就在我正噙着眼泪与这位面容枯槁的老人正面相觑的一刹那，他的眼睛突然一亮，就在这一秒钟，你听见了吗？就在这一瞬间老人认出了我，尽管他从我童年时代起就没再见过我了。他认出了我，我恨不得跪倒在他面前，亲吻他的双手。我只是把你用来打发我的钞票从暖手筒里掏出来，塞到了他的手里。他哆嗦着，惊慌而诧异地看着我——在这一瞬间，他对我的了解比你这一辈子对我的了解还要多。所有的人都娇纵我，宠爱我，大家对我都很好——只有你，只有你把我忘得一干二净，只有你从来没认出我来！

作者介绍

斯蒂芬·茨威格（1881-1942），奥地利著名作家、小说家、传记作家。他善于运用各种体裁，写过诗、小说、戏剧、文论、传记，还从事过文学翻译。他在诗、小说、戏剧和人物传记等写作方面均有过人的造诣，但他的作品中尤以小说和人物传记最为著称。其代表作有小说《最初的经历》、《马来狂人》、《恐惧》、《感觉的混乱》、《人的命运转折点》《一个陌生女人的来信》等；回忆录《昨日的世界》；传记《异端的权利》、《麦哲伦航海纪》、《断头王后》、《人类群星闪耀的时刻》等。

单词注解

glorious ['glɔ:riəs] *adj.* 光荣的，荣耀的；辉煌的

intellectual [ˌinti'lektjuəl] *adj.* 智力的；理智的

casual ['kæʒjuəl] *adj.* 偶然的；随便的

passionately ['pæʃənitli] *adv.* 热情地；激昂地

debase [di'beis] *v.* 降低；贬低

precipitate [pri'sipiteit] *v.* 使突然发生；加速；促使

kindness ['kaindnis] *n.* 仁慈；和蔼；好意

名句大搜索

此时一股突发的力量怂恿了我。

可是你的眼睛微笑着，亲切但却没有任何含义。

他这一瞬间里对我的了解比你这一辈子对我的了解还多。

The Scarlet Letter

红字

[美] 纳撒尼尔·霍桑（Nathaniel Hawthorne）

小说描写女主人公海丝特·白兰跟丈夫从英国移居美国波士顿。中途丈夫被印第安人俘虏。海丝特只身到了美国，被一青年牧师诱骗怀孕。此事，被当地虚伪的清教徒社会视为大逆不道。当局把海丝特抓起来并关入监狱，游街示众，还要终身佩带象征耻辱的红色的 A 字（Adultery：通奸女犯）。海丝特宁愿一人受辱，誓死也不招供。在远离社会，受尽屈辱的处境中，海丝特孤苦顽强地生活着，若干年后，珠儿，海丝特的女儿，长大成人，海丝特一人再回到波士顿，仍带着那个红色的 A 字，用自己的“崇高的道德和助人精神”，把耻辱的红字变成了道德与光荣的象征，直到老死。

The grass-plot before the jail, in Prison Lane, on a certain summer morning, not less than two centuries ago, was occupied by a pretty large number of the inhabitants of Boston; all with their eyes intently fastened on the iron-clamped oaken door. Amongst any other population, or at a later period in the history of New England, the grim rigidity that **petrified** the bearded physiognomies of these good people would have augured some awful business in hand. It could have betokened nothing short of the anticipated execution of some noted culprit on whom the sentence of a legal tribunal had but confirmed the verdict of public sentiment. But, in that early severity of the Puritan character, an inference of this kind could not so indubitably be drawn. It might be, that a sluggish bond-servant, or an undutiful child, whom his parents had given over to the civil authority, was to be corrected at the whipping-post. It might be, that an Antinomian, a Quaker, or other heterodox religionist, was to be scourged out of the town, or an idle and **vagrant** Indian, whom the white man's fire-water had made riotous about the streets, was to be driven with stripes into the shadow of the forest. It might be, too, that a witch, like old Mistress Hibbins, the bitter-tempered widow of the magistrate, was to die upon the gallows. In either case, there was very much the same solemnity of demeanour on the part of the spectators; as befitted a people amongst whom religion and law were almost identical, and in whose character both were so thoroughly interfused, that the mildest and the severest acts of public discipline were alike made venerable and awful. Meagre, indeed, and cold, was the sympathy that a transgressor might look for, from such bystanders, at the **scaffold**. On the other hand, a penalty which, in our days, would infer a degree of mocking infamy and ridicule, might then be invested with almost as stern a dignity as the punishment of death itself.

It was a circumstance to be noted, on the summer morning when our story begins its course, that the women, of whom there were several in the crowd, appeared to take a peculiar interest in whatever penal infliction might be expected to ensue. *The age had not so much refinement, that any sense of impropriety restrained the wearers of petticoat and farthingale from stepping forth into the public ways, and wedging their not unsubstantial persons, if occasion were, into the throng nearest to the scaffold at an execution.* Morally, as well as materially, there was a coarser fibre in those wives and maidens of old English birth and breeding, than in their fair descendants separated from them by a series of six or seven generations; for, throughout that chain of ancestry every **successive** mother has transmitted to her child a fainter bloom, a more delicate and briefer beauty, and a slighter physical frame, if not a character of less force and solidity, than her own. The women who were now standing about the prison-door stood within less than half a century of the period when the man-like Elizabeth had been the not altogether unsuitable representative of the sex. They were her country-women; and the beef and ale of their native land, with a moral diet not a whit more refined, entered largely into their composition. The bright morning sun, therefore, shone on broad shoulders and well-developed busts, and on round and ruddy cheeks, that had ripened in the far-off island, and had hardly yet grown paler or thinner in the atmosphere of New England. There was, moreover, a boldness and rotundity of speech among these **matrons**, as most of them seemed to be, that would startle us at the present day, whether in respect to its purport or its volume of tone.

"Goodwives," said a hard-featured dame of fifty, "I'll tell ye a piece of my mind. It would be greatly for the public behoof, if we women, being of mature age and church-members in good repute, should have the handling of such malefactresses as this Hester Prynne. What think ye, gossips? If the hussy stood up for judgment before us five, that are now here in a knot together, would she come off with such a sentence as the worshipful magistrates have awarded? Marry, I trow not!"

"People say," said another, "that the Reverend Master Dimmesdale, her godly pastor, takes it very **grievously** to heart that such a scandal should have come upon his congregation."

"The magistrates are God-fearing gentlemen, but merciful overmuch — that is a truth," added a third autumnal matron. "*At the very least, they should have put the brand of a hot iron on Hester Prynne's forehead.* Madam Hester would have winced at that, I warrant me. But she — the naughty baggage — little will she care what they put upon the bodice of her gown! *Why, look you, she may cover it with a brooch, or such like heathenish adornment, and so walk the streets as brave as ever!*"

两百多年前一个夏日的上午，波士顿监狱门前的那块草地上万人攒动，众人的眼睛都牢牢地盯着布满铁钉的栎木大门。要是在其他居民区，或者在时间上推迟至新英格兰后来的历史

时期，这些蓄着胡须的男子脸上的严峻表情，一定会被人认为是将要发生某种可怕事端的先兆，很可能预示着一个臭名昭著的罪犯要被押出来接受宣判，尽管当时对人的宣判只是确认一下公众舆论对他的裁决而已。但是在清教徒清规戒律非常严厉的早期，这种推测未免过于武断。也许，受惩罚的是一个偷懒的奴仆；或者是一个不守规矩的顽童，其父母把他交给当局，让他在笞刑柱上受管教。也许，是一位唯信仰论者、一位贵格派的教友，或者其他异端的教徒，他们要被鞭挞出城。也许，是一名游手好闲的印第安人，因为喝了白人的烈酒在大街上胡闹，要挨着鞭子给赶进树林。也完全可能是一个巫婆，就像那个地方官的遗孀西宾斯老太太那样恶毒的老巫婆，要被判处死刑，送上刑台。不管属于哪种情况，围观者总是摆出分毫不爽的庄严姿态；这倒十分符合早期移民的身份，因为他们把宗教和法律视为一体，二者在他们的品性中融二为一，凡涉及公共纪律的条款，不管是最轻微的还是最严重的，都令他们肃然起敬和望而生畏。确实，一个站在刑台上的罪人能从这些旁观者身上谋得的同情是少之又少，冷而又冷的。此外，在我们今天只会引起某种冷嘲热讽的惩罚，在当时却如死刑般被赋予令人望而生畏的威严。

就在我们故事发生的那个夏天的早晨，有一个情况颇值一书：挤在那人群中有好几个妇女，看来她们对即将发生的任何宣判惩处都抱有特殊的兴趣。那年月没有那么多的讲究，这些穿着衬裙和圈着环裙的女人毫不在乎地出入于大庭广众之间，而且只要有可能，还扭动她们那结实的身躯向前挤，挤到最靠近刑台的人群中去，也不会给人什么不成体统的感觉。在英国土生土长的那些妇女和少女，比之相隔六七代之后她们的漂亮后代，无论在体魄上还是在精神上，都具有一种更粗犷的品质，因为在世代繁衍的过程中，每代母亲遗传给她们女儿的，就体质而言，往往要比她们自己纤弱一些，容貌更为娇嫩，身材更为苗条，纵然在性格方面，其坚毅顽强的程度也未必逊色。当时站在狱门附近的妇女，跟那位堪称代表女性的、具有男子气概的伊丽莎白女王相距不足半个世纪。她们是那位女王的同胞乡亲，家乡的牛肉和麦酒，以及丝毫没有经过加工的精神食粮大量地进入她们的躯体滋养助长。因此，灿烂的晨曦所照射的是她们宽厚的肩膀、丰满的胸脯和又圆又红润的双颊——她们都是在遥远的祖国本岛上长大成人的，还没有受到新英格兰环境的熏陶而变得白皙或瘦削些呢！再者，这些妇女，至少是其中的大多数人，说起话来都是粗声粗气，直截了当，要是在今天，无论是她们说话的内容，还是嗓门的大小都会使我们瞠目结舌，叹为观止。

“娘儿们！”一个满脸横肉的50多岁的老女人说，“我要跟你们说说我的想法。要是我们这些上了年纪、在教会里有名声的妇道人家，能把像海丝特·白兰那样的坏女人处置了，倒是给公众办了一件大好事。你们是怎么想的，娘儿们？要是把那个破鞋交给我们眼下站在这儿的五个娘儿们来审判，她会获得像那些可敬的地方长官们给她的判决，而轻易地混过去吗？哼，我才不信呢！”

“听人说，”另一个妇女说：“她的教长、尊敬的丁梅斯代尔牧师，为他自己的教会里发生这样的丑事伤透了心。”

“那些地方长官都是些敬畏上帝的好好先生，心肠太软——那倒是实话。”第三个人老珠黄的婆娘接着说，“最起码，他们该在海丝特·白兰的额头上烙上个印记。我敢说，这个小贱人才会有点畏忌。但是，现在他们在她衣服的胸口上贴个什么东西，她——那个贱货——才不会在乎呢！嗨，你们等着瞧吧，她会别上一枚胸针，或者异教徒爱佩戴的其他什么装饰品，把它遮住，照样招摇过市！”

On earth there is nothing great but man; in the man there is nothing great but mind.

——A. Hamilton

地球上唯一伟大的是人，人身上唯一伟大的是心灵。

——哈密尔顿

实战提升
Practising & Exercise

作者介绍

纳撒尼尔·霍桑（1804–1864）是19世纪美国著名的浪漫主义小说家，出生在美国东部新英格兰地区某镇，是当地居民中一个有名望的家族后代。大学毕业后，除了在海关供职和出任驻英公使之外，一生致力于文学写作，写下了《红字》、《七个尖角阁的房屋》、《福谷传奇》、《玉石雕像》等四部长篇小说，为美国文学的发展做出了杰出的贡献。他称自己的作品是人的“心理罗曼史”，故文学史家常把他列为浪漫主义作家。

单词注解

petrify ['petri,fai] *v.* 使僵化，使丧失活力

vagrant ['veigrənt] *n.* 流浪者；漂泊者

scaffold ['skæfəld] *n.* 断头台；绞刑架

successive [sək'sesiv] *adj.* 连续的，相继的；依次的

matron ['meitrən] *n.* 已婚女子；遗孀

grievously ['gri:vəsli] *adv.* 极其痛苦地；令人悲伤地

heathenish ['hi:ðəniʃ] *adj.* 异教的，非基督教的

名句大搜索

那年月没有那么多的讲究，这些穿着衬裙和圈着环裙的女人毫不在乎地出入于大庭广众之间，而且只要有可能，还扭动她们那结实的身躯向前挤，挤到最靠近刑台的人群中去，也不会给人什么不成体统的感觉。

最起码，他们应该在海丝特·白兰的脑门上烙个记号。

嗨，你们等着瞧吧，她会别上一枚胸针，或者异教徒爱佩戴的其他什么装饰品，把它遮住，照样招摇过市！”

Sons and Lovers
儿子与情人

[英] 戴维·赫伯特·劳伦斯（D.H.Lawrence）

《儿子与情人》是一部带有自传性质的长篇小说。莫尔太太把儿子当作自己理想中的爱人，她照顾他，抚养他，她做的一切，都超出了一位母亲所能做的。她对儿子的这种爱，不是单纯的亲情之爱，更大程度上来说是一种爱情的体现。而保罗，也在心目中把自己的母亲当作了自己的爱人，以至于他觉得，只要他母亲在，他在此生就不可能找到自己的爱人。因为这个爱人就在他身边，那就是他的母亲。

When he was twenty-three years old Paul sent in a landscape to the winter exhibition at Nottingham Castle. Miss Jordan had taken a good deal of interest in him, had invited him to her house, where he met other artists. He was beginning to grow **ambitious**.

One morning the postman came just as he was washing in the scullery. Suddenly he heard a wild noise from his mother. Rushing into the kitchen, he found her standing on the hearthrug wildly waving a letter and crying "Hurrah!" as if she had gone mad. He was shocked and frightened.

"Why, mother!" he exclaimed.

She flew to him, flung her arms round him for a moment, then waved the letter, crying:

"Hurrah, my boy! I knew we should do it!

He was afraid of her — the small, severe woman with greying hair suddenly bursting out in such frenzy. The postman came running back, afraid something had happened. They saw his tipped cap over the short curtains. Mrs. morel rushed to the door.

"His picture's got first prize, Fred," she cried, "and is sold for twenty guineas."

"My word, that's something like!" said the young postman, whom they had known all his life.

"And Major Moreton has bought it!" she cried.

"It looks like meanin'something, that does, Mrs. Morel," said the postman, his blue eyes bright. He was glad to have brought such a lucky letter. Mrs. Morel went indoors and sat down, trembling. *Paul was afraid lest she might have misread the letter, and might be disappointed after all. He scrutinized it once, twice.* Yes, he became convinced it was true. Then he sat down, his heart beating with joy.

"Mother!" he exclaimed.

"Didn't I say we should do it!" she said, pretending she was not crying.

He took the kettle off the fire and mashed the tea.

"You didn't think, mother —" he began tentatively.

"No, my son — not so much — but I expected a good deal."

"But not so much," he said.

"No — no — but I knew we should do it."

And then she recovered her composure, apparently at least. He sat with his shirt turned back, showing his young throat almost like a girl's, and the towel in his hand, his hair sticking up wet.

"Twenty guineas, mother! That's just what you wanted to buy Arthur out. Now you needn't borrow any. It'll just do."

"Indeed, I shan't take it all," she said.

"But why?"

"Because I shan't."

"Well — you have twelve pounds, I'll have nine."

They cavilled about sharing the twenty guineas. She wanted to take only the five pounds she needed. He would not hear of it. So they got over the stress of emotion by **quarreling**.

Morel came home at night from the pit, saying:

"They tell me Paul's got first prize for his picture, and sold it to Lord Henry Bentley for fifty pound."

"Oh, what stories people do tell!" she cried.

"Ha!" he answered. "I said I wor sure it wor a lie. But they said tha'd told Fred hodgkisson."

"As if I would tell him such stuff!"

Ha! assented the miner.

But he was disappointed nevertheless.

"It's true he has got the first prize," said Mrs. Morel.

The miner sat heavily in his chair.

"Has he, beguy!" he exclaimed.

He stared across the room fixedly.

"But as for fifty pounds — such nonsense!" she was silent awhile. "Major Moreton bought it for twenty guineas, that's true."

"Twenty guineas! Tha niver says!" exclaimed Morel.

"Yes, and it was worth it."

"Ay!" he said. "I don't misdoubt it. But twenty guineas for a bit of a paintin' as he knocked off in an hour or two!"

He was silent with conceit of his son. Mrs. Morel sniffed, as if it were nothing.

"And when does he handle th' money?" asked the collier.

"That 1 couldn't tell you When the picture is sent home, I suppose."

There was silence. Morel stared at the sugar-basin instead of eating his dinner His black arm, with the hand all gnarled with work, lay on the table. His wife pretended not to see him rub the back of his hand across his eyes, nor the smear in the coal-dust on his black face.

"Yes, an' that other lad' ud' a done as much if they hadna ha' killed' im," he said quietly.

The thought of William went through Mrs. Morel like a cold blade. It left her feeling she was tired, and wanted rest.

Paul was invited to dinner at Mr Jordan's. Afterwards he said:

"Mother, I want an evening suit."

"Yes, I was afraid you would," she said. She was glad. There was a moment or two of silence "There's that one of William's," she continued, "that I know cost four pounds ten and which he'd only worn three times. "

"Should you like me to wear it, mother?" he asked.

" Yes, I think it would fit you — at least the coat The trousers would want shortening"

He went upstairs and put on the coat and vest Coming down, he looked strange in a flannel collar and a flannel shirt-front, with an evening coat and vest It was rather large.

"The tailor can make it right," she said, smoothing her hand over his shoulder "It's beautiful stuff. I never could find in my heart to let your father wear the trousers, and very glad I am now."

And as she smoothed her hand over the silk collar she thought of her eldest son. But this son was living enough inside the clothes. She passed her hand down his back to feel him. He was alive and hers. The other was dead.

He went out to dinner several times in his evening suit that had been William's. Each time his mother's heart was firm with pride and joy. He was started now. The studs she and the children had bought for William were in his shirt-front ; he wore one of William's dress shirts. But he had an elegant figure. His face was rough, but warm-looking and rather pleasing. He did not look particularly a gentleman, but she thought he looked quite a man.

He told her everything that took place, everything that was said. It was as if she had been there. And he was dying to introduce her to these new friends who had dinner at seven-thirty in the evening.

"Go along with you!" she said. "What do they want to know

me for?"

"They do! " he cried indignantly. "If they want to know me — and they say they do — then they want to know you, because you are quite as clever as I am."

"Go along with you, child!" she laughed.

But she began to spare her hands. They, too, were work-gnarled now. The skin was shiny with so much hot water, the knuckles rather swollen. But she began to be careful to keep them out of soda. She regretted what they had been — so small and **exquisite**. And when Annie insisted on her having more stylish blouses to suit her age, she submitted. She even went so far as to allow a black velvet bow to be placed on her hair. Then she sniffed in her sarcastic manner, and was sure she looked a sight. But she looked a lady, Paul declared, as much as Mrs. Major Moreton, and far, far nicer. The family was coming on. Only Morel remained unchanged, or rather, lapsed slowly.

Paul and his mother now had long discussions about life. Religion was fading into the background. He had shoveled away all the beliefs that would hamper him, had cleared the ground, and come more or less to the bedrock of belief that one should feel inside oneself for right and wrong, and should have the patience to gradually realize one's God. Now life interested him more.

"You know," he said to his mother, "I don't want to belong to the well-to-do middle class. I like my common people best. I belong to the common people."

"But if anyone else said so, my son, wouldn't you be in a tear. You know you consider yourself equal to any gentleman."

"In myself," he answered," not in my class or my education

or my manners. But in myself I am.'

"Very well, then. Then why talk about the common people?"

"Because — the difference between people isn't in their class, but in themselves. Only from the middle classes one gets ideas, and from the common people — life itself, warmth. You feel their hates and loves."

"It's all very well, my boy. But, then, why don't you go and talk to your father's pals?"

"But they're rather different."

Not at all. They're the common people. After all, whom do you mix with now — among the common people? Those that exchange ideas, like the middle classes. The rest don't interest you."

"But — there's the life —"

"I don't believe there's a lot more life from Miriam than you could get from any educated girl — say Miss Moreton? It is you who are snobbish about class."

She frankly wanted him to climb into the middle class, a thing not very difficult, she knew. And she wanted him in the end to marry a lady.

Now she began to combat him in his restless fretting. He still kept up his connexion with Miriam, could neither break free nor go the whole length of engagement. And this indecision seemed to bleed him of his energy. Moreover, his mother suspected him of an unrecognized leaning towards Clara, and, since the latter was a married woman, she wished he would fall in love with one of the girls in a better station of life. But he was stupid, and would refuse to love or even to admire a girl much, just because she was his social **superior**.

"My boy," said his mother to him, "All your cleverness,

your breaking away from old things, and taking life in your own hands, doesn't seem to bring you much happiness."

"What is happiness! " he cried. "It's nothing to me! How am I to be happy?"

The plump question disturbed her.

"That's for you to judge, my lad. But if you could meet some good woman who would make you happy — and you began to think of settling your life — when you have the means — so that you could work without all this fretting — it would be much better for you."

He frowned. His mother caught him on the raw of his wound of Miriam. He pushed the tumbled hair off his forehead, his eyes full of pain and fire.

"you mean easy, mother," he cried. "That's a woman's whole doctrine for life — ease of soul and physical comfort. And I do despise it."

"Oh, do you!" replied his mother. "And do you call yours a divine discontent?"

"Yes. I don't care about its divinity. But damn your happiness! *So long as life's full, it doesn't matter whether it's happy or not. I'm afraid your happiness would bore me.*"

"You never give it a chance," she said. Then suddenly all her passion of grief over him broke out. "But it does matter!" she cried. "And you ought to be happy, you ought to try to be happy, to live to be happy. How could I bear to think your life wouldn't be a happy one!

"Your own's been bad enough, mater, but it hasn't left you so much worse off than the folk who've been happier. I reckon you've done well. And I am the same. Aren't I well enough off?"

"You're not, my son. Battle — battle — and suffer. It's about all you do, as far as I can see."

"But why not, my dear? I tell you it's the best —"

"It isn't. And one ought to be happy, one ought.

By this time Mrs. Morel was trembling violently. Struggles of this kind often took place between her and her son, when she seemed to fight for his very life against his own will to die. He took her in his arms. She was ill and pitiful.

"Never mind, Little," he murmured. "So long as you don't feel life's paltry and a miserable business, the rest doesn't matter, happiness or unhappiness."

She pressed him to her.

"But I want you to be happy," she said **pathetically**.

Eh, my dear — say rather you want me to live.

Mrs. Morel felt as if her heart would break for him. At this rate she knew he would not live. *He had that poignant careless ness about himself, his own suffering, his own life, which is a form of slow suicide.* It almost broke her heart. With all the passion of her strong nature she hated Miriam for having in this subtle way undermined his joy. It did not matter to her that Miriam could not help it. Miriam did it, and she hated her.

保罗 23 岁时送了一幅风景画参加诺丁汉城堡举办的冬季画展。乔登小姐对他非常感兴趣，还邀请他去她家里，在那里他见到了其他的艺术家。他逐渐变得雄心勃勃了。

一天早上，他正在水槽旁洗脸，邮差来了。他突然听到母亲大叫了一声，他飞快地冲进厨房，只见她正站在炉前的地毯上，手里拿着一封信使劲挥舞着大喊“好哇！”就像发疯似的。他被吓住了。

“你怎么了，妈妈？”他喊道。

她朝他飞跑过来，猛地抱住他，紧紧地抱了一会儿，然后挥舞着信大声说：

“好哇，我的孩子！我就知道我们能成功！”

他心里发怵——这个身材矮小、神态严肃、头发斑白的女人怎么会突然这样疯头疯脑。邮差生怕出什么事，又跑了回来。母子俩从短窗帘上看到了他那顶翘着的帽子。莫尔太太就飞奔了过去。

“他的画得了一等奖，弗雷德，”她大声叫着说，“还卖了 20 几尼。”

“我的天，真了不起！”这位年轻的邮差说，他从小就认识他们。

“莫尔顿少校买下了那幅画。”她大声说道。

“看样子是件大好事，确实是这样的，莫尔太太。”邮差说道，他那对蓝眼睛也发亮了。他送来了一份喜报，心里可高兴呢。莫尔太太进屋坐下来，激动得身体直哆嗦。保罗生怕她看错信，到头来落得一场空欢喜。他仔细把这封信看了一遍又一遍。没错，他现在也相信了这一切是真的。这时他才坐下，兴奋不已，心怦怦直跳。

“妈妈！”他欢呼道。

“我以前不就说过我们会成功的吗！”她说着，不想让他看出自己在流泪。

他把水壶从炉子上拿下来，泡了杯茶。

“你没想到过，妈妈——”他试探着说。

“是的，我的儿子——我没想到——不过我对你期望很高。”

“可是你没想到，”他说。

“是的，我没想——真没想到——但我一直相信我们会成功的。”

她终于恢复了平静，至少看上去是这样。他敞开衬衫坐着，露出像女孩一般白皙的脖子，手里拿着毛巾，头发湿淋淋地竖着。

“20 几尼，妈妈！刚好可以把亚瑟赎出来。现在你不必去借钱了。这钱够了。”

“可是，我不会都拿去的，”她说。

“为什么？”

“因为我不应该用。”

“那好——你拿去 12 镑，9 镑我留着。”

为如何分这 20 几尼，他们争论不休。她只想拿 5 镑就够了，可他不听。因此，他们争执了起来，刚才的激动情绪也平息了。

晚上莫尔从矿井下班回来，说：

“他们告诉我，保罗的画拿了一等奖，亨利·本特利爵士还用 50 英镑把它买下了。”

“哟，瞧人家编的故事多离奇！”她大声说。

“哈！”他答道，“我就说他们一定在撒谎。可他们说那是你告诉弗雷德·霍奇金森的。”

“真像我会告诉他这番话似的！”

“哈！”这位煤矿工人附和着。

不过他还是有点失望。

“他得了一等奖没错，”莫尔太太说。

莫尔一屁股坐在椅子上。

“是吗？好小子！”他失声惊叫道。

他目不转睛地盯着他对面的墙壁。

“但那 50 英镑——纯属谣言！”她停了一下，“其实是莫尔顿少校用 20 几尼买了它。”

“20 几尼，真有那么多！”莫尔大声叫道。

“是的，它值这么多钱。”

“哎！”他说，“我就是不信，人们竟花了 20 几尼买他用一两个小时画出的小玩意儿！”

他为儿子暗暗感到自豪。莫尔太太若无其事地哼了一声。

“他什么时候能拿到钱？”矿工问。

“那我可说不上。我想，要在画送到以后吧。”

大家都沉默着。莫尔没在吃饭，两眼盯着糖罐看。他那黝黑的胳膊搁放在桌子上，那双手因劳动而粗糙不堪。他用手背擦了一下眼睛，在黑黑的脸上留下了一抹煤灰，他妻子假装没看见。

“是的，要是他们没把老大整死，他也能赚这么多，”他嘀咕着。

一想到威廉，莫尔太太心如刀割。这下她才觉得自己累了，要歇歇了。

保罗应邀到乔登家吃晚饭。于是保罗说：

“妈妈，我想要一套晚礼服。”

“好，我想你也该有一套了，”她说着，心里很高兴。他们俩沉默了一会儿。“威廉有一件，”她继续说，“我记得他花了四磅十先令买的，就穿过三次。”

“你想让我穿那件衣服，妈妈？”他问。

“是的，我想你穿着它会合身的——至少上衣肯定合身。裤子还需要改短一点。”

他上楼去穿上晚礼服的上衣和背心。下楼来时，只见他那晚礼服上衣和背心露出法兰绒衬衫的前襟和衣领，样子看起来很怪。衣服太肥了。

“裁缝改一下就好了，”她用手捋捋他肩膀，说“料子很不错。我不舍得让你爸爸穿这裤子，可现在我很高兴你能穿它了。”

她又整了整衣领，想起了她的大儿子。而现在，他的衣服却穿在了这个生龙活虎的儿子身上。她抚摸着她，他还活着，而且是属于她的。而另一个儿子却已经死了。

好几次，保罗晚上出去吃饭都穿着威廉的衣服。每次他妈妈都会很高兴，倍感骄傲。他现在有了新的开始。他衬衫的前襟钉着她和孩子们给威廉买的饰物；衬衫是威廉的。他的体态优雅，他的脸部线条粗犷，但他看上去很热情，挺讨人喜欢的。看上去虽不见得特别像绅士，但她觉得他很有男子汉的气概。

他把所见所闻统统都讲给她听。好像她也在场似的。他非常想在七点半吃晚饭的时候把她介绍给他的新朋友。

“去你的吧！”她说，“他们为什么想认识我？”

“他们想认识你！”他愤愤不平地说，“如果他们想认识我的话——而且他们说过他们想认识你——他们就会想认识你，因为你和我一样聪明能干。”

“去你的吧，傻孩子！”她笑着说道。

不过，她倒爱惜起自己的一双手来了。这双手干了太多家务活，如今也粗糙了。手上的皮肤用热水浸过后就闪闪发亮，关节也肿胀起来。她开始注意不让手浸到苏打水里。从前她的手是那么纤小而细嫩，一想起来就十分惋惜。当安妮坚持让她添一些适合她年龄穿的时髦点的衬衫时，她顺从了。她甚至同意给她在头上扎一个绸制的黑色蝴蝶结。她觉得自己的行为很滑稽，觉得自己看上去怪模怪样的。但保罗却总说她看上去像个贵妇人，可以和莫尔顿少校夫人相媲美，而且是有过之而无不及。全家境况日见好转。只有莫尔和原来一样没有变化，或者更确切地说，在慢慢退步。

保罗和他的母亲近来经常会长时间地谈论人生。宗教渐渐退居次要地位。所有牵制他的思想也被他铲除出去，他清扫场地，多少奠定了这样的信仰基础：人应该用自己的内心来判断是非曲直，应该耐心地逐渐认识自己心中的上帝。现在他对生活更感兴趣了。

“你要知道，”他对他母亲说，“我不想成为生活富足的中产阶级。我还是情愿做普通老百姓。我属于老百姓。”

“可是，如果是别人这样对你说，我的孩子，你听了不会难过吗？你要知道你向来认为自己和绅士没有什么差别。”

“从我本身来说是这样的，”他回答，“但这和我的阶级、我的教育和我的行为举止无关，就我的本身来说，确是平等的。”

“说得不错，可你干吗又要说什么老百姓呢？”

“因为——人的差别不在于阶级，而在于本身。你能从中产阶级那里得到的只是思想，而从普通老百姓那里——获得的是生活本身，还有他们强烈的情感。你感受到他们的爱和恨。”

“对倒是对，我的孩子。可是，那你为什么不去和你父亲的哥们聊聊呢？”

“可他们有些不同。”

“你错了。他们就是普通老百姓。最重要的是，你现在和谁混在一起——是和普通的老百姓？和那些爱交流思想的人才对，比如那些中产阶级。其他的人你是不会感兴趣的。”

“可是——还有生活——”

“我就不相信，米里亚姆的生活会比那些受过教育的小姐——比如莫尔顿小姐的生活要丰富得多。对阶级抱势利观点的人是你。”

坦白地说，她很想让他跻身于中产阶级，她知道，这并不是很难。她希望他最终能娶个名门淑女。

现在她开始跟满心烦恼的他进行斗争。他仍然跟米里亚姆藕断丝连；既不能彻底断掉，也没发展到订婚这一步。这种优柔寡断把他折磨得精疲力竭。而且他母亲怀疑他可能对有夫之妇克莱拉暗中倾心，她希望他能和一位生活条件优越一点的女子谈恋爱。他太傻，竟然因为女孩子社会地位比他高就不愿去爱慕她们，甚至不愿去对她们表达爱慕之情。

“我的孩子，”母亲对他说，“你聪明，你不受旧事物羁绊，而且能掌握自己的未来，这一切看来并没有带给你很多幸福。”

“幸福是什么东西！”他叫道，“它对我来说什么东西都不是！我怎么做才能幸福？”

这句鲁莽的话把她问得心烦意乱。

“这要由你来判断了，我的孩子。但如果你遇到某个好姑娘，她能令你幸福——你开始想安定下来——你有了收入后——

那你就会安安心心地工作，没那么多烦恼——你就会比现在好多了。”

他皱了皱眉头。母亲触到他和米里亚姆关系的痛处。他把额前乱蓬蓬的头发拨开，两眼冒火，十分痛苦。

“你说得容易，妈妈，”他喊道，“那只是女人的全部的生活教条——精神上的安宁和肉体上的舒适。我看不起这些东西。”

“噢，你这么想！”他母亲回答，“你把你的生活教条叫做一种神圣的缺憾？”

“是的，我不关心它是否神圣。让你的幸福见鬼去吧！只要生活充实，幸福不幸福又有什么关系。反而你的幸福会让我厌烦。”

“你从来没去尝试过，”她说。一下子，她对他的悲痛之情全部都爆发出来。“幸福很重要！”她喊道，“而且你应该得到幸福，你应该努力使自己幸福，幸福地去生活。我怎么忍心眼看你过得不幸福！”

“你自己的生活很不幸，妈妈，但你并没有比那些生活得比你幸福的人更糟。我认为你做得很好。我和你一样。我不是也很好吗？”

“不好，我的儿子。搏斗——搏斗——然后受苦。这就是我所看到的你生活的全部。”

“为什么不，亲爱的妈妈？我要告诉你这样最好——”

“不是的。每个人都应该生活幸福，每一个人都应该这样。”

此刻，莫尔太太浑身剧烈地颤抖。她常常和她儿子为这样的问题争论不休，就好像是在力图保全他这条命而竭力打消他只求一死的念头似的。他抱着她。她气色不好，怪可怜的。

“没事的，好妈妈，”他喃喃地说，“只要生活对你来说不是毫无价值，不是贫乏得不值得一提的话，幸福也罢不幸福也罢，都无关紧要。”

她紧紧地抱住他。

“可是我希望你能幸福，”她可怜巴巴地说。

“嗯，亲爱的妈妈——你还不如说你希望我能活着。”

莫尔太太感到自己的一颗心为他操碎了。再这样下去，她知道他可能都不愿再活下去。他已经对他自己，他所遭受的痛苦，他的生命漠不关心，这简直就是一种慢性自杀。这让她的心都碎了。性情刚强的她用她所有情感来痛恨米里亚姆，恨她在一步一步悄无声息地摧残着他的快乐。她不管米里亚姆是不是有意这样做。米里亚姆摧残了他的快乐，因此她痛恨她。

All happy families are like one another; each unhappy family is unhappy in its own way.

——Leo Tolstoy

所有幸福的家庭都是相似的，而不幸的家庭各有各的不幸。

——俄国文学家　托尔斯泰

作者介绍

戴维·赫伯特·劳伦斯（1885–1930），英国著名小说家、散文家，当过会计，小学教师，曾游历意大利、南美、美国、澳洲等地，并在国外居住多年。著名小说有《虹》、《恋爱中的女人》、《查泰莱夫人的情人》、《袋鼠》、《雨蛇》等，著名散文有《意大利的黄昏》、《大海与萨丁岛》、《启示录》等。其散文语言优美流畅、气势宏大、富含智慧和洞察力，堪称世界一流。戴维·赫伯特·劳伦斯是二十世纪杰出的小说家，被称为“英国文学史上最伟大的人物之一”。

单词注解

ambitious [æm'biʃəs] *adj.* 有雄心的；野心勃勃的

exquisite ['ekskwizit] *adj.* 精美的；精致的；制作精良的

superior [sju:'piəriə] *adj.* 较高的，上级的

pathetically [pə'θetikəli] *adv.* 可怜地，可悲地

名句大搜索

保罗生怕她看错信，到头来落得一场空欢喜。他仔细把这封信看了一遍又一遍。

只要生活充实，幸福不幸福又有什么关系。反而你的幸福会让我厌烦。

他已经对他自己，他所遭受的痛苦，他的生命漠不关心，这简直就是一种慢性自杀。

Lady Chatterley's Lover

查泰莱夫人的情人

[英] 戴维·赫伯特·劳伦斯（D.H.Lawrence）

康妮的丈夫克利福德·查泰莱在1917年的大战中身负重伤，被送回英国后腰部以下永远瘫痪了，战后他们回到克利福德的老家拉格比，克利福德继承了爵位，康斯坦丝成了查泰莱男爵夫人。在康斯坦丝的眼里，二十七岁的自己已经老了！她突然开始憎恨克利福德，憎恨他的写作和谈话以及骗人的精神生活。后来梅乐士出现在她的生活中，他们两人越来越融洽，越来越和谐。康斯坦丝终于离开勒格贝去了苏格兰。梅乐士去了乡间，期待再次相聚。

Ours is essentially a tragic age, so we refuse to take it tragically. The cataclysm has happened, we are among the ruins, we start to build up new little habitats, to have new little hopes. It is rather hard work: there is now no smooth road into the future: but we go round, or scramble over the obstacles. We've got to live, no matter how many skies have fallen.

This was more or less Constance Chatterley's position. The war had brought the roof down over her head. And she had realized that one must live and learn.

She married Clifford Chatterley in 1917, when he was home for a month on leave. They had a month's honeymoon. Then he went back to Flanders: to be shipped over to England again six months later, more or less in bits. Constance, his wife, was then twenty-three years old, and he was twenty-nine.

His hold on life was marvellous. He didn't die, and the bits seemed to grow together again. For two years he remained in the doctor's hands. Then he was pronounced a cure, and could return to life again, with the lower half of his body, from the hips down, **paralysed** for ever.

This was in 1920. They returned, Clifford and Constance, to his home, Wragby Hall, the family 'seat'. His father had died, Clifford was now a baronet, Sir Clifford, and Constance was Lady Chatterley.They came to start housekeeping and married life in the rather forlorn home of the Chatterleys on a rather inadequate income. Clifford had a sister, but she had departed. Otherwise there were no near relatives. The elder brother was dead in the war. Crippled for ever, knowing he could never have any children, Clifford came home to the smoky Midlands to keep the Chatterley name alive while he could.

He was not really downcast. He could wheel himself about in a wheeled chair, and he had a bath-chair with a small motor attachment, so he could drive himself slowly round the garden and into the line melancholy park, of which he was really so proud, though he pretended to be **flippant** about it.

Having suffered so much, the capacity for suffering had to some extent left him. He remained strange and bright and cheerful, almost, one might say, chirpy, with his ruddy, healthy-looking face, arid his pale-blue, challenging bright eyes. His shoulders were broad and strong, his hands were very strong. He was expensively dressed, and wore handsome neckties from Bond Street. Yet still in his face one saw the watchful look, the slight vacancy of a cripple.

He had so very nearly lost his life, that what remained was wonderfully precious to him. It was obvious in the **anxious** brightness of his eyes, how proud he was, after the great shock, of being alive. But he had been so much hurt that something inside him had perished, some of his feelings had gone. There was a blank of insentience.

Constance, his wife, was a ruddy, country-looking girl with soft brown hair and sturdy body, and slow movements, full of unusual energy. She had big, wondering eyes, and a soft mild voice, and seemed just to have come from her native village. It was not so at all. Her father was the once well-known R. A., old Sir Malcolm Reid. Her mother had been one of the cultivated Fabians in the palmy, rather pre-Raphaelite days. Between artists and cultured socialists, Constance and her sister Hilda had had what might be called an **aesthetically** unconventional upbringing. They had been taken to Paris and Florence and Rome to breathe in art, and they had been taken also in the other direction, to the Hague and Berlin, to great Socialist conventions, where the speakers spoke in every civilized tongue, and no one was **abashed**. The two girls, therefore, were from an early age not the least haunted by either art or ideal politics. It was their natural atmosphere. They were at once cosmopolitan and provincial, with the cosmopolitan provincialism of art that goes with pure social ideals.

They had been sent to Dresden at the age of fifteen, for music among other things. And they had had a good time mere. They lived freely among the students, they argued with the men over philosophical, sociological and artistic matters, they were just as good as me men themselves: only better, since they were women. And they tramped off to the forests with sturdy youths bearing guitars, twang–twang! They sang the Wandervogel songs, and they were free. Free! That was the great word. Out in the open world, out in the forests of the morning, with lusty and splendid–throated young fellows, free to do as they liked, and—above all—to say what they liked. It was the talk that mattered supremely: the impassioned **interchange** of talk. Love was only a minor accompaniment.

这是一个真正的悲剧时代，而我们正置身其中。但我们不能因此绝望而消极地对待这个时代。近乎毁灭性的打击已成事实，废墟环绕在四周。我们开始重建小小的栖身之地，祈祷新的、小小的愿望。道路上满是荆棘，没有一条可能前进的光明之途，我们在路上蹒跚而行。即便是没有希望，我们仍要坚持活下去。

现实对于康斯坦丝·查泰莱来说，似乎就是这个样子的。战争对于她来说是一个晴天霹雳。她明白，除了坚强地活下去，别无他法。

1917 年，她成为了克利福德·查泰莱的妻子，共度了一个月的蜜月之后，他又返回佛兰德前线，在六个月后他那已近乎散了架的身体被运回了英国。那时，23 岁的康斯坦丝要面对这样的一个丈夫，而她的丈夫也才 29 岁。

克利福德坚持着每一丝生存的希望。经过医生足足两年的治疗，他和身体奇迹般的复合了，随后，被宣布重生的他又可以正常地生活了。但是，胯以下永久地失去了知觉。

1920 年，克利福德和康斯坦丝返回了拉格比庄园，回到家族的生息之地。克利福德继承了已经过世的父亲的爵位，成为克利福德男爵，康斯坦丝成了查泰莱夫人。在日渐败落的查泰莱家族，夫妻二人只能凭着并不丰厚的收入维持他们的生活。查泰莱兄妹三人，姐姐搬出了家，而哥哥已经被战争夺去了性命，家中只剩下克利福德了。残疾的克利福德永久性地失去了生育的能力，他回到这座烟雾笼罩的米德兰庄园，只是为了尽可能地撑起查泰莱家族，让这个姓氏继续延续一段时日。

事实上，他并没有彻底绝望。他可以坐在轮椅上，来去自由。他还有一个有小马达的轮椅，他可以驾驶着开进花园，还有那个他引以为傲的葱翠蓊郁而又悲凉的猎苑。虽然，从表面上看他满不在乎，其实是非常在意的。

一连串的重创，他好似已麻木了痛苦的感受，可他却依然这样奇特、活泼、愉快，那满面红光的脸和炯炯有神的淡蓝色的眼睛，好似一切都没有发生过一样。他的肩膀宽厚，双手厚实，穿着讲究，他只系邦德街买来的名贵领带。但是，他的脸上仍然有一个残废者的呆视状态和有点空虚的样子。

经历了九死一生的磨难，他完全理解了生命的珍贵之处。劫后余生，在他警惕的明亮眸子里满是欣喜，承受这样沉重的打击，使他内心中最私密的情感也已逝去，剩下的只是失措的迷茫。

他的夫人康斯坦丝如一个农村姑娘般富有青春活力，一头黑褐色的柔发，饱满的身体，优雅的举止，永远保持着旺盛的生命力。她的声音轻柔而有质感，一双迷人的美目，犹如刚从乡下殷实人家出来的闺秀。但那是错觉，她父亲是著名的皇家艺术学会的马尔科姆·理德爵士；她母亲在前拉斐尔派风行时代是费边社的一位才女。康斯坦丝和姐姐希尔达在一些艺术家和社会主义学者们组成的圈子中耳濡目染，形成了与传统教育大不一样的美学思维。她们俩曾在巴黎、佛罗伦萨、罗马自由地呼吸着艺术气息，也曾参加过在海牙、柏林举办的社会主义者的大会，在这些大会上，演讲者用各种优雅的方式表达自己的理念，没有一丝刻意造作。因此两个年轻的姑娘，很早就对艺术以及理想主义政治处之坦然。艺术和政治的气息在她俩的思维中并不矛盾。

在康斯坦丝 15 岁那年，她和姐姐为了学习音乐一同去了德国的德累斯顿。那是一段快乐无比的时光。她们愉快地在校园中穿梭，十足地显示着作为女性的优秀，她们与男子们的辩论涉及哲学、社会学和艺术等许多方面的问题，见解独到，更胜于男子。当她们漫步于森林，勇敢的男孩背着吉他，尾随其后。他们畅快地欢唱着，自由自在。自由自在——绝好的形容。清晨的森林是自由的世界，在歌声中做着大家都喜欢的事，无拘无束，无所顾忌地畅谈是最自由的表达。这时，爱情不过是件小小的陪衬品。

Treat other people as you hope they will treat you.

——Aesop

你希望别人如何对待你，你就如何对待别人。

——古希腊寓言家　伊索

作者介绍

戴维·赫伯特·劳伦斯（1885-1930），英国著名小说家、诗人、作为 20 世纪英国最独特和最有争议的作家，被称为“英国文学史上最伟大的人物之一”。他生于诺丁汉一个矿工家庭，21 岁时入诺丁汉大学学习，一生中创作了 40 余部小说、诗歌、游记等作品，《儿子与情人》被认为是其最好的小说。劳伦斯在国内外漂泊 10 多年。他写过诗，但主要写长篇小说，共有十部，最著名的为《虹》、《爱恋中的女人》和《查泰莱夫人的情人》。

单词注解

tragically ['trædʒikəli] *adv.* 悲剧地；悲惨地

paralysed ['pærəlaizd] *adj.* 瘫痪的

flippant ['flipənt] *adj.* 轻率的；不认真的；无礼的

anxious ['æŋkʃəs] *adj.* 焦虑的，挂念的

aesthetically [iːs'θetikli] *adv.* 审美地

abashed [ə'bæʃt] *adj.* 窘的，尴尬的，羞惭的

interchange [ˌintə'tʃeindʒ] *v.* 交换，互换

名句大搜索

这是一个真正的悲剧时代，而我们正置身其中。但我们不能因此绝望而消极地对待这个时代。

一连串的重创，他好似已麻木了痛苦的感受。

经历了九死一生的磨难，他完全理解了生命的珍贵之处。

Pride and Prejudice
傲慢与偏见

[英] 简·奥斯汀（Jane Austen）

小乡绅班纳特有五个待字闺中的千金，班纳特太太整天操心着为女儿物色称心如意的丈夫。新来的邻居彬格莱在一次舞会上，对班纳特家的大女儿简一见钟情，班纳特太太为此欣喜若狂。彬格莱的好友达西对伊丽莎白产生了好感，在另一次舞会上主动请她同舞，却遭到伊丽莎白的拒绝，达西狼狈不堪。经过了一系列的变化后，伊丽莎白对达西的偏见转化成了真诚之爱。一对曾因傲慢和偏见而延搁婚事的有情人终成了眷属。

This was enough to prove that her approbation need not be doubted: and Elizabeth, rejoicing that such an effusion was heard only by herself, soon went away. But before she had been three minutes in her own room, her mother followed her.

"My dearest child," she cried, "I can think of nothing else! Ten thousand a year, and very likely more! Tis as good as a Lord! And a special **licence**. You must and shall be married by a special licence. But my dearest love, tell me what dish Mr. Darcy is particularly fond of, that I may have it tomorrow."

This was a sad omen of what her mother's behaviour to the gentleman himself might be ; and Elizabeth found that, though in the certain possession of his warmest affection, and secure of her relations' consent, there was still something to be wished for. But the morrow passed off much better than she expected ; for Mrs. Bennet luckily stood in such awe of her intended son-in-law that she ventured not to speak to him, unless it was in her power to offer him any attention, or mark her **deference** for his opinion.

Elizabeth had the satisfaction of seeing her father taking pains to get acquainted with him ; and Mr. Bennet soon assured her that he was rising every hour in his esteem.

"I admire all my three sons-in-law highly," said he. "Wickham, perhaps, is my favourite ; but I think I shall like your husband quite as well as Jane's."

Elizabeth's spirits soon rising to playfulness again, she wanted Mr. Darcy to account for his having ever fallen in love with her. "How could you begin?" said she. "I can comprehend your going on **charmingly**, when you had once made a beginning ; but what could set you off in the first place?"

"I cannot fix on the hour, or the spot, or the look, or the words, which laid the foundation. It is too long ago. *I was in the middle before I knew that I had begun*."

"My beauty you had early withstood, and as for my manners — my behaviour to you was at least always bordering on the uncivil, and I never spoke to you without rather wishing to give you pain than not. Now be sincere; did you admire me for my impertinence?"

"For the liveliness of your mind, I did."

"You may as well call it impertinence at once. It was very little less. The fact is, that you were sick of civility, of deference, of officious attention. You were disgusted with the women who were always speaking and looking, and thinking for your **approbation** alone. I roused, and interested you, because I was so unlike them. Had you not been really amiable, you would have hated me for it; but in spite of the pains you took to disguise yourself, your feelings were always noble and just; and in your heart, you thoroughly despised the persons who so assiduously courted you. There — I have saved you the trouble of accounting for it; and really, all things considered, I begin to think it perfectly reasonable. To be sure, you knew no actual good of me — but nobody thinks of that when they fall in love."

"Was there no good in your affectionate behaviour to Jane, while she was ill at Netherfield?"

"Dearest Jane! Who could have done less for her? But make a virtue of it by all means. My good qualities are under your **protection**, and you are to exaggerate them as much as possible; and, in return, it belongs to me to find occasions for teasing and quarrelling with you as often as may be; and I shall begin directly by asking you what made you so unwilling to come to the point at last.What made you so shy of me, when you first called, and afterwards dined here? Why, especially, when you called, did you look as if you did not care about me?"

"Because you were grave and silent, and gave me no encouragement."

"But I was embarrassed."

"And so was I."

"You might have talked to me more when you came to dinner."

"A man who had felt less, might."

"*How unlucky that you should have a reasonable answer to give, and that I should be so reasonable as to admit it!* But I wonder how long you would have gone on, if you had been left to yourself. I wonder when you would have spoken, if I had not asked you! My resolution of thanking you for your kindness to Lydia had certainly great effect. Too much, I am afraid ; for what becomes of the moral, if our comfort springs from a breach of promise? for I ought not to have mentioned the subject. This will never do."

"You need not distress yourself. The moral will be perfectly fair. Lady Catherine's unjustifiable endeavours to separate us were the means of removing all my doubts. I am not indebted for my present happiness to your eager desire of expressing your gratitude. I was not in a humour to wait for any opening of yours. My aunt's intelligence had given me hope, and I was determined at once to know everything."

"Lady Catherine has been of infinite use, which ought to make her happy, for she loves to be of use. But tell me, what did you come down to Netherfield for? Was it merely to ride to Longbourn and be embarrassed? Or had you intended any more serious consequence?"

"*My real purpose was to see you, and to judge, if I could, whether I might ever hope to make you love me.* My **avowed** one, or what I avowed to myself, was to see whether your sister were still partial to Bingley, and if she were, to make the confession to him which I have since made."

"Shall you ever have courage to **announce** to Lady Catherine, what is to befall her?"

"I am more likely to want more time than courage, Elizabeth. But it ought to be done, and if you will give me a sheet of paper, it shall be done directly."

"And if I had not a letter to write myself, I might sit by you and admire the evenness of your writing, as another young lady once did. But I have an aunt, too, who must not be longer neglected."

这番话足以表明她已完全同意了这门婚事；令伊丽莎白欣慰的是，只有她一人听见了母亲那些得意忘形的话，然后她便回到自己的房间里，可不到三分钟，母亲又跟来了。

"我的宝贝，"母亲大声叫道，"我真的什么也不奢求了！每年有一万镑的收入，还可能比这更多！啊，富比王侯啊，而且还有特许结婚证！你必须要用特许结婚证结婚。不过，我的心肝儿，告诉妈妈，达西先生最爱吃什么菜，我明天好准备啊。”

这句话可不是什么好兆头啊，不知道明天母亲要在那位先生面前做出什么样的事来；伊丽莎白心想，现在虽然已经确切地得到了他最热烈的爱，而且家里人也都同意了，但仍然有些美中不足。好在第二天的情形比她想象的要好得多，因为班纳特太太对这位未来的女婿太敬畏了，不敢贸然与他说话，只是偶尔大着胆子向他献点殷勤，表示她如何尊重他的意见。

伊丽莎白见父亲也煞费苦心地和他亲近，心中很是高兴。而且班纳特先生也对她说，他愈来愈器重达西先生了。

“我的三个女婿我都非常欣赏，”父亲说道，“或许威克姆是我最欣赏的一位。不过我想，你的丈夫和简的丈夫我会同样喜欢的。”

这时，伊丽莎白情绪高涨，变得调皮起来，她便要求达西先生讲一讲是怎样爱上她的。她问：“你最开始是怎样想的？我知道你一旦决定了，便会坚持下去；可你最初是怎么爱上我的呢？”

“我也说不清究竟是在什么时间，什么地点，看见了你什么样的神情，或是听到了你什么样的谈吐，让我爱上了你。那都是很久以前的事了。当我意识到我真爱上你的时候，我已经爱得无可救药了。”

“可之前你并没有为我的美丽而倾心啊。至于说到我的举止嘛，我对你从来都是比较粗鲁的；再说，我跟你说话就是存心想让你难受。现在你老实说，你是不是因为我的莽撞无礼才爱上我的？”

“我爱你头脑活跃，思维敏捷。真的。”

“还不如说是无礼呢，而且是相当无礼。事实是你厌倦了彬彬有礼、谦逊恭谨的那一套。你很讨厌那些无论是说话、做事，都只为博得你赞许的女人。我之所以会引起你注意，能够打动你，是因为我跟她们不一样。如果你不是一个真正和蔼可亲的人，你一定会讨厌我的；可尽管你想尽了办法来遮掩自己，但你的真实情感一直都是高尚而公正的。其实，你根本就看不起那些一味向你献媚的人。我都为你解释清楚了，你就轻松多了；总的来说，我觉得你爱上我完全是合情合理的。毫无疑问，你当时并不知道我有些什么实际的优点，不过，凡是坠入情网的人，谁都不会考虑那个问题的。”

“不对，当简在尼日斐花园生病时，你把她照顾得体贴入微，难道那不算是你的优点吗？”

“简是那么讨人喜欢！谁都会好好待她的。你姑且把它当做我的一个优点吧。不过我的所有美德都靠你来夸奖，你爱怎么说就怎么说吧；不过，我会反过来尽量找机会跟你打趣，跟你争辩。我现在就要开始了，听好了：你为什么总是不愿意直截了当、开门见山地表示你喜欢我呢？在你第一次来访时，以及后来的吃饭，为什么总是见到我就觉得害臊呢？尤其是你来拜访的那一次，你为什么要摆出一副对我一点都不感兴趣的样子呢？”

“因为你那时看起来很严肃，而且一句话也不说，我根本没有勇气跟你说话。”

“那时我也觉得难为情呀。”

“我还不是一样啊。”

“那么，你来吃饭的那一次，为什么不跟我多谈谈？”

“要是不那么爱你，话就可以说得多些了。”

“你的解释总是那么合情合理，而我偏偏又这样懂道理，那我就接受你这个解释吧！但我在想，要是当时我不理你，不知你要拖到什么时候；要是我不和你说话，不知你什么时候才肯开口。幸好我拿定了主意，要来感谢你对莉迪亚的帮助，这毫无疑问起了很大的作用。如果说，我们是因为违背了当初的诺言，才获得了目前的慰藉，那我的道德品质是不是有问题啊？我实在不应该提起那件事的，那事本不该提的。”

“你不用自责。你的道德品质一丁点儿问题都没有。凯瑟琳夫人蛮不讲理地想拆散我们，倒是帮了我们的大忙，使我们彻底消除了一切疑虑。别以为我会因为现在的幸福，而对你当初说的那些话表示感激。我本来就不打算等你先开口。我姨妈带来的那个消息给了我希望，于是我决定立刻把事情弄个水落石出。”

“凯瑟琳夫人确实帮了大忙，她自己也应该为此感到高兴，因为她总是喜欢帮人家的忙。不过，请你告诉我，你这次来尼日斐花园究竟是要干什么？难道就只是为了骑着马到浪搏恩来让自己难堪吗？还是打算正儿八经地做件大事呢？”

“我到这儿来的真正目的就是为了看你。如果可能的话，我还想知道，是否有希望让你也爱上我。可我总是自欺欺人地说，到这里来主要是为了看看你姐姐是否对宾利仍然一往情深，要是她还深爱着他的话，我就老老实实地将实情告诉宾利，我就决定把这事的原委向他讲明。”

“那你是否有勇气向凯瑟琳夫人说明这一切呢？”

“我并不是没有勇气，而是没有时间，伊丽莎白。可是这件事是应该要做的；如果你给我一张纸，我马上就做。”

“要不是我自己也有信要写，我一定会像其他小姐一样，坐在你身旁欣赏你那工整的书法。可惜我要给舅妈回信，不能再拖了。”

作者介绍

简·奥斯汀（1775–1817），出生于乡村小镇斯蒂文顿，父亲是当地教区牧师。奥斯汀没有上过正规学校，但接受了很好的家庭教育，主要教材就是父亲的文学藏书。她20岁左右开始写作，共发表了6部长篇小说。《理智与情感》是她的处女作，随后又接连发表了《傲慢与偏见》、《曼斯菲尔德花园》和《爱玛》。简·奥斯汀是世界上为数不多的著名女性作家之一，介于新古典主义和浪漫运动的抒情主义之间的“小幅画家”和“家庭小说”家。她在英国小说的发展史上有承上启下的作用，被誉为地位“可与莎士比亚平起平坐”的作家。

单词注解

licence ['laisəns] *n.* 许可，特许
deference ['defərəns] *n.* 服从；遵从
charmingly ['tʃa:minli] *adv.* 迷人地；愉悦地
approbation [ˌæprə'beiʃən] *n.* 许可，认可，核准
protection [prə'tekʃən] *n.* 保护，防护；警戒
reasonable ['ri:znəbl] *adj.* 通情达理的，讲道理的
avowed [ə'vaʊd] *adj.* 公然宣称的；公开承认的；公然的

名句大搜索

等我意识到我是真爱上你的时候，我已经爱得无可救药了。

你的解释总是那么合情合理，而我偏偏又这样懂道理，那我就接受你这个解释吧！

我到这儿来的真正目的就是为了看你。如果可能的话，我还想知道，是否有希望让你也爱上我。

Wuthering Heights

呼啸山庄

［英］艾米莉·勃朗特（Emily Bronte）

在英格兰北部荒凉的山区里，有座呼啸山庄。主人恩萧收养了一个孤儿，取名希斯克利夫。在后来的相处中，他爱上了主人的女儿凯瑟琳，但身份的悬殊使他们不能在一起。希斯克利夫带着仇恨离家。等他衣锦返乡时，凯瑟琳已经成为画眉山庄的女主人。但最终悔恨离世，留下了女婴凯蒂。报复心很强的希斯克利夫在孩子身上继续着他疯狂的报复。但对凯瑟琳的爱化解了他心头的恨，在饱尝人间的辛酸后愤然离世。

They lifted their eyes together, to **encounter** Mr. Heathcliff: perhaps you have never remarked that their eyes are precisely similar, and they are those of Catherine Earnshaw. The present Catherine has no other likeness to her, except a breadth of forehead, and a certain arch of the nostril that makes her appear rather haughty, whether she will or not. With Hareton the resemblance is carried farther: it is singular at all times, then it was particularly striking ; because his senses were alert, and his mental faculties wakened to unwonted activity. I suppose this resemblance disarmed Mr. Heathcliff: he walked to the hearth in evident agitation ; but it quickly subsided as he looked at the young man: or, I should say, altered its character ; for it was there yet. He took the book from his hand, and glanced at the open page, then returned it without any observation ; merely signing Catherine away: her companion lingered very little behind her, and I was about to depart also, but he bid me sit still.

"It is a poor conclusion, is it not?" he observed, having brooded awhile on the scene he had just witnessed: "an **absurd** termination to my violent exertions? I get levers and mattocks to demolish the two houses, and train myself to be capable of working like Hercules, and when everything is ready and in my power, I find the will to lift a slate off either roof has vanished! My old enemies have not beaten me ; now would be the precise time to revenge myself on their representatives: I could do it ; and none could hinder me. But where is the use? I don't care for striking: I can't take the trouble to raise my hand! That sounds as if I had been labouring the whole time only to exhibit a fine trait of magnanimity. It is far from being the case: I have lost the faculty of enjoying their destruction, and I am too idle to destroy for nothing."

"Nelly, there is a strange change approaching; I'm in its shadow at present. I take so little interest in my daily life that I hardly remember to eat and drink. Those two who have left the room are the only objects which retain a distinct material appearance to me; and that appearance causes me pain, amounting to agony. About her I won't speak; and I don't desire to think; but I earnestly wish she were invisible: her presence invokes only maddening sensations. He moves me differently: and yet if I could do it without seeming insane, I'd never see him again! You'll perhaps think me rather inclined to become so," he added, making an effort to smile, "if I try to describe the thousand forms of past associations and ideas he awakens or embodies. *But you'll not talk of what I tell you; and my mind is so eternally secluded in itself, it is tempting at last to turn it out to another.*"

"*Five minutes ago Hareton seemed a personification of my youth, not a human being*; I felt to him in such a variety of ways, that it would have been impossible to have accosted him rationally. In the first place, his startling likeness to Catherine connected him fearfully with her. That, however, which you may suppose the most potent to arrest my imagination, is actually the least: for what is not connected with her to me? And what does not recall her? I cannot look down to this floor, but her features are shaped in the flags! In every cloud, in every tree — filling the air at night, and caught by glimpses in every object by day—I am surrounded with her image! The most ordinary faces of men and women — my own features–mock me with a resemblance. The entire world is a dreadful collection of memoranda that she did exist, and that I have lost her! Well, Hareton's aspect was the ghost of my immortal love; of my wild **endeavours** to hold my right; my degradation, my pride, my happiness, and my anguish."

"But it is frenzy to repeat these thoughts to you: only it will let you know why, with a **reluctance** to be always alone, his society is no benefit; rather an aggravation of the constant torment I suffer: and it partly contributes to render me regardless how he and his cousin go on together. I can give them no attention any more."

"But what do you mean by a change, Mr. Heathcliff?" I said, alarmed at his manner: though he was neither in danger of losing his senses, nor dying, according to my judgment: he was quite strong and healthy; and, as to his reason, from childhood he had a delight in dwelling on dark things, and entertaining odd fancies. He might have had a monomania on the subject of his departed idol; but on every other point his wits were as sound as mine.

"I shall not know that till it comes," he said; "I'm only half **conscious** of it now."

"You have no feeling of illness, have you?" I asked.

"No, Nelly, I have not," he answered.

"Then you are not afraid of death?" I pursued.

"Afraid? No!" he replied. "I have neither a fear, nor a presentiment, nor a hope of death. Why should I? With my hard constitution and temperate mode of living, and unperilous occupations, I ought to, and probably shall, remain above ground till there is scarcely a black hair on my head. And yet I cannot continue in this condition! I have to remind myself to breathe —

almost to remind my heart to beat! And it is like bending back a stiff spring: it is by compulsion that I do the slightest act not prompted by one thought ; and by compulsion that I notice anything alive or dead, which is not associated with one universal idea. I have a single wish, and my whole being and faculties are yearning to attain it. They have yearned towards it so long, and so unwaveringly, that I'm convinced it will be reached — and soon — because it has devoured my existence: I am swallowed up in the anticipation of its fulfilment. *My confessions have not relieved me ; but they may account for some otherwise unaccountable phases of humour which I show. O, God! It is a long fight ; I wish it were over*!"

He began to pace the room, muttering terrible things to himself, till I was inclined to believe, as he said Joseph did, that conscience had turned his heart to an earthly hell. I wondered greatly how it would end. Though he seldom before had revealed this state of mind, even by looks, it was his habitual mood, I had no doubt: he asserted it himself ; but not a soul, from his general bearing, would have **conjectured** the fact. You did not when you saw him, Mr. Lockwood: and at the period of which I speak, he was just the same as then ; only fonder of continued solitude, and perhaps still moke laconic in company.

他们俩同时抬起眼睛，看到了希斯克利夫先生。你也许从来没有注意过他们的眼睛竟这么相像，都是凯瑟琳•恩肖那样的眼睛。现在的小凯瑟琳除了宽额和翘鼻子外，再没有别的地方像她了，而这个拱形线条不管她内心怎样总使她显得颇为高傲。而哈里顿，就更像他姑姑了，平常已经像得出奇，这时候更像了。因为他的感觉很锐敏，思维也异常活跃。我想这种相貌的相似使希斯克利夫先生心软了。他走到炉边看起来很激动，但是当他望着这对年轻人时，那激动很快就平静下来了，或者，我应该说，是改变了性质，因为那份激动并未消除。他从哈里顿手中拿过那本书，瞅了瞅翻开的那一页，然后把书还给他，一句话也没说，只是挥手让凯瑟琳走开。她的同伴在她走后不久，也就离开了；当我正要走开时，他却要我坐着别动。

"这是一个很糟糕的结局，对不对吗？"他对他刚刚目睹的情况思索了片刻后说，"我那狂暴的努力的可笑下场？我准备好了杠杆铁锄要摧毁这两座房子，把自己锻炼成了大力士，当一切就绪，都在我掌握之中时，却发现连掀掉那两个屋顶上片瓦的劲头都没有了！我往日的仇人没有把我打垮，现在正好是在她们的后代身上报仇的时机，我能做到这一点，没有人能阻挡我。可有什么用呢？我不想打人了。我连拳头都不想举了！好像我苦干了一辈子为的就是到头来表现这点宽宏大量的好风格似的，其实并非如此。我已经丧失了欣赏这种毁灭的能力，我懒得去毫无目的地毁灭什么东西了。"

"耐莉，有一种奇怪的变化要发生了；我眼下正在它的阴影之下。我对日常生活毫无兴趣，甚至都不记得吃喝。刚刚离开这间屋子的那两个人，对我来说，是唯一还保留着清晰具体形象的东西；那形象使我痛苦，极度地痛苦。关于她，我就不想说些什么了；我想都不愿意想；但我真心希望不再见她。她在我面前令人发狂。他给我的感觉就完全不同了；但是我也宁愿永远不再见他，如果我能做到这一点，而不显得是神经错乱了的话。”他又强作笑颜说，“如果我试着跟你描述一下他在我心头唤起的，或是他所体现的，那千百种联想和思绪，也许你会认为我很可能神经错乱了。不过，你不要把我告诉你的说出去。我的想法总是深藏在自己心里，一直这样隐蔽着，不过，到头来还是忍不住要向一个人倾诉。”

“五分钟前，哈里顿似乎是我青春的化身，而不是一个人。我对他有各种不同的感觉，以至于我不能理性地对待他。首先，他和凯瑟琳那么相像，这就把他和她紧紧联系在一起了。或许你会认为这是最能引起我想象的东西，可实际上这是最微不足道的，因为对我来说，有什么东西不是跟她联系在一起的呢？有什么东西不使我想起她来呢？我每次望着地面，她的形貌就出现在地板上！每一朵云，每一棵树——晚上充满在空气里，白天在每一件东西上，我眼光所到之处，全是她的影子！普通的男女，连我自己的相貌——都好像她，都在捉弄我。整个世界就是一个惊人的缩影，证实她确实存在过，而我却失去了她！唉，哈里顿的模样就是我永恒的爱的幽灵；是我为维护自己的权利所作的狂热努力的幽灵，是我的贬损、我的骄傲、我的幸福和我痛苦的幽灵。”

“不过，我这岂不是发疯了。把这些想法说给你听，也只是让你知道为什么我并不想单独一个人，而他的陪伴对我来说却没有任何好处，反而加深了对我的折磨，这也是我对他和他表妹在一起的情况不再加以考虑的部分原因，我不再注意他们了。”

“你说的变化是什么意思，希斯克利夫先生？”我说。我对他的态度感到惊慌，虽然根据我的看法，他既不会发疯，也不会死，他很健康、结实，至于他的神志，他从小就喜欢注意阴暗的东西，抱着古怪的幻想。他在对待他失去偶像这件事上也许有一些偏执，但在其他事情上，他跟我一样，脑子是很清醒的。

“我要等，事到临头了才会知道，”他说，“我现在只是朦朦胧胧地意识到了它。”

“你没有生病的感觉吧，有吗？”我问道。

“没，耐莉，我没有。”他回答道。

“那么你不怕死吗？”我追问道。

“怕？不！”他答道。“我对死既不怕，也没有预感，也不存希望，为什么呢？我体质结实，生活有节制，又不干危险活儿，我应该，也许一定会，长命百岁。可是，我不能继续这样下去了！我得提醒自己要呼吸——几乎得提醒我的心脏要跳动！凡不是由那唯一的思想推动我去干的事，哪怕是举手之劳，都是像扳弯一根硬邦邦的弹簧一样硬逼着自己去干的，凡不是与那无处不在的想法相联系的东西，不论是死的，活的，都是我硬逼着自己去注意的。我只有一个愿望，我的全部生命、全部力量都渴望去达到它。它们对它长期以来这么坚定不移地孜孜以求。我相信会达到它的——而且为期不远了——因为它已经耗尽了我的生命，我期待它的实现，而在期待中我已经被吞没了。我向你道出了我的心事，但并未感到轻松。不过，这也许可以解释我表现出来的某些心情，否则那是无法解释的。啊，上帝呀！这真是一场长期的斗争，但愿它快点结束吧！”

他开始在屋里踱来踱去，嘴里还念叨着一些可怕的东西，到后来我完全相信约瑟夫说的那句话了：他的天良把他的内心世界闹腾成了一座人间地狱。我真不知道会是个什么结局。虽然他极少透露过他的这种思想情况，在外表上根本看不出，我却毫不怀疑这是他经常的心境。这话是他自己说的，但从他的平时的行为举止来看，没有一个人能猜到这一实情。你看到他的时候，洛乌德先生，就没有想到吧。就在这一段时间里，他还是跟往常一样，只是更喜欢一个人待着，有人在一起时，他说的话也比以前更少了。

What makes life dreary is the want of motive.

——George Eliot

没有了目的，生活便郁闷无光。

——艾略特

作者介绍

艾米莉·勃朗特（1818–1848），这位女作家在世界上仅仅度过了30年便默默无闻地离开了人间。艾米莉性格内向，娴静文雅，从童年时代起就酷爱写诗。《呼啸山庄》是她唯一的一部小说。她们三姐妹的三部小说——夏洛蒂的《简·爱》、艾米莉的《呼啸山庄》和小妹妹安妮的《艾格尼斯·格雷》是同一年问世的。除《呼啸山庄》外，艾米莉还创作了193首诗，被认为是英国一位天才的女作家。三人并称勃朗特三姐妹。在十九世纪文坛上焕发异彩。

单词注解

encounter [in'kauntə] *v.* 遭遇；遇到
absurd [əb'səːd] *adj.* 不合理的，荒谬的；可笑的，
distinct [dis'tiŋkt] *adj.* 明显的，清楚的
eternally [i'tɜːnəli] *adv.* 永恒地；常常；不绝地
endeavour [in'devə] *v.* 努力，力图
reluctance [ri'lʌktəns] *n.* 不情愿；勉强
conscious ['kɔnʃəs] *adj.* 神志清醒的，有知觉的
conjecture [kən'dʒektʃə] *n.* 推测，猜测

名句大搜索

不过，你不要把我告诉你的说出去。我的想法总是深藏在自己心里，一直这样隐蔽着，不过，到头来还是忍不住要向一个人倾诉。

五分钟前，哈里顿似乎是我青春的化身，而不是一个人。

不过，这也许可以解释我表现出来的某些心情，否则那是无法解释的。啊，上帝呀！这真是一场长期的斗争，但愿它快点结束吧

I Am Willing That It Is a Torrent
我愿意是激流

［匈牙利］裴多菲（Petöfi Sándor）

《我愿意是激流》是裴多菲献给未婚妻尤丽亚的一首情诗。诗人热情、真挚地向爱人倾诉衷肠，咏唱着对爱情的渴望与坚贞。这首诗运用比喻和对比手法，形象鲜明，寓意深长。

I am willing that it is a torrent,
the river in the mountain,
pass the rock on the rugged mountain path
Only my spouse
It is a small fish,
swim happily in my spray.

I willing **neglect** woods,
two sides in river,
to a burst of blast,
Fight bravely ?
Only my spouse
It is a bird
Dense in mine
Make the nest among the branch Pipe.

I am willing that it is the ruins,
on high and steep mountain and rock,
this ruin mourned in silence does not make me **dejected**?
Only my spouse
It is the blue and green blue and green Chinese ivy,
along my bleak and desolate volume,
climb up by holding on to and rise on intimate terms with each otherly.

I am willing that it is the thatched cottage,
in the deep mountain valley bottom, endure the strike of the trials and hardship to the fullest extent on the top of the thatched cottage?

Only my spouse

It is the lovely flame，in my stove,

flash slowly happily.

I am willing that it is a cloud,

it is the grey breaking the flag,

swing too lazy to feel like floatingly in the vast sky,

Only my spouse

Coral's the setting sun,

draw near me **pale** face and show bright-colored brilliance.

我愿意是激流，

山里的小河，

在崎岖的路上、岩石上经过……

只要我的爱人，

是一条小鱼，

在我的浪花中，

快乐地游来游去。

我愿意是荒林，

在河流的两岸，

对一阵阵狂风，

勇敢地作战……

只要我的爱人，
是一只小鸟，
在我稠密的
树枝间做巢、鸣叫。

我愿意是废墟，
在峻峭的山岩上，
这静默的毁灭
并不使我恼丧……
只要我的爱人，
是青青的常春藤，
沿着我荒凉的额，
亲密地攀援上升。

我愿意是草屋，
在深深的山谷底，
草屋的顶上，
饱受风雨的打击……
只要我的爱人，
是可爱的火焰，
在我的炉子里，
愉快地缓缓闪现。

我愿意是云朵，
是灰色的破旗，
在广漠的空中，

懒懒地飘来飘去，
只要我的爱人，
是珊瑚似的夕阳，
傍着我苍白的脸，
显出鲜艳的辉煌。

Every man is a poet when he is in love.

——Plato

每个恋爱中的人都是诗人。

——古希腊哲学家　柏拉图

实战提升
Practising & Exercise

作者介绍

裴多菲（1823-1849），是匈牙利 19 世纪最伟大的诗人，资产阶级民主主义革命家。他 15 岁开始写诗，题材多取自人民生活，一生共写了 800 多首诗和 8 篇长篇叙事诗，著名长诗有《使徒》、《亚诺什勇士》等。他的诗歌充满革命激情，风格清新，语言通俗，富有民歌味。其作品对匈牙利民族文学发展影响很大。

单词注解

path [pɑːθ] *n.* 小径，小路

neglect [ni'glekt] *v.* 忽视，忽略

dejected [di'jektid] *adj.* 沮丧的，情绪低落的，气馁的

flame [fleim] *n.* 火焰；光辉，光芒

pale [peil] *adj.* 苍白的，灰白的

名句大搜索

我愿意是激流，山里的小河，在崎岖的路上、岩石上经过……

只要我的爱人，是青青的常春藤，沿着我荒凉的额，亲密地攀援上升。

只要我的爱人，是可爱的火焰，在我的炉子里，愉快地缓缓闪现。

Jane Eyre

简·爱

［英］夏洛蒂·勃朗特（Charlotte Bronte）

简父母早亡，自小寄居在舅舅里德家里，舅母在舅舅病逝后，对简百般虐待，还把她关在恐怖的红屋子里，但是简却坚决反抗，于是被送到了条件更为恶劣的劳渥德学校。后来她受聘到桑菲尔德庄园当家庭教师，期间她和男主人罗切斯特摩擦出了爱的火花。简强烈的自尊心迫使她毅然决然地离开了已婚的罗切斯特。继承遗产后的简回到了罗切斯特的身边，而此刻的他在经历了一场大火后眼瞎肢残。后来他们如愿以偿地生活在一起。

"Never," said he, as he ground his teeth, "never was anything at once so frail and so indomitable. A mere reed she feels in my hand!"(And he shook me with the force of his hold.)"I could bend her with my finger and thumb: and what good would it do if I bent, if I uptore, if I crushed her? Consider that eye: consider the **resolute**, wild, free thing looking out of it, defying me, with more than courage — with a stern triumph. Whatever I do with its cage, I cannot get at it — the savage, beautiful creature! If I tear, if I rend the slight prison, my **outrage** will only let the captive loose. Conqueror I might be of the house ; but the inmate would escape to heaven before I could call myself possessor of its clay dwelling-place. And it is you, spirit — with will and energy, and virtue and purity — that I want: not alone your brittle frame. Of yourself you could come with soft flight and **nestle** against my heart, if you would: seized against your will, you will **elude** the grasp like an essence — you will vanish ere I inhale your fragrance. Oh! come, Jane, come!"

As he said this, he released me from his clutch, and only looked at me. The look was far worse to resist than the **frantic** strain: only an idiot, however, would have succumbed now. I had dared and baffled his fury ; I must elude his sorrow: I retired to the door.

"You are going, Jane?"

"I am going, sir."

"You are leaving me?"

"Yes."

"*You will not come? You will not be my comforter, my rescuer?* My deep love, my wild woe, my frantic prayer, are all nothing to you?"

What unutterable pathos was in his voice! How hard it was to reiterate firmly, "I am going."

"Jane!"

"Mr. Rochester!"

"Withdraw, then—I consent; but remember, you leave me here in anguish. Go up to your own room; think over all I have said, and, Jane, cast a glance on my sufferings — think of me."

He turned away; he threw himself on his face on the sofa. "Oh, Jane! my hope—my love— my life!" broke in anguish from his lips. Then came a deep, strong sob.

I had already gained the door; but, reader, I walked back—walked back as determinedly as I had retreated. I knelt down by him; I turned his face from the cushion to me; I kissed his cheek; I smoothed his hair with my hand.

"God bless you, my dear master!" I said, "God keep you from harm and wrong — direct you, solace you — **reward** you well for your past kindness to me."

"Little Jane's love would have been my best reward," he answered; "without it, my heart is broken. But Jane will give me her love: yes— nobly, generously."

Up the blood rushed to his face; forth flashed the fire from his eyes; erect he sprang; he held his arms out; but I evaded the **embrace**, and at once quitted the room.

"Farewell!" was the cry of my heart as I left him. Despair added, "Farewell for ever!"

“从来没有，”他咬牙切齿地说，“从来没有什么东西像这样既纤弱又不屈不挠的。在我看来她只不过像根芦苇！（他边说边用抓住我的手使劲摇我）我可以轻而易举地把这它弄弯，但我即使是把它弄弯了，拨起来，捏碎了，又有什么用呢？看看那对眼睛，看看那里面流露出来的坚决、大胆、什么也不顾的神气，不仅带着勇气，还带着坚定的胜利感对我公然蔑视。这野性难驯的美丽的东西，不管我怎么做，都无法靠拢这个笼子！即使我拆掉、捣毁那纤脆的牢笼，我的暴行也只会放走囚徒。我也许可以征服那房子，但我还来不及称自己是这泥屋的主人，里边的居住者就会飞上天去。而我要的正是你，你的精神——富有意志、能量、德行和纯洁——而不仅仅是你那脆弱的身躯。如果你愿意，你会悄然朝我飞来，偎依在我的怀中。倘若不顾你的意愿硬把你抓住，你就像香气似的从我手中消失——在我还没有闻到你的芬芳时，就消失的无影无踪了。哦，来吧！简，来吧！”

他一边这么说着，一边松开他那紧握的手，只是那样地看着我。这眼神远比发疯时的紧扯更让人难受。然而，现在只有白痴才会屈服。我已面对他的怒火，并把它挫败了。我得避开他的忧愁。我朝门口退去。

“你要走了，简？”

“我要走了，先生。”

“你要离开我了？”

“是的。”

“你不愿意来了？你不愿做我的安慰者，我的拯救者了？——

面对我这深沉的爱，剧烈的痛苦，疯狂的祈求，你都无动于衷吗？”

他的声音中带有一种难以言说的悲哀！而要毅然决然重复说出“我走了”，这句话是多么困难啊！

“简！”

“罗切斯特先生！”

“那么，去吧——我同意——但是记着，你把我一个人撇在痛苦之中。到楼上你的房间再好好想想我说过的话，简，看一看我所承受的痛苦吧——想想我吧。”

他转过身去，一头扎进了沙发里，“哦，简！我的希望——我的爱——我的生命啊！”他痛苦地脱口而出。随后便听到了他那深沉而强烈的哭泣声。

我那时已经走到了门口，可我的读者呀，我又走了回去——就像我刚刚走出时那样坚决。我跪在他身旁，把他的脸从沙发垫里捧起来，并转向我；我吻了吻他的脸颊，理了理他的头发。

“上帝保佑你，我亲爱的主人！”我说，“上帝会保佑你不受伤害，不做错事——他会指引你，安慰你——会好好报答你过去对我的恩情。”

“可简的爱情才是对我最好的酬谢，”他答道，“没有了它，我的心就碎了，不过简一定会把她的爱给我的，会的——会高尚、慷慨地给我的！”

血色一下子泛在他的脸上，眼睛里射出了火一般的光芒。他猛地跳了起来，站直了身子，张开了双臂。但我躲开了他的拥抱，立即跑出了房间。

“别了！”就在我离开他时，我的心在狂喊。绝望又使我加了一句：“永别了！”

实战提升

Practising & Exercise

作者介绍

夏洛蒂·勃朗特（1816–1855），英国十九世纪著名的女作家。《简·爱》是一部具有自传色彩的作品。她的作品包括《简·爱》、《雪莉》、《维莱特》等。

单词注解

resolute ['rezəlju:t] *adj.* 坚决的，坚定的；果敢的；

outrage ['autreidʒ] *n.* 恶行，暴行

nestle ['nesl] *v.* 依偎，贴靠

elude [i'lu:d] *v.* 逃避，躲避；使困惑

frantic ['fræntik] *adj.* 狂暴的，狂乱的

reward [ri'wɔ:d] *n.* 报答；报偿；奖赏；

embrace [im'breis] *v.* 拥抱，包含

名句大搜索

你不愿意来了？你不愿做我的安慰者，我的拯救者了？

他的声音中带有一种难以言说的悲哀！而要毅然决然重复说出“我走了”，这句话是多么困难啊！

“别了，”就在我离开他时，我的心在狂喊。绝望又使我加了一句话“永别了。”

A Rose for Emily

献给爱米丽的玫瑰

[美] 威廉·福克纳（William Faulkner）

故事发生在美国的内战时期，战争给南方人造成了致命的打击。小镇居民沉浸在对辉煌过去的回忆之中，他们迫切需要一座代表传统的“偶像”给他们精神上的支撑和慰藉，于是，她永远成为他们的“纪念碑”和梦想中的“南方淑女”。爱米丽的大院就成了“神龛”，爱米丽小姐既是全镇人的偶像，也是全镇人的玩物。因此，她必须是一个无欲的南方贵族，她必须要为保持自己高贵的身份舍弃超越了阶级的爱情。

So the next day we all said, "She will kill herself"; and we said it would be the best thing. When she had first begun to be seen with Homer Barron, we had said, "She will marry him." Then we said, "She will persuade him yet," because Homer himself had **remarked**—he liked men, and it was known that he drank with the younger men in the Elk's Club—that he was not a marrying man. Later we said, "Poor Emily," behind the jalousies as they passed on Sunday afternoon in the glittering buggy, Miss Emily with her head high and Homer Barron with his hat cocked and a cigar in his teeth, reins and whip in a yellow glove.

Then some of the ladies began to say that it was a disgrace to the town and a bad example to the young people. The men did not want to interfere, but at last the ladies forced the Baptist minister—Miss Emily's people were Episcopal—to call upon her. He would never divulge what happened during that interview, but he refused to go back again. The next Sunday they again drove about the streets, and the following day the minister's wife wrote to Miss Emily's relations in Alabama.

So she had blood-kin under her roof again and we sat back to watch developments. At first nothing happened. Then we were sure that they were to be married. We learned that Miss Emily had been to the jeweler's and ordered a man's toilet set in silver, with the letters H. B. on each piece. Two days later we learned that she had brought a complete **outfit** of men's clothing, including a nightshirt, and we said, "They are married." We were really glad. We were glad because the two female cousins were even more Grierson than Miss Emily had ever been.

So we were not surprised when Homer Barron—the streets had been finished some time since—was gone. We were a little disappointed that there was not a public blowing-off , but we believed that he had gone on to prepare for Miss Emily's coming, or to give her a chance to get rid of the cousins. (By that time it was a cabal, and we were all Miss Emily's allies to help circumvent the cousins.) Sure enough, after another week they departed. And, as we had expected all along, within three days Homer Barron was back in town. A neighbor saw the Negro man admit him at the kitchen door at dusk one evening.

And that was the last we saw of Homer Barron. And of Miss Emily for some time. The Negro man went in and out with the market basket, but the front door remained closed. Now and then we would see her at a window for a moment, as the men did that night when they **sprinkled** the lime, but for almost six months she did not appear on the streets. Then we knew that this was to be expected too ; as if that quality of her father which had thwarted her woman's life so many times had been too virulent and too furious to die.

When we next saw Miss Emily, she had grown fat and her hair was turning gray. During the next few years it grew grayer and grayer until it attained an even pepper-and-salt iron-gray, when it ceased turning. Up to the day of her death at seventy-four it was still the vigorous iron-gray, like the hair of an active man.

From that time on her front door remained closed, save for a period of six or seven years, when she was about forty, during which she gave lessons in china-painting. She fitted up a studio in one of the downstairs rooms, where the daughters and grand-daughters of Colonel Sartoris' contemporaries were sent to her with the same regularity and in the same spirit that they were sent on Sundays with a twenty-five cent piece for the collection plate. Meanwhile her taxes had been remitted.

Then the newer generation became the backbone and the spirit of the town, and the painting pupils grew up and fell away and did not send their children to her with boxes of color and tedious brushes and pictures cut from the ladies' magazines. The front door closed upon the last one and remained closed for good. *When the town got free postal delivery Miss Emily alone refused to let them fasten the metal numbers above her door and attach a mailbox to it.* She would not listen to them.

Daily, monthly, yearly we watched the Negro grow grayer and more stooped, going in and out with the market basket. Each December we sent her a tax notice, which would be returned by the post office a week later, unclaimed. Now and then we would see her in one of the downstairs windows—she had evidently shut up the top floor of the house—like the carven torso of an idol in a niche, looking or not looking at us, we could never tell which. *Thus she passed from generation to generation—dear, inescapable, impervious, tranquil, and perverse.*

And so she died. Fell ill in the house filled with dust and shadows, with only a doddering Negro man to wait on her. We did not even know she was sick; we had long since given up trying to get any information from the Negro. He talked to no one, probably not even to her, for his voice had grown harsh and rusty, as if from disuse.

She died in one of the downstairs rooms, in a heavy walnut bed with a curtain, her gray head propped on a pillow yellow and **moldy** with age and lack of sunlight.

于是，第二天我们大家都说："她要自杀了。"我们也都说这是再好不过的事了。我们第一次看到她和荷默·伯隆在一块儿时，我们都说："她要嫁给他了。"后来又说："她还得说服他呢。"因为荷默自己说他喜欢和男人来往，大家都知道他和年轻人在麋鹿俱乐部一起喝酒，他本人也说过，他是无意于成家的人。以后每逢礼拜天下午他们乘着漂亮的轻便马车路过时，爱米丽小姐昂着头，荷默歪戴着帽子，嘴里叼着雪茄，戴着黄手套握着马缰和马鞭。我们在百叶窗后面不禁要说一声："可怜的爱米丽。"

后来有些妇女开始说，这是这个镇子的耻辱，在年轻人间中造成了很坏的影响。男人们不想干涉，但妇女们终于迫使浸礼会牧师——爱米丽小姐一家人都是属于圣公会的——去拜访她。关于访问经过，他从未透露，但他再也不愿去第二趟了。第二个礼拜天他们又驾着马车出现在了街上，于是牧师夫人在第二天就写信告知爱米丽那在亚拉巴马的亲属。

原来她家里还有近亲，于是我们坐待事态的发展。起先没有动静，随后我们确定，他们即将结婚。我们还听说爱米丽小姐去过首饰店，订购了一套银质男人盥洗用具，每件上面都刻着"荷·伯"。两天之后人家又告诉我们她买了全套男人服装，包括睡衣，因此我们说："他们已经结婚了。"我们着实高兴。我们高兴的是两位堂姐妹跟爱米丽小姐比起来，更有格里尔生家族的风度。

因此当荷默·伯隆离开本城——街道铺路工程已经竣工好一阵子了——时，我们一点也不惊奇。倒是因为缺少一番送行告别的热闹，不无失望之感。不过我们都相信他此去是为了迎娶爱米丽小姐做一番准备，或者是让她有个机会打发走两个堂姐妹（这时已经形成了一个秘密小集团，我们都站在爱米丽小姐一边，帮她踢开这一对堂姐妹）。真是这样的，一星期后她们就走了。而且，正如我们一直所期待的那样。荷默·伯隆又回到镇上来了。一位邻居亲眼看见那个黑人在一个黄昏时分打开厨房门让他进去了。

这是我们最后一次看到荷默·伯隆。至于爱米丽小姐，我们则有一段时间没有见过她。黑人拿着购货篮进进出出，可是前门却总关着。偶尔可以看到她的身影在窗口晃过，就像人们在撒石灰那天夜晚曾经见过的那样，但却整整 6 个月，她没有出现在大街上。我们明白这也并非出乎意料，她父亲的性格给她那作为女性的一生平添了许多波折，而这种性格仿佛太恶毒，太狂暴，但却消失不了。

等到我们再见到爱米丽小姐时，她已经发胖了，头发也灰白了。以后几年中，头发越来越灰，最后变成了像胡椒盐似的铁灰色。直到她 74 岁去世时，还保持着那旺盛的铁灰色，像是一个活跃的男子的头发。

打那时起，她的前门就一直关着，除了在她 40 岁左右的六七年的时间之外。在那段时期，她开授瓷器彩绘课。在楼下的一个房间里，她临时布置了一个画室。沙多里斯上校的那一代人全都把女儿、孙女儿送到她那里学画，那样的守时，那样的认真，简直同礼拜天去教堂去，还给她们二角伍分钱的硬币准备放在捐献盆子里的情况是一模一样的。这时，她的捐税已经被赦免了。

后来，新的一代成了全镇的骨干，学画的学生们也长大成人，渐次离开了，他们没有让自己的孩子带着颜色盒、令人生厌的画笔和从妇女杂志上剪下来的图片到爱米丽小姐那里去学画。最后一个学生离开后，前门就关上了，而且是永远地关上了。全镇实行免费邮递制度之后，只有爱米丽小姐一人拒绝在她门口钉上金属门牌号，附设一个邮件箱。她对他们不理不睬。

日复一日，月复一月，年复一年，我们眼看着那黑人的头发白了，背也驼了，还照旧提着购货篮进进出出。每年12月我们都寄给她一张纳税通知单，但一星期后又被邮局退了回来，因为无人收信。不时我们在楼下的一个窗口——她显然是把楼上封闭起来了——见到她的身影，像神龛中的一个偶像的雕塑躯干，我们说不上她是不是在看着我们。她就这样度过了一年又一年——高贵，宁静，无法逃避，无法接近，怪僻乖张。

她就这样与世长辞了。在一栋尘埃遍地、鬼影幢幢的屋子里得了病，侍候她的只有一个老态龙钟的黑人。我们甚至连她病了也不知道，也早已不想从黑人那里去打听什么消息了。他跟谁也不说话，恐怕对她也是如此，他的嗓子似乎由于长久不用而变得嘶哑了。

她死在楼下的一间屋子里，笨重的胡桃木床上还挂着床帷。她的枕头由于多年不见阳光，已经黄得发霉了。

作者介绍

美国作家威廉·福克纳 (l897–1962)，出身名门望族，全名威廉·卡斯伯特·福克纳。福克纳其他重要作品还有《圣殿》、《标塔》、《没有被征服的》、《野棕榈》、《坟墓的闯入者》、《修女安魂曲》、《寓言》、《掠夺者》等。斯诺普斯三部曲（《村子》、《小镇》、《大宅》）也很重要。1950 年，福克纳获得了诺贝尔文学奖。

单词注解

remark [ri'mɑ:k] *v.* 谈到；评论；说

outfit ['autfit] *n.* 全套装备；全套工具

sprinkle ['spriŋkl] *v.* 洒，喷淋；撒

refuse [ri'fju:z] *v.* 拒绝；拒受；拒给

moldy ['məuldi] *adj.* 发霉的；陈腐的；乏味的

名句大搜索

后来有些妇女开始说，这是这个镇子的耻辱，在年轻人间中造成了很坏的影响。

全镇实行免费邮递制度之后，只有爱米丽小姐一人拒绝在她门口钉上金属门牌号，附设一个邮件箱。

她就这样度过了一年又一年——高贵，宁静，无法逃避，无法接近，怪僻乖张。

Tess of the d'Urbervilles
德伯家的苔丝

[英] 托马斯·哈代（Thomas Hardy）

德贝菲尔在偶尔得知自己是古老的武士后裔时，这个小贩高兴得手舞足蹈。他幻想着让苔丝去认毫无渊源的“本家”，这样能帮他摆脱经济上的困境。苔丝在被“本家”亚雷奸污后，遭到了社会的耻笑和指责。后来，苔丝遇到了“真命天子”安玑，但这段姻缘在新婚之夜突变，爱人远走巴西。由于生活所迫，苔丝杀死了乘虚而入的亚雷。

On an evening in the latter part of May a middle-aged man was walking homeward from Shaston to the village of Marlott, in the adjoining Vale of Blakemore or Blackmoor. The pair of legs that carried him were rickety, and mere was a **bias** in his gait which inclined him somewhat to the left of a straight line. He occasionally gave a smart nod, as if in confirmation of some opinion, though he was not thinking of anything in particular. An empty egg-basket was slung upon his arm, the nap of his hat was ruffled, a patch being quite worn away at its brim where his thumb came in taking it off. Presently he was met by an elderly parson **astride** on a gray mare, who, as he rode, hummed a wandering tune. "Good night t'ee," said the man with the basket.

"Good night, Sir John," said the parson.

The pedestrian, after another pace or two, halted, and turned round.

"Now, sir, begging your pardon ; we met last market-day on this road about this time, and I said 'Good-night', and you made reply 'Good night, Sir John', as now."

"I did," said the parson.

"And once before that near a month ago."

"I may have."

"Then what might your meaning be in calling me 'Sir John' these different times, when I be plain Jack Durbeyfield, the haggler?"

The parson rode a step or two nearer.

"*It was only my whim*," he said, and, after a moment's hesitation:

"It was on account of a discovery I made some little time ago, whilst

I was hunting up pedigrees for the new county history. I am Parson Tringham, the **antiquary**, of Stagfoot Lane. Don't you really know, Durbeyfield, that you are the lineal representative of the ancient and knightly family of the d'Urbervilles, who derived their descent from Sir Pagan d'Urberville, that renowned knight who came from Normandy with William the Conqueror, as appears by Battle Abbey Roll?"

"Never heard it before, sir!"

"Well it's true. Throw up your chin a moment, so that I may catch me **profile** of your face better. Yes, that's the d'Urberville nose and chin — a little debased. Your ancestor was one of the twelve knights who assisted the Lord of Estremavilla in Normandy in his conquest of Glamorganshire. Branches of your family held manors over all this part of England; their names appear in the Pipe Rolls in the time of King Stephen. In the reign of King John one of them was rich enough to give a manor to the Knights Hospitallers; and in Edward the Second's time your forefather Brian was summoned to Westminster to attend the great Council there. You declined a little in Oliver Cromwell's time, but to no serious extent, and in Charles the Second's reign you were made Knights of the Royal Oak for your loyalty. Aye, there have been generations of Sir Johns among you, and if knighthood were **hereditary**, like a baronetcy', as it practically was in old times, when men were knighted from father to son, you would be Sir, John now."

"Ye don't say so!"

"In short," concluded the parson, decisively smacking his leg with his switch, "there's hardly such another family in England."

"Daze my eyes, and isn't there?" said Durbeyfield. "And here have I been knocking about, year after year, from pillar to post, as if I was no more than the commonest feller in the **parish**... And how long hev this news about me been knowed, Pa'son Tringham?"

The clergyman explained that, as far as he was aware, it had quite died out of knowledge, and could hardly be said to be known at all. His own investigations had begun on a day in the preceding spring when, having been engaged in tracing the vicissitudes of the d'Urberville family, he had observed Durbeyfield's name on his wagon, and had thereupon been led to make inquiries about his father and grandfather till he had no doubt on the subject.

"At first I resolved not to disturb you with such a useless piece of information," said he. "*However, our impulses are too strong for our judgment sometimes.* I thought you might perhaps know something of it all the while."

"Well, I have heard once or twice,'tis true, that my family had seen better days afore they came to Blackmoor. But I took no notice o't, thinking it to mean that we had once kept two horses where we now keep only one. I've got a wold silver spoon, and a wold graven seal at home, too ;but, Lord, what's a spoon and seal?... And to think that I and these noble d'Urbervilles were one flesh all the time. 'Twas said that my gr't-grandfer had secrets, and didn't care to talk of where he came from... And where do we raise our smoke, now, parson, if I may make so bold ;I mean, where do we d'Urbervilles liver?"

"You don't live anywhere. You are extinct as a county family."

"That's bad."

"Yes what the mendacious family chronicles call extinct in the male line that is，gone down gone under."

五月下旬的一个傍晚，一位中年男子正从沙斯顿赶回自己的家乡——马洛特。该村庄坐落在与沙斯顿毗邻的布雷克摩(或布莱克摩）山谷里。这位中年人拖着两条蹒跚的腿，步态倾斜，整个身子总是向左边歪着。他偶尔也把头轻巧地一点，仿佛是对什么事情表示赞同，其实他什么都没想。他胳膊上挎着一只盛鸡蛋的空篮子，帽子的绒面皱皱巴巴的，摘帽子时大拇指接触的那个地方已经磨损了一大块。不一会儿，一个骑着灰色母马、随口哼着小调的老牧师迎面而来。

"你好。"挎着篮子的男子说。

"你好，约翰爵士。"牧师说道。

步行的男子又走了一两步，站住了，转过身来。

"呃，先生，俺真不明白，上回赶集的那天，差不多也是在这个时候，俺俩在这条路上相遇了，俺对你说了一声'你好'，你也是像方才一样回答：'你好，约翰爵士。'"

"不错，我是这么说的。"牧师说道。

"在那以前还有过一回，大概一个月以前。"

"或许是的。"

"那么，你干吗三番两次地叫俺'约翰爵士'呀？俺只不过是个普普通通的小贩，名叫杰克•德贝菲尔呀。"

牧师拍马走近了一两步。

"那是我的一时兴起。"牧师说道，然后又迟疑了一会儿说，"那是因为不久前我为编写新郡志而考查各个家谱时，偶尔发现了这件事。我是斯塔福特路的特林厄姆牧师。德贝菲尔，你真的不知道你是古老高贵的爵士世家德伯维尔的直系子孙吗？德伯维尔的始祖是佩根•德伯维尔爵士，根据《功臣谱》的记载，这位著名的武将是跟随征服王从诺曼底来的。"

"以前俺可从来没听说过这事呀，先生！"

"这是真的。把你的下巴抬起来一点点，让我好好看看你的脸。不错，这正是德伯维尔的鼻子和下巴——但有一点儿衰落。辅佐诺曼底的埃斯特玛维拉勋爵征服格拉摩根郡有 12 个武将，你的祖先就是其中一个。你家族的分支在英格兰这一带拥有好多庄园，他们的名字出现在斯蒂芬王朝时代的《国库年报》里。在约翰王统治时代，其中有几个富豪还把受封领地捐赠给了僧兵团。在爱德华二世时代，你的祖先布赖恩被召到威斯敏斯特参加过大议会。在克伦威尔时代，你们家族有所衰败，但不算严重。在查理二世时代，你们家由于忠于君主，被封为'御橡爵士'。呃，你的家族中已有好几代约翰爵士了，假如爵士封号也像男爵那样，可以世袭相传，那么，你现在不就是约翰爵士了吗？实际上，在过去，爵士封号就是世袭的。"

"可你没有这样说过呀！"

"简而言之，"牧师态度坚决地用马鞭抽了一下自己的腿，下结论说，"在英格兰，你们这样的家族简直找不出第二家。"

"真令我吃惊，在英格兰找不出第二家吗？"德贝菲尔说，"可是我一直在这一带四处漂泊，一年又一年的，糟糕透顶了，好像我同这个教区里的最普通的人没什么两样……特林汉姆牧师，关于我们家族的这件事，大家知道吗，有多久了？"

牧师解释说，据他所知，这件事儿已经被大家遗忘了，很难说有什么人知道。他自己的调查是从去年春天开始的，他碰巧看到了刻在马车上的德贝菲尔这个姓氏，由于对德伯维尔家族的盛衰变迁极感兴趣，他就展开了对德贝菲尔父亲和祖父的调查，直至彻底弄清楚了这个问题。

“起初，我并不想把这个毫无价值的事实讲给你听，免得打扰了你，”他说，“但是，我们的冲动有时候强于我们的判断力。我本以为你或多或少知道一些情况呢。”

“是啊，的确是的，有过一两回，俺听说俺家在来布莱克摩山谷之前，日子要好过得多。可俺却没在意，只是以为俺家曾经有过两匹马儿，而不像现在这样，只有一匹。俺家里倒是有一把古老的银匙，也有一个古老的印章，可是，先生，银匙和印章又能说明什么呢？……哪里想到俺会和这些高贵的德伯维尔血肉相连。据说俺老爷子有些秘密事儿，他不肯说出他是打哪儿来的……那么，俺冒昧地问一句，眼下俺家的人在哪儿呢？俺是说，俺德伯维尔家的人眼下住在哪儿呢？”

“哪儿都没有了。作为郡里的贵族人家，已经绝嗣了。”

“真是伤心呐。”

“是啊，那些编造家史的人，总是把衰败了的男系世家称作绝嗣家族。”

实战提升
Practising & Exercise

作者介绍

托马斯·哈代（1840–1928），英国伟大的小说家和诗人，在文坛上享有盛誉。哈代共发表了 14 部长篇小说，4 个短篇小说集，8 卷诗和两部诗剧。就哈代的整个小说创作来说，可以分为三个阶段。第一个阶段的小说是抒发田园理想的颂歌，带有浪漫主义风格，主要有《绿荫下》、《远离尘器》等。第二个阶段的作品描写威塞克斯社会的悲剧，主要有《还乡》、《卡斯特桥市长》等。第三个阶段的作品描写威塞克斯破产农民的前途和命运，主要有《德伯家的苔丝》、《无名的裘德》等。

单词注解

bias ['baiəs] *n.* 偏见，成见；偏心

astride [əs'traid] *prep.* 在……两旁；在其上；横过

antiquary ['æntikwəri] *n.* 古董商；古籍商

profile ['prəufail] *n.* 轮廓，外形；外观；形象

hereditary [hi'reditəri] *adj.* 世袭的，传代的

parish ['pæriʃ] *n.* 教区

mendacious [men'deiʃəs] *adj.* 虚伪的；说谎的

名句大搜索

那是我的一时兴起。

但是，我们的冲动有时候强于我们的判断力。

是啊，那些编造家史的人，总是把衰败了的男系世家称作绝嗣家族。”

。

Madame Bovary

包法利夫人

[法]居斯塔夫·福楼拜(Gustave Flaubert)

平庸的医学学生查理·包法利，在他那年长而衰弱的太太去世后和心爱的爱玛结婚。浪漫的爱玛对这个不懂生活情趣的丈夫日渐厌倦，查理为了妻子能高兴，搬到了勇维尔·拉贝。在这里爱玛接连遭到了赖昂和罗道尔弗的抛弃。绝望的爱玛委身于读书归来的赖昂，陷入了堕落的快乐中。为了维持与这些男人的关系，爱玛一再举债，直至破产。在绝望之余，她服砷自杀了。

We were in class when the head-master came in, followed by a "new fellow," not wearing the school **uniform**, and a school servant carrying a large desk. *Those who had been asleep woke up, and every one rose as if just surprised at his work.*

The headmaster made a sign to us to sit down. Then, turning to the classmaster, he said to him in a low voice—

"Monsieur Roger, here is a pupil whom I recommend to your care ; he'll be in the second. If his work and conduct are **satisfactory**, he will go into one of the upper classes, as becomes his age."

The "new fellow," standing in the corner behind the door so that he could hardly be seen, was a country lad of about fifteen, and taller than any of us. His hair was cut square on his forehead like a village chorister's ; he looked **reliable**, but very ill at ease. Although he was not broad-shouldered, his short school jacket of green cloth with black buttons must have been tight about the arm-holes, and showed at the opening of the cuffs red wrists accustomed to being bare. His legs, in blue stockings, looked out from beneath yellow trousers, drawn tight by braces, He wore stout, ill-cleaned, hob-nailed boots.

We began repeating the lesson. He listened with all his ears, as attentive as if at a sermon, not daring even to cross his legs or lean on his elbow ; and when at two o'clock the bell rang, the master was obliged to tell him to fall into line with the rest of us.

When we came back to work, we were in the habit of throwing our caps on the ground so as to have our hands more free ; we used from the door to toss them under the form, so that they hit against the wall and made a lot of dust: it was the thing.

But, whether he had not noticed the trick, or did not dare

to **attempt** it, the "new fellow", was still holding his cap on his knees even after prayers were over. It was one of those head-gears of composite order, in which we can find traces of the bearskin, shako, billycock hat, sealskin cap, and cotton night-cap ; one of those poor things, in fine, whose dumb ugliness has depths of expression, like an imbecile's face. Oval, stiffened with whalebone, it began with three round knobs ; then came in succession lozenges of velvet and rabbit-skin separated by a red band ; after that a sort of bag that ended in a cardboard polygon covered with **complicated** braiding, from which hung, at the end of a long thin cord, small twisted gold threads in the manner of a tassel. The cap was new ; its peak shone.

"Rise," said the master.

He stood up ; his cap fell. The whole class began to laugh. He stooped to pick it up. A neighbor knocked it down again with his elbow ; he picked it up once more.

"Get rid of your helmet," said the master, who was a bit of a wag.

There was a burst of laughter from the boys, which so thoroughly put the poor lad out of **countenance** that he did not know whether to keep his cap in his hand, leave it on the ground, or put it on his head. He sat down again and placed it on his knee.

"Rise," repeated the master, "and tell me your name."

The new boy articulated in a stammering voice an unintelligible name.

"Again!"

The same sputtering of syllables was heard, drowned by the tittering of the class.

"Louder!" cried the master ; "louder!"

The "new fellow" then took a supreme resolution, opened an inordinately large mouth, and shouted at the top of his voice as if calling someone in the word "Charbovari."

A hubbub broke out, rose in crescendo with bursts of shrill voices (they yelled, barked, stamped, repeated "Charbovari! Charbovari"), then died away into single notes, growing quieter only with great difficulty, and now and again suddenly recommencing along the line of a form whence rose here and there, like a damp cracker going off, a stifled laugh.

However, amid a rain of impositions, order was gradually re-established in the class ; and the master having succeeded in catching the name of "Charles Bovary," having had it dictated to him, spelt out, and re-read, at once ordered the poor devil to go and sit down on the **punishment** form at the foot of the master's desk. He got up, but before going hesitated.

我们正在上自习，校长进来了，后面跟着一个没有穿学生装的“新生”，还有一个小校工，扛着一张大书桌。正在打瞌睡的学生也醒过来了，个个站了起来，仿佛功课受到了打扰似的。

校长朝我们挥挥手，让我们坐下，然后转过身去，低声对班主任说：

“罗杰先生，我把这个学生交给你了，让他上五年级的课吧。如果他的学习和品德都不错，再让他进高年级，按他的岁数应该上高年级才是。”

这个“新生”坐在门背后的角落里，门一开，谁也看不见他，他是一个小乡巴佬，大约有 15 岁，个子比我们都高。他的头发顺着前额剪齐，像乡下教堂里的歌童，看样子老实听话，连手脚都不知往哪儿搁。他的肩并不宽，可那件黑纽扣绿呢子上装却仿佛被他的肩绷得紧紧的，活动不便，袖饰开衩处露出了经常风吹日晒的手腕，红红的。两根背带把他那条浅黄色的裤子吊得很高，露出穿着蓝袜子的双脚。脚上穿了一双不常擦油的钉鞋。

我们开始背诵课文。他竖起耳朵听着，全神贯注，就像在教堂里听传道，连腿也不敢跷，胳膊也不敢放在书桌上。两点钟下课铃响的时候，要不是班主任提醒他，他也不知道和我们一起排队。

我们平时有个习惯，一进教室，就把帽子扔在地上，以免拿在手里碍事；因此，一跨过门槛，就得把帽子扔到长凳底下，掀起一片尘土，拍打在墙壁上；这已习以为常了。

不知道这个新生是没有注意到我们这一套，还是不敢跟大家一样做，课前的祷告做完之后，他还把鸭舌帽放在膝盖上。他的帽子像是一盘大杂烩，看不出到底是皮帽、军帽、圆顶帽、尖嘴帽还是睡帽，反正是便宜货，说不出的难看，好像哑巴吃了黄连后的苦脸。帽子是鸡蛋形的，里面用铁丝支撑着，帽口有三道滚边；往上是交错的菱形丝绒和兔皮，中间有条红线隔开；再往上是口袋似的帽筒；帽顶是多边的硬壳纸，纸上蒙着复杂的彩绣，还有一根细长的饰带，末端吊着一个金线结成的小十字架作为坠子。帽子是新的，帽檐还闪光呢。

“站起来，”老师说。

他一起立，鸭舌帽就掉了。全班同学都笑了起来。他弯腰去拣帽子。旁边一个学生用胳膊捅了他一下，帽子又掉了，他又拣了一回。

“不必担心，你的王冠不会摔坏。”老师很风趣地说。

同学们都哈哈大笑起来，可怜的新生更加手足无措了，不知道帽子应该拿在手里，还是让它掉在地下，还是把它戴在头上。他坐下，仍然把帽子搁在并拢的双膝上。

“站起来，”老师又说了一遍，“告诉我，你叫什么名字。”

新生嘟嘟囔囔地说了个名字，根本听不清楚他说的是什么。

“再说一遍！”

还是嘟嘟囔囔含混不清的声音，全班笑得更厉害了。

“声音高点！”老师喊道，“声音高点！”

于是“新生”狠下决心，张开血盆大口，像在呼救似的，使出了吃奶的力气说道：“夏包华里！”

这下好了，笑声叫声直线上升，越闹越凶，有的声音尖得刺耳，有的像狼嚎，有的像狗叫，有人跺脚，有人学舌：‘下坡花力！下坡花力！”好不容易平息下来，但是一排板凳好像一串爆竹，说不准什么时候还会爆发出一两声压制不住的笑声，犹如死灰复燃的爆竹一样。

然而，在暴雨般的作业重罚下，课堂次序渐渐恢复，老师让新生一个字母一个字母地反复拼读，由他写在黑板上，这才弄清楚新生的名字叫夏尔·包法利，他当即命这个可怜虫坐到讲台前懒学生的凳子上去。

作者介绍

居斯塔夫·福楼拜（1821–1880），19 世纪中叶法国现实主义作家。生于法国诺曼底卢昂医生世家。福楼拜在中学时从事文学习作。早期习作有浓厚的浪漫主义色彩。1857 年，福楼拜出版了轰动文坛的长篇小说《包法利夫人》。但作品受到当局指控，罪名是败坏道德，毁谤宗教。此后，他一度转入古代题材创作，于 1862 年发表长篇小说《萨朗波》。他的作品语言精练、准确、铿锵有力，是法国文学史上的“模范散文”之作。

单词注解

uniform ['ju:nifɔ:m] *adj.* 相同的，一致的

satisfactory [ˌsætis'fæktəri] *adj.* 令人满意的；符合要求的

reliable [ri'laiəbl] *adj.* 可信赖的；可靠的；确实的

attempt [ə'temp] *v.* 试图；企图；试图做

complicated ['kɔmplikeitid] *adj.* 复杂的；难懂的；结构复杂的

countenance ['kauntinəns] *n.* 面容，脸色；表情

punishment ['pʌniʃmənt] *n.* 处罚，惩罚；刑罚

名句大搜索

正在打瞌睡的学生也醒过来了，个个站了起来，仿佛功课受到了打扰似的。

“不必担心，你的王冠不会摔坏。”老师很风趣地说。

新生嘟嘟囔囔地说了个名字，根本就听不清楚他说的是什么。

The Kite Runner

追风筝的人

[美]卡勒德·胡赛尼(Khaled Hosseini)

这是一个身在美国的阿富汗移民童年的往事，和他成人后的心灵救赎的故事。全书类似自传体小说，主人公的经历和背景跟作者本人的经历背景非常相似。主人公儿时出身阿富汗上流社会，父亲经商积德，在当地非常有声望。而主人公由于孩童的自私，非常想获得父亲全部的爱，总是因为父亲对仆人孩子的温情而心生嫉妒。主人公儿时性格懦弱，仆人的孩子勇敢忠诚，心态失衡的主人公后来用不光彩的手段陷害了仆人一家，导致仆人一家流落异乡。后来阿富汗爆发战争，主人公一家被迫出走美国。后来父亲的合伙人在临过世前鼓励主人公回阿富汗寻找当年仆人的小孩，并通过努力去平复自己多年的负罪感。已经是事业有成的主人公鼓起勇气，找到了老朋友。在得知惊人的秘密后，他赎罪般的努力，最终完成了一个男人的成长。

I became what I am today at the age of twelve, on a frigid overcast day in the winter of 1975. I remember the **precise** moment, crouching behind a crumbling mud wall, **peeking** into the alley near the frozen creek. That was a long time ago, but it's wrong what they say about the past, I've learned, about how you can bury it. Because the past claws its way out. *Looking back now, I realize I have been peeking into that deserted alley for the last twenty-six years.*

One day last summer, my friend Rahim Khan called from Pakistan. He asked me to come see him. Standing in the kitchen with the receiver to my ear, I knew it wasn't just Rahim Khan on the line. It was my past of unatoned sins. After I hung up, I went for a walk along Spreckels Lake on the northern edge of Golden Gate Park. *The early afternoon sun sparkled on the water where dozens of miniature boats sailed, propelled by a crisp breeze.* Then I glanced up and saw a pair of kites, red with long blue tails, soaring in the sky. They danced high above the trees on the west end of the park, over the windmills, floating side by side like a pair of eyes looking down on San Francisco, the city I now call home. *And suddenly Hassan's voice whispered in my head: For you, a thousand times over.* Hassan the harelipped kite runner.

I sat on a park bench near a willow tree. I thought about something Rahim Khan said just before he hung up, almost as an after thought. There is a way to be good again. I looked up at those twin kites. I thought about Hassan. Thought about Baba. Ali. Kabul. I thought of the life I had lived until the winter of 1975 came and changed everything. And made me what I am today.

我成为今天的我，是在 1975 年某个阴云密布的寒冷冬日，那年我 12 岁。我清楚地记得当时我趴在一堵坍塌的泥墙后面，窥视着那条小巷，旁边是结冰的小溪。许多年过去了，人们说陈年旧事可以被埋葬，然而我终于明白这是错的，因为往事会自行爬上来。回首往事，我意识到在过去的这 26 年里，自己始终在窥视着那荒芜的小径。

去年夏季的一天，朋友拉辛汗从巴基斯坦打来电话，要我回去探望他。我站在厨房里，听筒贴在耳朵上，我知道电话线连着的，并不只是拉辛汗，还有我过去那些未曾赎还的罪行。挂了电话，我离开家门，到金门公园北边的斯普瑞柯湖边散步。晌午的骄阳照在波光粼粼的水面上，数十艘轻舟在和风的吹拂中漂行。我抬起头，望见两只红色的风筝，带着长长的蓝色尾巴，在天空中冉冉升起。它们舞动着，飞越公园西边的树林，飞越风车，并排漂浮着，如同一双眼睛俯视着旧金山，这个我现在当成家园的城市。突然间，哈桑的声音在我脑海中响起：为你，千千万万遍。哈桑，那个兔唇的哈桑，那个追风筝的人。

我在公园里柳树旁的长凳上坐下，想着拉辛汗在电话里说的那些事情，再三思量。那儿有再次成为好人的路。我抬头看了看那比翼齐飞的风筝。我忆起哈桑。我缅怀爸爸。我想念阿里。我思念喀布尔。我想起曾经的生活，想起 1975 年那个改变了一切的冬天。所有那一切造就了今天的我。

实战提升
Practising & Exercise

作者介绍

卡勒德·胡赛尼，1965 年 3 月 4 日出生于阿富汗喀布尔市，后随父亲移居美国。胡赛尼毕业于加州大学圣地亚哥医学系，现居加州执业。《追风筝的人》是他的第一本小说，因书中角色刻画生动，故事情节震撼感人，出版后大获好评，获得各项新人奖，并跃居全美各大畅销排行榜榜首。在 2006 年由梦工厂买下电影版权，同名电影于 2007 年上映。《灿烂千阳》是他的第二本小说，2007 年 5 月 22 日于美国首发。

单词注解

precise [pri'sais] *adj.* 精确的；准确的；确切的

peek [pi:k] *v.* 偷看，窥视

dozen ['dʌzn] *n.* 一打，十二个

whisper ['(h)wispə] *v.* 低语，耳语；私语

名句大搜索

回首往事，我意识到在过去 26 年里，自己始终在窥视着那荒芜的小径。

晌午的骄阳照在波光粼粼的水面上，数十艘轻舟在和风的吹拂中漂行。

突然间，哈桑的声音在我脑海中响起：为你，千千万万遍。

爱之光芒，驱走生命的黑暗

Love will consume all the darkness

The Old Man and the Sea
老人与海

［美］欧内斯特·米勒尔·海明威（Ernest Miller Hemingway）

《老人与海》的故事发生在二十世纪中叶的古巴。一位圣地亚哥风烛残年的渔夫一连 84 天都没有钓到一条鱼，几乎都快饿死了；但他仍然不肯认输，终于在第 85 天钓到一条身长 18 尺，体重 1,500 磅的大马林鱼。大鱼拖着船往海里走，但老人依然死拉着不放。经过两天两夜的努力后，他终于杀死大鱼，把它拴在船边。但许多小鲨立刻前来抢夺他的战利品；他一一地杀死它们，但大鱼仍难逃被吃光的命运，最终，老人精疲力竭地拖回一副鱼骨头。他只好在梦中去寻回那往日美好的岁月，以忘却残酷的现实。

He was an old man who fished alone in a skiff in the Gulf Stream and he had gone eighty-four days now without taking a fish. In the first forty days a boy had been with him. But after forty days without a fish the boy's parents had told him that the old man was now **definitely** and finally salao, which is the worst form of unlucky, and the boy had gone at their orders in another boat which caught three good fish the first week. It made the boy sad to see the old man come in each day with his skiff empty and he always went down to help him carry either the coiled lines or the gaff and harpoon and the sail that was furled around the mast. *The sail was patched with flour sacks and, furled, it looked like the flag of permanent defeat.*

The old man was thin and gaunt with deep wrinkles in the back of his neck. The brown blotches of the **benevolent** skin cancer the sun brings from its reflection on the tropic sea were on his cheeks. The blotches ran well down the sides of his face and his hands had the deep-creased scars from handling heavy fish on the cords. *But none of these scars were fresh. They were as old as erosions in a fishless desert.*

Everything about him was old except his eyes and they were the same color as the sea and were cheerful and undefeated.

"Santiago," the boy said to him as they climbed the bank from where the skiff was hauled up. "I could go with you again. We've made some money."

The old man had taught the boy to fish and the boy loved him.

"No," the old man said. "You're with a lucky boat. Stay with them."

"But remember how you went eighty-seven days without fish and then we caught big ones every day for three weeks."

"I remember," the old man said. "I know you did not leave me because you doubted."

"It was papa made me leave. I am a boy and I must obey him."

"I know," the old man said. "It is quite normal."

"He hasn't much faith."

"No," the old man said. "But we have. Haven't we?"

"Yes," the boy said. "Can I offer you a beer on the Terrace and then we'll take the stuff home."

"Why not?" the old man said. "Between fishermen."

They sat on the Terrace and many of the fishermen made fun of the old man and he was not angry. Others, of the older fishermen, looked at him and were sad. But they did not show it and they spoke politely about the current and the depths they had drifted their lines at and the steady good weather and of what they had seen. The successful fishermen of that day were already in and had **butchered** their marlin out and carried them laid full length across two planks, with two men staggering at the end of each plank, to the fish house where they waited for the ice truck to carry them to the market in Havana. Those who had caught sharks had taken them to the shark factory on the other side of the cove where they were hoisted on a block and tackle, their livers removed, their fins cut off and their hides skinned out and their flesh cut into strips for salting.

When the wind was in the east a smell came across the harbour from the shark factory; but today there was only the faint edge of the odour because the wind had backed into the north and then dropped off and it was **pleasant** and sunny on the Terrace.

"Santiago," the boy said.

"Yes," the old man said. He was holding his glass and thinking of many years ago.

"Can I go out to get sardines for you for tomorrow?"

"No. Go and play baseball. I can still row and Rogelio will throw the net."

"I would like to go. If I can't fish with you, I would like to werve in some way."

"You bought me a beer," the old man said. "You are already a man."

"How old was I when you first took me in a boat?"

"Five and you nearly were killed when I brought the fish in too great and he nearly tore the boat to pieces. Can you remember?"

"I can remember the tail slapping and banging and the thwart breaking and the noise of the clubbing. I can remember you throwing me into the bow where the wet coiled lines were and feeling the whole boat shiver and the noise of you clubbing him like chopping a tree down and the sweet blood smell all over me."

"Can you really remember that or did I just tell it to you?"

"I remember everything from when we first went together."

The old man looked at him with his sun-burned, confident loving eyes.

老人独自划着小船在墨西哥湾暖流钓鱼。整整84天过去了，他还是一条鱼也没逮着。头40天里，有个男孩一直跟着他。可是过了40天，老人还没抓到一条鱼，孩子的父母就对孩子说，老人如今真是倒霉透顶了，这个男孩于是听从了他们的吩咐，上了另外一条船。这条船在头一个礼拜就捕到了三条大鱼。看着老人每天回来时船总是空的，孩子感到很难过。他总是走到岸边，帮老人拿成卷的渔线，或者渔钩和渔叉，还有绕在桅杆上的帆。老人用面粉袋的布片在帆上打满了补丁，帆收拢后看上去就像是一面永远失败的旗子。

老人消瘦而憔悴，脖颈上布满了深深的皱纹。肋帮上有些黄褐斑，一直从脸的两侧蔓延下去，这是老人长时间在热带海洋上捕鱼时受太阳反光照射形成的。他的双手被绳索磨出了一条条深深的伤疤，那是老人在对付大鱼时留下的。但是这些伤疤中没有一块是新的，它们像是沙漠中枯裂的岩石。

老人身上的一切都显得很苍老，除了他那双眼睛。它们像海水一样蓝，总是透着股乐观向上、永不服输的劲头。

“桑地亚哥爷爷！”当他俩从小船停靠的地方爬上岸时，孩子大声对他说，“我又可以和你一起去打鱼了。我在那条船上已经赚了一点儿钱了。”

老人一直在教孩子捕鱼，孩子很喜欢他。

“不，”老人说，“你上了一条运气不错的船。跟他们在一起吧。”

“但是您还记得有一次，您87天都没钓到一条鱼，后来连着三个礼拜我们天天都抓到大鱼吗？”

“我当然记得。”老人说，“我知道，你不是因为信不过我才离开的。”

“是爸爸叫我走的。我是他儿子，不能不听他的。”

“我明白，”老人说，“孩子应该听大人的话。”

“他对您没什么信心。”

“是啊，”老人说，“可是我们有信心，不是吗？”

“对！”孩子说，“我请您到露台餐馆喝杯啤酒，然后我们一起把打鱼的东西拿回去，好吗？”

“好啊，”老人说，“咱俩还说什么呢。”

他们坐在餐馆的露台上，不少年轻的渔夫拿老人开玩笑，老人并不生气。另外一些上了年纪的渔夫看着他，感到很难受。不过他们并没流露出来，只是有分寸地谈论着海流，谈他们放渔线的深度，谈多日来的好天气和他们的所见所闻。当天捕到鱼的渔民们都已回来，他们把大马林鱼剖开，整片儿平放在两块木板上，每块木板的一头由两个人抬着，摇摇晃晃地把鱼送到鱼仓里，在那里等冷藏车来把它们运往哈瓦那的市场出售。捕到鲨鱼的人们已把它们送到海湾另一边的鲨鱼加工厂里。在那里，人们用滑轮车把鲨鱼吊起来，挖出肝脏，割掉鱼鳍，剥下鱼皮，把鱼肉切成条状，以备腌制。

刮风的时候，人们总能够闻到从隔着海湾的鲨鱼加工厂飘来的一股鱼腥味；但今天只是淡淡的一丝气味，因为风转了方向，最后风渐渐停了。现在露台餐馆这边阳光明媚，让人感觉很舒服。

“桑地亚哥爷爷！”孩子叫道。

“嗯。”老人应了一声。他拿着酒杯，想着好多年前的事儿。

“我去给您准备好明天用的沙丁鱼好吗？”

“不用了，你去打棒球吧。我还划得了船，罗吉立奥会帮我撒网的。”

“可我很想去。我不能和您一起钓鱼，就让我做点别的事吧。”

“你已经请我喝了啤酒了呀。”老人感谢道，“你都是个男子汉了。”

“您第一次带我上船时，我几岁呀？”

“五岁。还记得那次我捕的那条鱼吗？它又大又壮，差一点把咱们的船撞个粉碎，你也差一点送了小命。”

“我记得鱼尾巴噼啪噼啪地拍打着，船上的座板都给打断了，船上的木棍也当当地响。我记得您怕我摔出去，还把我推倒在船头那堆湿漉漉的渔线上。我感到整条船都在摇晃，而您用棍子打鱼时发出的啪啪声，就像是风在吹树的声音。鱼血溅了一身，弄得我浑身上下都是血腥味儿。”

“是你自己记得那回事儿，还是我刚跟你说的？”

“从我们头一回一起出海到现在，那些事儿我可都记得清清楚楚。”

老人用他那双有着晒斑的眼睛看着孩子，眼里充满了信任和慈爱。

作者介绍

厄内斯特·米勒尔·海明威（1899–1961），美国著名小说家。出生于一个医生家庭。第一次世界大战时任红十字会救护车司机，在意大利前线受伤。他的作品包括《在我们的时代里》、《太阳照样升起》、《没有女人的男人》、《胜者无所得》，反战小说《永别了，武器》和《丧钟为谁而鸣》被誉为现代世界文学名著，中篇小说《老人与海》获得普利策奖。其他作品还有《死在午后》、《非洲的青山》、《有的和没有的》、《过河入林》等。 海明威的作品具有独特的风格，不仅文体简洁，而且语言生动明快，对美国文学界产生了很大影响。1954 年海明威获诺贝尔文学奖。

单词注解

definitely ['definitli] *adv.* 明确地；明显地，清楚地

benevolent [bi'nevələnt] *adj.* 仁慈的，厚道的，有爱心的

butcher ['butʃə] *v.* 屠杀，残杀

pleasant ['plezənt] *adj.* 令人愉快的；舒适的

confident ['kɔnfidənt] *adj.* 确信的；有信心的，自信的

名句大搜索

老人用面粉袋的布片在帆上打满了补丁，帆收拢后看上去就像是一面永远失败的旗子。

但是这些伤疤中没有一块是新的，它们像是沙漠中枯裂的岩石。

老人用他那双有着晒斑的眼睛看着孩子，眼里充满了信任和慈爱。

The Memory Keeper's Daughter

不存在的女儿

[美] 金·爱德华兹 (Kim Edwards)

医生戴维亲自为妻子接生，发现双胞胎中的女婴患有唐氏症。不忍面对女儿为智障的现实，他让护士将女儿送走，并对妻子诺拉谎称她已经夭折。善意的欺骗竟成了一家人的梦魇……25 年间，诺拉不能承受丧女之痛，开始出走、酗酒，而戴维终日被满心愧疚纠缠却无法言说，只能带着一架“记忆守护者”牌相机去寻找女婴、女孩、少女的影子，仿佛要为他那不存在的女儿留下成长的记录。暗恋戴维的护士卡罗琳并没有送走女孩，她搬到另一个城市隐姓埋名，以一己之力对抗社会的不公，尽力给女儿一个温暖的家……多年后，戴维和卡罗琳再次相遇，她对他说：“你逃过了很多心痛，但你也错过了无数的喜悦。”

March 1964

The snow started to fall several hours before her labor began. A few flakes first, in the dull gray late-afternoon sky, and then wind-driven swirls and eddies around the **edges** of their wide front porch. He stood by her side at the window, watching sharp gusts of snow billow, then swirl and drift to the ground. All around the neighborhood, lights came on, and the naked branches of the trees turned white.

After dinner he built a fire, venturing out into the weather for wood he had piled against the garage the previous autumn. The air was bright and cold against his face, and the snow in the driveway was already halfway to his knees. He gathered logs, shaking off their soft white caps and carrying them inside. The kindling in the iron grate caught fire immediately, and he sat for a time on the hearth, cross-legged, adding logs and watching the flames leap, blue-edged and hypnotic. Outside, snow continued to fall quietly through the darkness, as bright and thick as static in the cones of light cast by the streetlights. By the time he rose and looked out the window, their car had become a soft white hill on the edge of the street. Already his footprints in the driveway had filled and disappeared.

He brushed ashes from his hands and sat on the sofa beside his wife, her feet propped on pillows, her swollen ankles crossed, a copy of Dr. Spock balanced on her belly. Absorbed, she licked her index finger **absently** each time she turned a page. Her hands were slender, her fingers short and sturdy, and she bit her bottom lip lightly, intently, as she read. Watching her, he felt a surge of love and wonder: that she was his wife, that their baby, due in just three weeks, would soon be born. Their first child, this would be. They had been married just a year.

She looked up, smiling, when he tucked the blanket around her legs. "You know, I've been wondering what it's like," she said. "Before we're born, I mean. It's too bad we can't remember." She opened her robe and pulled up the sweater she wore underneath, revealing a belly as round and hard as a melon. *She ran her hand across its smooth surface, firelight playing across her skin, casting reddish gold onto her hair.* "Do you suppose it's like being inside a great lantern? The book says light-permeates my skin, that the baby can already see."

"I don't know," he said.

She laughed. "Why not?" she asked. "You're the doctor."

"I'm just an orthopedic surgeon," he reminded her. "I could tell you the ossification pattern for fetal bones, but that's about it." He lifted her foot, both **delicate** and swollen inside the light blue sock, and began to massage it gently: the powerful tarsal bone of her heel, the metatarsals and the phalanges, hidden beneath skin and densely layered muscles like a fan about to open. Her breathing filled the quiet room, her foot warmed his hands, and he imagined the perfect, secret, symmetry of bones. In pregnancy she seemed to him beautiful but fragile, fine blue veins faintly visible through her pale white skin.

It had been an excellent pregnancy, without medical restrictions. Even so, he had not been able to make love to her for several months. He found himself wanting to protect her instead, to carry her up flights of stairs, to wrap her in blankets, to bring her cups of custard. "I'm not an invalid," she protested each time, laughing. "I'm not some fledgling you discovered on the lawn." Still, she was pleased by his attentions. Sometimes he woke and watched her as she slept: the flutter of her eyelids, the slow even movement of her chest, her outflung hand, small enough that he could enclose it completely with his own.

She was eleven years younger than he was. He had first seen her not much more than a year ago, as she rode up an escalator in a department store downtown, one gray November Saturday while he was buying ties. He was thirty-three years old and new to Lexington, Kentucky, and she had risen out of the crowd like some kind of **vision**, her blond hair swept back in an elegant chignon, pearls glimmering at her throat and on her ears. She was wearing a coat of dark green wool, and her skin was clear and pale. He stepped onto the escalator, pushing his way upward through the crowd, struggling to keep her in sight. She went to the fourth floor, lingerie and hosiery. When he tried to follow her through **aisles** dense with racks of slips and brassieres and panties, all glimmering softly, a sales clerk in a navy blue dress with a white collar stopped him, smiling, to ask if she could help. *A robe, he said, scanning the aisles until he caught sight of her hair, a dark green shoulder, her bent head revealing the elegant pale curve of her neck.* A robe for my sister who lives in New Orleans. He had no sister, of course, or any living family that he acknowledged.

The clerk disappeared and came back a moment later with three robes in sturdy terry cloth. He chose blindly, hardly glancing down, taking the one on top. Three sizes, the clerk was saying, and a better selection of colors next month, but he was already in the aisle, a coral-colored robe draped over his arm, his shoes squeaking on the tiles as he moved impatiently between the other shoppers to where she stood.

She was shuffling through the stacks of expensive stockings, sheer colors shining through slick cellophane windows: taupe, navy, a maroon as dark as pig' s blood. The sleeve of her green coat brushed his and he smelled her perfume, something delicate and yet pervasive, something like the dense pale petals of lilacs outside the window of the student rooms he'd once occupied in Pittsburgh. The squat windows of his basement apartment were always grimy, opaque with steel-factory soot and ash, but in the spring there were lilacs blooming, sprays of white and lavender pressing against the glass, their scent drifting in like light.

1964 年 3 月

她临盆前几小时下起了雪。起先只是午后阴沉的天上飘下几朵雪花，而后大风吹得雪花滚滚飞扬，盘旋在他们家宽敞前廊的边际。他站在她身旁，倚在窗边，看着雪花在强风中翻腾、回旋，缓缓飘落到地面。附近家家户户点亮了灯火，光秃秃的树枝变得雪白。

晚餐后，他生了一炉火。他鼓起勇气走入风雪中，去拿秋季堆积在车库旁边的柴火。冷冽的寒风打着他的脸颊，车道上的积雪已经深及腿肚。他捡起木头，抖去上面松软的白雪，抱着木头走回屋内。壁炉里的火花马上引燃熊熊火光，他在壁炉前盘腿坐了一会，一面添加木头，一面看着火花跃动，火焰周围带着一圈蓝光，令人昏昏欲睡。屋外，白雪在黑暗中静静地持续飘落，在街灯的照耀下，既静谧，又明亮、厚实。等到他起身往窗外一看，他们的车已经变成街角的一座白色小山丘，先前印在车道上的脚印已被填满，不见踪迹。

他拍去双手上的灰烬，坐到沙发上的妻子身旁。她双脚垫在靠枕上，肿胀的脚踝交叠放着，一本斯波克医生的育儿宝典四平八稳地摆在她肚子上。她读得出神，每次翻页就不自觉地舔一下食指。她双手纤细，五指短而强壮，阅读时心无旁骛地轻咬着下唇。他看着她，心中顿时充满了挚爱与惊叹：她是他的妻子，他们的宝宝即将诞生，预产期只剩 3 个星期。这是他们第一个宝宝，而他俩结婚才一年。

他拿了条毯子盖住她的双腿，她微笑地抬起头。“你知道吗？我始终想不通那是什么感觉。”她说，“我是说出生之前。真可惜我们不记得。”她拉开袍子，脱下穿在里面的毛衣，露出像西瓜般圆硬的腹部。她伸手抚过它圆滑的表面，火光映在她的脸上，在她的发际洒下金红色的光影。“你猜那种感觉像不像置身一个大灯笼里？书上说灯光能透过我的皮肤，小宝宝能看得见。”

“我不知道。”他说。

她笑了笑说，“怎么不知道？”她问道，“你是个医生。”

“我只是个骨科医生。”他提醒她，“我可以告诉你小宝宝在胚胎时期的骨化历程，但仅此而已。”他抬高她一只脚，裹在浅蓝色袜子里的双脚细腻而肿胀，他轻轻地按摩：她脚后跟的跗骨强劲有力，脚掌骨和趾骨隐藏在肌肤之下，密密相迭的肌肉仿佛是把即将展开的扇子。房间里静得能听到她的呼吸声，她的脚温暖了他的双手，他脑海中浮现出骨头的完美、隐秘与匀称。在他眼里，怀孕的她显得美丽而脆弱，苍白的肌肤上隐约可见细微的蓝色血管。

怀孕过程非常顺利，医生也没有给出什么限制。尽管如此，他已好几个月没有跟她燕好。他发现自己只想保护她，抱她上楼、替她盖被子、帮她端布丁等等。“我不是病人，”她每次都笑着抗议，“也不是你在草坪上发现的雏鸟。”虽说如此，他的关爱其实令她相当开心。有时他醒来看着沉睡中的她，她的眼睫毛轻轻眨动，胸脯缓慢而平稳地起伏，一只手伸到一旁，小巧得能让他完全握住。

她比他小 11 岁。一年前，他们初次相逢。当时是 11 月的一个星期六，天气阴沉，他到市区的一家百货商店买领带，刚好看到她乘电扶梯上楼。33 岁的他刚搬到肯塔基州的莱克星顿。她从人群中脱颖而出，仿佛美景般，一头金发在脑后盘成优雅的髻，珍珠在她颈部与耳际闪闪发光。她穿着一件深绿色的毛外套，肌肤澄净而洁白。他踏上电扶梯，推开人群往上走，力图让她不要离开自己的视线。她走到四楼的内衣与丝袜柜台，他试图跟随着她，穿过一排排挂满内衣、胸罩、内裤的货架，件件衣物散发出柔软的光泽。有位穿白领和天蓝色外套的售货小姐拦下了他，微笑着询问有何需要服务之处，他说想找件睡袍，同时双眼不停地在货架间搜寻，直至看到她的金发及深绿色的身影为止。她微微低头，露出洁白优美的颈线。我想帮住在新奥尔良的妹妹买件睡袍，他当然没有妹妹，或是任何他所认识的、尚在人间的亲人。

售货小姐离开没多久，拿来了三件质料结实的绒布睡袍，他漫不经心地挑拣，几乎连看都没看就拿起最上面那件。售货小姐说有三种尺寸，下个月还有更多颜色可供挑选，但他已经走向货架之间，手臂上搭着那件珊瑚色的睡袍，皮鞋在地砖上发出刺耳的声响，焦急地迈过其他顾客朝她走去。

她正在看一叠昂贵的丝袜，丝袜细致的色彩映着光滑的玻璃柜台闪闪发亮：灰褐、天蓝，还有像猪血般暗沉的红栗。她绿色外套的衣袖扫过他的袖口，他闻到她的香水，气味淡雅却弥漫各处，好像他以前在匹兹堡学生宿舍窗外浓密、洁白的紫丁香花瓣。当年他住在地下室，低矮的窗户外面一片灰暗，总是蒙着钢铁工厂的煤灰。但到了春天紫丁香盛开时，洁白与淡紫色的花瓣紧贴着窗面，香气如同光线般飘进室内。

If you fight for yourself, only you can win; when you fight for your marriage, you both win.

——Pearsall Paul

如果你只为自己奋斗，只有你一个人是赢家；若为婚姻奋斗，夫妻两人都是赢家。

——美国哲学家　保罗

作者介绍

金·爱德华兹：生于德州，长于纽约，现为肯塔基大学英文系助理教授，常在各地举办写作工作坊，著有短篇小说集《火王的秘密》。《不存在的女儿》是她出版的第一部长篇小说。她是美国各大文学奖项的常客。2002 年她获得怀丁基金会的怀丁作家奖，1998 年则入选海明威文学奖。她还得过芝加哥论坛报举办的倪尔森爱格林奖、全国杂志奖等。

单词注解

edge [edʒ] *n.* 边，棱；边缘

absently ['æbsəntli] *adv.* 心不在焉地

delicate ['delikit] *adj.* 脆的，易碎的；娇贵的

vision ['viʒən] *n.* 视力；视觉

Aisle [ail] *n.* 通道，走道

名句大搜索

她伸手抚过它圆滑的表面，火光映在她的脸上，在她的发际洒下金红色的光影。

同时双眼不停地在货架间搜寻，直至看到她的金发及深绿色的身影为止。她微微低头，露出洁白优美的颈线。

她正在看一叠昂贵的丝袜，丝袜细致的色彩映着光滑的玻璃柜台闪闪发亮：灰褐、天蓝，还有像猪血般暗沉的红栗。

I Am Legend

我是传奇

[美] 理查德·马瑟森 (Richard Matheson)

恐怖的生化战争席卷而来，人类为自己掘下了死亡的坟墓。世纪末日随即而来，人类快要灭绝了，唯一存活下来的是纽约一个才华横溢的病原体学者，罗伯特·奈维尔。这种通过空气传播的病毒快速地笼罩了整个城市。血液天生的免疫力使罗伯特成了仅存的人类。作为人类最后的希望，他用自己血液中的免疫系统，寻找逆转病毒的方法。他别无选择，因为他的时间不多了。

On those cloudy days, Robert Neville was never sure when sunset came, and sometimes they were in the streets before he could get back.

If he had been more analytical, he might have **calculated** the approximate time of their arrival ; but he still used the lifetime habit of judging nightfall by the sky, and on cloudy days that method didn't work. That was why he chose to stay near the house on those days.

He walked around the house in the dull gray of afternoon, a cigarette dangling from the corner of his mouth, trailing threadlike smoke over his shoulder. He checked each window to see if any of the boards had been loosened. After violent attacks, the planks were often split or partially pried off, and he had to replace them completely ; a job he hated. Today only one plank was loose. Isn't that amazing? he thought.

In the back yard he checked the hothouse and the water tank. Sometimes the **structure** around the tank might be weakened or its rain catchers bent or broken off. Sometimes they would lob rocks over the high fence around the hothouse, and occasionally they would tear through the overhead net and he'd have to replace panes.

Both the tank and the hothouse were undamaged today. He went to the house for a hammer and nails. As he pushed open the front door, he looked at the **distorted** reflection of himself in the cracked mirror he'd fastened to the door a month ago. In a few days, jagged pieces of the silver-backed glass would start to fall off. Let'em fall, he thought. It was the last damned mirror he'd put there ; it wasn't worth it. He'd put garlic there instead. Garlic always worked.

He passed slowly through the dim silence of the living room, turned left into the small hallway, and left again into his bedroom. Once the room had been warmly **decorated**, but that was in another time. Now it was a room entirely functional, and since Neville's bed and bureau took up so little space, he had converted one side of the room into a shop.

A long bench covered almost an entire wall, on its hardwood top a heavy band saw ; a wood lathe, an emery wheel, and a vise. Above it, on the wall, were haphazard racks of the tools that Robert Neville used.

He took a hammer from the bench and picked out a few nails from one of the disordered bins. Then he went back outside and nailed the plank fast to the shutter. The unused nails he threw into the rubble next door.

For a while he stood on the front lawn looking up and down the silent length of Cimarron Street. He was a tall man, thirty-six, born of English-German stock, his features undistinguished except for the long, determined mouth and the bright blue of his eyes, which moved now over the charred ruins of the houses on each side of his. He'd burned them down to prevent them from jumping on his roof from the **adjacent** ones.

After a few minutes he took a long, slow breath and went back into the house. He tossed the hammer on the living-room couch, then lit another cigarette and had his midmorning drink.

Later he forced himself into the kitchen to grind up the five-day **accumulation** of garbage in the sink. He knew he should burn up the paper plates and utensils too, and dust the furniture and wash out the sinks and the bathtub and toilet, and change the sheets and pillowcase on his bed ; but he didn't feel like it.

For he was a man and he was alone and these things had no importance to him.

It was almost noon. Robert Neville was in his hothouse collecting a basketful of garlic.

In the beginning it had made him sick to smell garlic in such quantity his stomach had been in a state of constant turmoil. Now the smell was in his house and in his clothes, and sometimes he thought it was even in his flesh.

He hardly noticed it at all.

When he had enough bulbs, he went back to the house and dumped them on the drainboard of me sink. As he flicked the wall switch, the light flickered, then flared into normal brilliance. A disgusted hiss passed his clenched teeth. The generator was at it again. He'd have to get out that damned manual again and check the wiring. And, if it were too much trouble to repair, he'd have to install a new generator.

Angrily he jerked a high-legged stool to the sink, got a knife, and sat down with an exhausted grunt.

First, he separated the bulbs into the small, sickle-shaped cloves. *Then he cut each pink, leathery clove in half, exposing the fleshy center buds.* The air thickened with the musky, **pungent** odor. When it got too oppressive, he snapped on the air-conditioning unit and suction drew away the worst of it.

Now he reached over and took an icepick from its wall rack. He punched holes in each clove half, then strung them all together with wire until he had about twenty-five necklaces.

In the beginning he had hung these necklaces over the windows. But from a distance they'd thrown rocks until he'd been forced to cover the broken panes with plywood scraps. Finally one day he'd torn off the plywood and nailed up even rows of planks instead. It had made the house a gloomy **sepulcher**, but it was better than having rocks come flying into his rooms in a shower of splintered glass. And, once he had installed the three air-conditioning units, it wasn't too bad. A man could get used to anything if he had to.

When he was finished stringing the garlic cloves, he went outside and nailed them over the window boarding, taking down the old strings, which had lost most of their potent smell.

He had to go through this process twice a week. *Until he found something better, it was his first line of defense.*

Defense? he often thought. For what?

在阴天，罗伯特·奈维尔判断日落的时间就不准了。有时在他赶回家之前，天就黑了。

如果他仔细分析一下，或许能推测出日落的大概时间。但他已经习惯了根据天色来判断时间。一到阴天，这方法就不灵了，所以一到阴天，他就呆在自家附近。

一个阴晦的下午，他正绕着房屋散步，嘴角叼着香烟，细丝状的烟雾在他身后缭绕上升。他仔细检查每扇窗户，看是否有木板松动。疯狂袭击过后，那些厚实的木板总会出现裂痕甚至被掀起一角，他只好换掉它们。一个讨厌的活儿。今天只有一块窗板松脱，真让人吃惊！他暗自想着。

他检查后院的温室和贮水池，贮水池周围的桁架总是失去力度，接雨装置要么弯曲要么断裂。有时他们把石头扔过温室周围的高大围栏，石块偶尔会撕开上面的天棚，他不得不替换它们。

今天温室和贮水池都没损坏。他进屋拿锤子和钉子。推开前门，他看到自己在破裂的镜子里的扭曲影像。镜子是他上个月钉在门上的。可没几天，镀银玻璃就开始剥落，由它们落吧，他想。他再也不往那地方放混蛋镜子了，不值，还不如放大蒜。大蒜总是管用。

他缓慢地穿过昏暗寂静的客厅，左转进入狭窄的走廊，然后来到他的卧室。那房间曾经装饰得很漂亮，但那是过去。现在它只是个实用性房间，奈维尔的衣橱和床没占多大空间，于是他把房间一头改成了工作坊。

一个长凳占据了几乎整面墙，在它的硬木表面放着重锯齿、车床、砂轮、锤子和老虎钳，在长凳上方的壁架上，散乱堆放着罗伯特·奈维尔常用的各种工具。

他从长凳上拿起锤子，又从杂物箱里摸出了几个钉子。他来到屋外，把松动的木板钉好。剩余的钉子随手丢到了挨门的石堆里。

他在门口草坪上站了一会，前后打量着西马伦大街。他是个高个儿男子，今年 36 岁，英德血统。他的长相一般，只有细长的嘴唇和湛蓝的眼睛还算有型。现在这双蓝眼睛正盯着他房子两边的一堆烧毁的房屋废墟。是他自己烧的，以防有人通过邻近的房屋跳上他的屋顶。

几分钟后，他伸了个懒腰，走回屋去。他把锤子丢在客厅沙发上，又点了支烟，开始喝上午茶。

过后，他强迫自己进了厨房，在水槽里碾碎已经积累了 5

天的垃圾。他知道他应该烧掉纸餐具和炊具。应该掸去家具上的灰尘，应该清洗水槽，清洗浴缸和厕所。应该换洗他的床单枕套。但他讨厌做这些事。

因为他是男人，而且独自生活，这些破事对他来说无关紧要。

快到中午时，罗伯特·奈维尔在他的温室里收了满满一篮子大蒜。

想当初，闻到这么重的大蒜味时，他肯定会恶心得想吐，胃里会持续地翻腾。可现在，这种味道弥漫了他的房间、衣服，有时他甚至觉得这味道已经渗透进了他的肉体和血液里。

这味道再也不能引起他的注意了。

摘了足够多的大蒜后，他回到房间把它们全部倒在水槽里。他轻弹了下墙上的开关，灯光闪烁了一阵，才恢复正常光亮。他发出厌烦的嘶嘶声。一定是发电机的毛病。他又要找手册，又要检查线路。要是太难修理，又得去换新的。

他气愤地拎了个高脚凳放到水槽旁，拿了把小刀，带着疲惫的咕哝声坐下。

首先，他把大蒜剥成月牙状的小蒜瓣。然后把每个粉色皮革般坚韧的蒜瓣切开，露出里面的蒜肉。空气中顿时充满浓郁的刺激性气味。当他实在忍受不了这味道时，便打开空调抽掉这浑浊的气体。

他起身从壁架上抽出一个碎冰锥，在蒜片上打孔，然后把它们穿在金属丝上，直到他拥有 25 条项链为止。

先前他把大蒜项链挂在窗户上，但是有人总是从远处扔石头，他不得不用废钢夹板盖住损坏的窗户。后来，他又扯掉夹板，钉上一排厚木板。房子弄得像一个阴沉的墓穴，但总比石头夹着冰雹般的玻璃碎片飞进屋来要强。在他安装了三台空调后，发现状况还不错。一个男人可以适应任何事情，如果他必须这么做的话。

串好蒜瓣，他走出去将它们钉到窗板上，换下原来的旧项链，那些早已没了浓烈的气味。

这事他每周都要做两次。在找到更好的方法以前，这是他最好的第一防线。

防线？他经常想，防什么？

Goals determine what you are going to be.

——Julius Erving

目标决定你将成为什么样的人。

——欧　文

作者介绍

理查德·马瑟森被誉为“20 世纪最伟大的作家之一”,《 我是传奇》小说问世以来，已经于 1964 和 1971 年两度被搬上荧屏。除了一些魔幻、科普、恐怖风格的小说，马瑟森还是一个多产的影视剧作家，他的很多小说都被改编成影视剧本，如《奇怪的收缩人》、《重返的时刻》等。

单词注解

calculated ['kælkjuleitid] *adj.* 预先计划的；可能的

structure ['strʌktʃə] *n.* 结构；构造；组织

decorate ['dekəreit] *v.* 装饰，修饰

adjacent [ə'dʒeisənt] *adj.* 毗连的，邻接的

accumulation [əkju:mjʊ'leiʃ(ə)n] *n.* 积累；积聚；堆积

pungent ['pʌndʒənt] *adj.* 辛辣的；尖刻的

sepulcher ['sepəlkə] *n.* 坟墓，墓穴

名句大搜索

因为他是男人，而且独自生活，这些破事对他来说无关紧要。

然后把每个粉色皮革般坚韧的蒜瓣切开，露出里面的蒜肉。

在找到更好的方法以前，这是他最好的第一防线。

The Song of Kahunsha

没有悲伤的城市

[加] 阿诺什·艾拉尼（Anosh Irani）

在 1993 年的孟买，十岁的祥弟，自幼在孤儿院长大。他在脑海中构筑出一个祥和美好的乐土“卡洪莎”，意即“没有悲伤的城市”。面临孤儿院的拆迁，祥弟从院长口中得知父亲下落，随即带着自己沾染血迹的婴儿衣，展开了寻父之旅。他面对的不是梦想中的乐园，而是充满暴力与黑暗的孟买大街。祥弟与一对流浪街头的姐弟结伴同行，却又落入了黑道老大阿能拜的魔掌，更在当地一座印度教神庙的爆炸事件后，参与一场谋害无辜穆斯林家庭的血腥复仇行动。童年终要结束，美梦也总会清醒，哪个城市没有悲伤？身处残酷修罗场的祥弟被迫快快长大，他能否找到亲生父亲？

Guddi throws the twig away and wipes her hands on her brown dress.

And begins to sing.

What follows is something Chamdi has never imagined.

Guddi's voice suggests that her throat contains magical things, impossible things. It is as though colours are singing, and each colour is a note. Chamdi's skin breaks into ripples, and if he could fly he would go straight into the glass windows of the nearby classroom and come out unharmed. Such is the beauty of Guddi's voice.

The leaves in the trees move gently, as though the trees have felt her song, and dust rises in the air, and swirls about in a playful dance.

By the time Guddi finishes, Chamdi knows that this song is the beginning of something unearthly. So he will use unearthly words to tell her how lovely the song is. He leans towards her and whispers in her ear, "Khile Soma Kafusal."

"What?" she says, slowly catching her breath.

"Khile Soma Kafusal," he repeats softly.

"What does that mean?"

"It is spoken in the Language of Gardens. Someday I will tell you what it means."

"Where is that language spoken?"

"In Kahunsha."

"Kahunsha?"

"The city of no sadness. One day, all sadness will die, and Kahunsha will be born."

As Chamdi whispers his secret to Guddi, he forgets, for a second, that it is night. Everything around him is luminous—the leaves, the red hair ribbon, the gravel is waiting to burst.

Guddi flicks the hair off her face and her brown eyes widen. Her eyelashes seem to lengthen—they stretch out as if to reach Ghamdi.

"Don't be an idiot," she says. "How can such a place exist?"

"Because of your song. Your song is so beautiful that it has the power to create a whole new city.

"Have you lost your mind?"

"Yes. And I will lose it again, and again, and again, until we are happy. You, me, Sumdi, Amma, the baby, even Dabba. Someday, we will all live together in Kahunsha."

NINE

A group of boys sit on a handcart and smoke. Sumdi is amongst them, seated next to the smallest boy, whose head is shaved. Chamdi watches the boys pass a cigarette from hand to hand, and wait for it to come back to them. One of the boys has a tin can and he drums on it. The bald one who sits next to Sumdi starts drumming too, but he does so on Sumdi's polio leg, and then puts his ear to it, as though he expects it to emit a sound. The boys have a good laugh. Then Sumdi starts to speak and Chamdi realizes that Sumdi is telling them a story. It is about how his ribs will one day turn into tusks. Chamdi chuckles because Sumdi is doing is a terrible job of telling the story.

Chamdi wishes Mrs. Sadiq were next to him right now, so she could offer him.good advice. He knows what she would say, that it is wrong to steal. Jesus would have been of no use right now. Jesus always stayed silent.

“Go to sleep,” says Sumdi.

“No, I’ll stay awake for a while.”

“And do what?”

“Think.”

“About what?”

“Anything. I’ll dream.”

“How can you dream while you’re awake?”

“That’s the best kind of dream.”

“You have to be drunk for that to happen. Or on ganja. But you must not even know what ganja is.

“No.”

“Ganja is what poor people use to distract themselves from their miserable lives. But even that costs money.”

“That’s why I dream. Dreams are free.”

“Why are you so strange? Why can’t you be normal and spit on the road or shit in your pants?”

“Tell me, what’s the one thing you really want in your life?” asks Chamdi.

“I want to leave Bombay.”

“That’s not a dream.”

“Why not?”

“Running away is not a dream. Anyway that is Bulbul’s dream.”

“Who the hell is Bulbul?”

Chamdi looks at Guddi. She smiles and then closes her eyes quickly as though a massive bout of sleep has suddenly come over her.

“She is Bulbul?” asks Sumdi. “That terror, you called her a nightingale? You really are a dreamer. Now go to sleep.”

"Not before you answer my question."

"Why can't you let me be? Go and talk to the rat if you are lonely. Here, I'll lift the box and you can enter that hole and dream in the dark."

"What's the one thing you really want?"

"You won't let me sleep till I answer your question, will you?"

"No."

"Okay, I'll tell you."

"Truthfully."

"Yes, truthfully." Sumdi glances over at his sister. Her eyes stay closed. Amma stirs and then settles. A police jeep rushes past the bus stop. Ghamdi quickly imagines three blue-and-yellow-striped tigers roaring behind the jeep, serving as its siren. The police-tigers go to places the jeep cannot. They pick out the scent of thieves much better than any policeman. And they will look after the children of Bombay, treat them as their own cubs.

"Okay," says Sumdi, holding his stiff leg. "I'll tell you."

"Good."

"But you can never repeat this to anyone. Not even back to me. And after we have had this stupid conversation, you'll let me sleep in peace. Even if God comes and starts cooking mutton biryani in the middle of the road you'll not wake me."

I promise. "You see this leg of mine? I've never been able to run. Even when I walk, I feel heavy. It's as though all my anger collects in this leg and it gets heavier and heavier. Even when my father died, I couldn't run to him. I got there last, after Amma and my sister. Sometimes I just wish that I wouldn't feel so heavy So I really wish, you know, a waking dream just like yours in a way, that I will one day... No, it's stupid. I'm sleeping."

"Go on, Sumdi."

"What's the point? What I wish for is impossible."

"Why wish for what's possible?"

"Is that so?"

"Yes, it's like that."

"I want to fly," he whispers. "That's my dream. I, Sumdi, will one day fly all over Bombay, see every gulley, see all the shops, movie theatres, gambling dens, brothels, cock fights, cricket matches, and once I am done, I will fly over the sea like a champion bird, and never ever stop. I will keep on flying for the rest of my life."

"That's a wonderful dream," says Chamdi.

"But it can never come true, so what's the use?"

Chamdi does not say anything. He wants to tell Sumdi about Kahunsha. How police-tigers will patrol the streets to keep them safe, how there will be flowers everywhere, how all the water taps will gush forth pure rainwater, and how, most of all, no one will be deformed and people will not hurt each other.

古蒂把那根小树枝扔出去，在棕色裙子上擦了擦手。

然后她开始唱起歌来。

古蒂的歌声有着不可思议的魔力，好像是五颜六色的，每个音符都是一种颜色。祥弟的心整个荡漾了起来，如果他能飞的话，他会直接朝旁边教室的窗户飞进去，然后又原样飞出来，这就是古蒂的歌声的美妙之处。

树叶轻轻地摇着，好像也听到了古蒂的歌声，地上的尘土飞到空中旋转，像是在顽皮地跳舞。

古蒂唱完一首歌，祥弟觉得这首歌一定来自另一个世界，因此他决定用另一个世界的语言告诉古蒂这首歌有多么好听。他凑过去在古蒂耳边说："Khile Soma Kafusal。"

"什么？"古蒂说，慢慢地喘着气。

"Khile Soma Kafusal。"祥弟又轻轻地说了一遍。

"这是什么意思？"

"这是花园语言，我以后告诉你是什么意思。"

"这种语言在哪儿用啊？"

"在卡洪莎。"

"卡洪莎？"

"没有悲伤的城市。有一天这个世界所有的悲伤会消失，而卡洪莎就会出现。"

祥弟在把他的秘密偷偷告诉古蒂的时候，他有一刻忘了那是在夜晚。他周围的一切都染上了光晕——树叶、红发带和碎石子。

古蒂把垂到脸上的头发抹开，睁大了褐色的眼睛。她的眼睫毛好像变长了，好像要伸出来碰到祥弟一样。

"别傻了，"她说，"怎么可能有这样的地方呢？"

"因为你唱的歌，那首歌太美了，它能创造出一个崭新的城市。"

"你是不是精神不正常了？"

“对，我还会一次又一次地这样，直到我们过上快乐的生活。你，我，桑迪，艾玛，艾玛的孩子，还有达巴，有一天我们会在没有悲伤的城市生活在一起。”

一帮孩子坐在手推车上抽着烟，桑迪也在里面，他坐在那个最小的孩子旁边，那个孩子头剃得光光的。祥弟看见那帮孩子轮着抽一支香烟，有个孩子在敲着一个马口铁罐，桑迪旁边的那个光头孩子也开始敲，不过他敲打的是桑迪那条坏腿，敲完了又趴在上面听，好像是想听听会发出什么声音。男孩们哈哈大笑，然后桑迪开始说话，祥弟意识到桑迪是在给他们讲故事，讲的是他的肋骨怎么突然变成了长牙。祥弟偷偷笑了，因为桑迪讲的可不怎么样。

祥弟希望萨迪克夫人这时候就在他身边，能给他点忠告。他知道萨迪克夫人会说什么，偷东西是不对的。耶稣这时候没什么用，他总是沉默着。

“睡吧。”桑迪说。

“不，我还想再待会儿。”

“做什么。”

“想事情。”

“想什么？”

“什么都想，我喜欢梦想。”

“你醒着的时候怎么梦想？”

“那是最好的梦。”

“你得喝醉了才能梦得到，或者抽印度大麻，但是你没准连大麻是什么都不知道。”

“的确不知道。”

“大麻是穷人用来逃避悲惨命运的东西，但这也要花钱。”

“这就是我要梦想的原因，梦想不要钱。”

“你怎么这么怪？你为什么不能正常点，在路上吐痰，或者拉在裤子里？”

“告诉我你真正想要的是什么？”

“我想离开孟买。”

“这不是梦想。”

“为什么不是？”

“逃离不是梦想，不管怎么样吧，那是布布的梦想。”

“布布到底是谁？”

祥弟看着古蒂，她突然笑了一下，然后赶快闭上眼睛，好像沉重的睡意突然来袭一样。

“她是布布？”桑迪问，“真可怕，你给她起了个夜莺的名字，你可真够能做梦的。现在去睡吧。”

“你先回答我的问题。”

“你为什么要缠着我？如果你闲得慌，就去跟老鼠说话吧。看，我把盒子拿起来，然后你就钻进洞里做梦了。”

“有什么东西是你真正梦想要得到的吗？”

“我不回答你的问题，你就不让我睡了，是吗？”

“对。”

“好，那我就告诉你。”

“讲实话。”

“好，讲实话，”桑迪瞅了他妹妹一眼，古蒂闭着眼睛，艾玛动了一下又安静下来了。一辆警车冲过公共汽车站，祥弟马上想到三只蓝黄相间条纹的老虎跟在警车后面吼叫着，像警车的警报器一样。警察虎能到警车去不了的地方，它们比警察更能闻出贼的气味，它们还能照看孟买的孩子们，像对自己的虎崽一样。

“好，”桑迪说，他抓着那条僵硬的腿，“我告诉你。”

“好的。”

“但是你不能跟别人说，也不许再跟我重复。我们胡扯完之后，你就得让我好好睡觉，就算上帝来了，开始在路当中做羊肉比亚尼菜，你也不能叫醒我。”

“我答应你。”

“看到我这条腿了吗？我从来都不能跑，就算走路都觉得沉重，就好像我的怒气都积聚在这条腿上一样，它变得越来越重。连我爸爸死的时候，我都没法朝他跑过去，最后我总算在艾玛和我妹妹后面到了那儿。有时候我只希望不会觉得这么沉重，你知道，就像你做白日梦一样，我希望有一天……算了，太傻了，我去睡了。”

“讲啊，桑迪。”

“这有什么意思啊？我希望的东西是不可能实现的。”

“为什么要希望能实现的东西呢？”

“难道不是这样吗？”

“不是的。”

“那我想飞，”桑迪小声说，“这是我的梦想。我，桑迪，有一天能飞遍孟买，看到每一条水沟，看到所有的商店、影剧院、赌场、妓院、斗鸡、板球赛，一旦我看完了这些，我就像一只冠军鸟一样，飞过大海，一直不停，我这辈子就在天上飞着了。”

“这真是个很棒的梦想。”祥弟说。

“但这永远也不会成真，所以又有什么用呢？”

祥弟没说话，他想跟桑迪说没有悲伤的城市，警察虎怎么在街上巡逻，保护他们，怎样到处都是花，水龙头怎样喷出纯净的雨水，而且最主要的是，没有人会变成残疾，人们也不会彼此伤害。

Genius is formed in quiet, character in the stream of life.

——Goethe

天才形成于平静中，性格来自于生活的激流。

——歌　德

作者介绍

阿诺什·艾拉尼，印度裔作家，在孟买长大，1998 年移民加拿大。他不仅写小说，也写舞台剧。2004 年，他的首部长篇《那残废和他的护身符》引起文坛瞩目。两年后的第二部作品《没有悲伤的城市》更是大放异彩，获美国图书馆协会 2008 年最佳青少年好书提名，2007 年加拿大广播公司的“全民读好书”选书，在加拿大和意大利均攻占畅销排行榜，售出美国、法国、意大利、西班牙、希腊、以色列等 9 国版权。

单词注解

basket [bɑ:skit] *n.* 篮，篓，筐
afraid [ə'freid] *adj.* 害怕的，怕的
cement [si'ment] *n.* 水泥
eventually [i'ventjuəli] *adv.* 最后，终于
sewage ['sju(:)idʒ] *n.* 污水；污秽物

名句大搜索

古蒂的歌声有着不可思议的魔力，好像是五颜六色的，每个音符都是一种颜色。

古蒂唱完一首歌，祥弟觉得这首歌一定来自另一个世界。

祥弟没说话，他想跟桑迪说没有悲伤的城市，警察虎怎么在街上巡逻，保护他们，怎样到处都是花，水龙头怎样喷出纯净的雨水，而且最主要的是，没有人会变成残疾，人们也不会彼此伤害。

The Silence of the Lambs
沉默的羔羊

［美］托马斯•哈里斯（Thomas Harris）

克拉丽丝是联邦调查局的见习特工，他所在的城市出现了一个专剥女性皮的变态杀人犯“野牛”比尔。克拉丽丝的任务是去一所戒备森严的监狱访问精神病专家汉尼拔博士，同他交谈以获取罪犯的心理行为资料来帮助破案。汉尼拔被关在地牢里，他是一位智商极高、思维敏捷但有些精神变态的中年男子，并且是个食人狂。博士对她进行心理分析，克拉丽丝说出童年的最痛苦的回忆是常常听到羔羊的惨叫……经过一番心理分析，汉尼拔了解了克拉丽丝为什么总会听到羔羊的惨叫。克拉丽丝把对象锁定在一个叫詹米·冈的人身上。克拉丽丝找到并击中了比尔，然而更危险的人物却又出现了。

Behavioral Science, the FBI section that deals with serial murder, is on the bottom floor of the Academy building at Quantico, half-buried in the earth. Clarice Starling reached it **flushed** after a fast walk from Hogan's Alley on the firing range. She had grass in her hair and grass stains on her FBI Academy windbreaker from diving to the ground under fire in an arrest problem on the range.

No one was in the outer office, so she fluffed briefly by her reflection in the glass doors. She knew she could look all right without primping. Her hands smelled of gunsmoke, but there was no time to wash — Section Chief Crawford's summons had said now.

She found Jack Crawford alone in the cluttered suite of offices. He was standing at someone else's desk talking on the telephone and she had a chance to look him over for the first time in a year. What she saw disturbed her.

Normally, Crawford looked like a fit, middle-aged engineer who might have paid his way through college playing baseball — a crafty catcher, tough when he blocked the plate. Now he was thin, his shirt collar was too big, and he had dark **puffs** under his reddened eyes. Everyone who could read the papers knew Behavioral Science section was catching hell. Starling hoped Crawford wasn't on the juice. That seemed most unlikely here.

Crawford ended his telephone conversation with a sharp "No". He took her file from under his arm and opened it.

"Starling, Clarice M., good morning," he said.

"Hello." Her smile was only polite.

"Nothing's wrong. I hope the call didn't spook you."

"No." Not totally true, Starling thought.

"Your **instructors** tell me you're doing well, top quarter of the class."

"I hope so, they haven't posted anything."

"I ask them from time to time."

That surprised Starling ; she had written Crawford off as a two-faced recruiting sergeant son of a bitch.

She had met Special Agent Crawford when he was a guest lecturer at the University of Virginia. The quality of his criminology seminars was a factor in her coming to the Bureau. She wrote him a note when she qualified for the Academy, but he never replied, and for the three months she had been a trainee at Quantico, he had ignored her.

Starling came from people who do not ask for favors or press for friendship, but she was puzzled and regretful at Crawford's behavior. Now, in his presence, she liked him again, she was sorry to note.

Clearly something was wrong with him. There was a peculiar cleverness in Crawford, aside from his intelligence, and Starling had first noticed it in his color sense and the **textures** of his clothing, even within the FBI-clone standards of agent dress. Now he was neat but drab, as though he were molting.

"A job came up and I thought about you," he said. "It's not really a job, it's more of an interesting errand. Push Berry's stuff off that chair and sit down. You put down here that you want to come directly to Behavioral Science when you get through with the Academy."

"I do."

"You have a lot of forensics, but no law enforcement background. We look for six years, minimum."

"My father was a **marsha**, I know the life."

Crawford smiled a little. "What you do have is a double major in psychology and criminology, and how many summers working in a mental health center — two?"

"Two."

"Your counselor's license, is it current?"

"It's good for two more years. I got it before you had the seminar at UVA — before I decided to do this."

"You got stuck in the hiring freeze."

Starling nodded. "I was lucky though — I found out in time to qualify as a Forensic Fellow. Then I could work in the lab until the Academy had an opening."

"You wrote to me about coming here, didn't you, and I don't think I answered — I know I didn't. I should have."

"You've had plenty else to do."

"Do you know about VI-CAP?"

"I know it's the Violent Criminal Apprehension Program. The Law Enforcement Bulletin says you're working on a **database**, but you aren't operational yet."

Crawford nodded. "We've developed a questionnaire. It applies to all the known serial murderers in modern times." He handed her a thick sheaf of papers in a **flimsy** binding. "There's a section for investigators, and one for surviving victims, if any. The blue is for the killer to answer if he will, and the pink is a series of questions an examiner asks the killer, getting his reactions as well as his answers. It's a lot of paperwork."

Paperwork, Clarice Starling's self-interest snuffled ahead like a keen beagle. She smelled a job offer coming — probably the drudgery of feeding raw data into a new computer system. It was tempting to get into Behavioral Science in any capacity she could, but she knew what happens to a woman if she's ever pegged as a secretary—it sticks until the end of time. *A choice was coming, and she wanted to choose well.*

行为科学部是联邦调查局处理系列凶杀案的部门，位于昆迪可学院大楼的底层，有一半在地下。克拉丽丝·史达琳从联邦调查局模拟射击训练中心的靶场上一路快步走来，到这儿时已是满脸通红。她的头发里有草，那件联邦调查局学员的防风衣上也都沾着草迹，那是在射击场的抓捕训练中她冒着火力猛扑到地上时沾上的。

外面的办公室空无一人，所以她就对着玻璃门，就着自己的影子，将头发简单地拂弄了一下。她知道自己不用过分打扮看上去也是可以的。她的手上有火药味，可来不及洗了，该部的头儿克劳福德说，现在就要召见她。

她发现杰克·克劳福德独自一人在一个杂乱无序的办公套间里。他正站在别人的桌子边打电话。一年来，这是她第一次有机会好好地打量他。他的样子，让她觉得很是不安。

平日里，克劳福德看上去像一位体魄强健的中年工程师。他读大学时的费用很可能是靠打棒球支付的——他像是个机灵的接手，由他来挡投手板，对方可就头疼了。而如今，他瘦了，衬衫的领子那么大，红肿的双眼下有黑眼圈。每个看报纸的人都知道，行为科学部眼下正大遭骂名。史达琳希望克劳福德不要开足马力拼老命，可在这儿，那看来是根本不可能的。

克劳福德突然“不”的一声结束了他的电话谈话。他从腋下取出她的档案，打了开来。

“克拉丽丝·M·史达琳，早上好！”他说。

“你好。”她只是礼貌的微微一笑。

“也没出什么事，但愿叫你来并没有把你吓着。”

“没有。”史达琳想，这么说并不完全是真的。

“你的老师告诉我你学得不错，班上排前 15 名。”

“希望如此。成绩他们还没有张榜公布呢。”

“我时不时会问他们。”

这使史达琳有些吃惊；她原以为克劳福德是个招募新手的警察小队长，两面派的耍滑头角色，成不了什么大器。

克劳福德曾以特工身份应邀到弗吉尼亚大学讲过课，史达琳就是在那儿遇见他的。他开的犯罪学课程质量高，她之所以来联邦调查局，就有这个因素。她获得进入学院的资格后曾给他写过一个条子，可他一直没有回音；在昆蒂科当实习生 3 个月了，也没有引起他的注意。

史达琳是那种不求人施恩、不强求他人友谊的人，但克劳福德这种做法还是叫她感到困惑和后悔。可此刻，她很遗憾地注意到，当着他的面，自己竟又喜欢上他了。

显然是出什么事了。克劳福德身上除了他那才智之外，还有一种特别的机敏，史达琳看出这一点首先是从他的着装搭配及其衣服的质地上，即使衣服是联邦调查局工作人员的统一制服。此刻的他整洁却了无生气，仿佛人正在蜕皮换骨似的。

“来了件活儿，我就想到了你。”他说，“其实也不是什么活儿，更确切地说是一份有趣的差使。你把那椅子上贝利的东西拿开坐下。这儿你写着，学院的实习一结束，你就想直接来行为科学部。”

“是的。”

“你的法医学知识很丰富，但没有执法方面的经历。我们需要有 6 年执法经历的人，至少 6 年。”

“我爸曾是个司法官，那生活什么样我知道。”

克劳福德微微笑了笑。“你真正具备的是心理学和犯罪学这一双专业，还有就是在一个心理健康中心干过，几个夏天？是两个吗？”

“两个。”

“你那心理咨询员证书现在还能用吗？”

“还可以管两年，我是在你到弗吉尼亚大学讲课之前拿到这证书的，那时我还没有决定要干这个。”

“雇用单位冻结不招人，你就被困住了。”

史达琳点了点头。“不过我的运气还不错——及时发现了结果并获得了法医会员的资格。接下来我可以到实验室干，直到学院有空缺的职位。”

“你曾写信给我说要上这儿来是吧？我想我没有回信——我知道我没有回。应该回的。”

“你有许多别的事要忙。”

“你知不知道有关 VI-CAP 的情况？”

“我知道那是指‘暴力犯罪分手拘捕计划’。《执法公报》上说你们正在处理数据，尚未进入实施阶段。”

克劳福德点点头。“我们设计了一份问卷，它适用于当今所有已知的系列凶犯。”他将装在簿封皮里的厚厚一叠文件递给了她。“其中有一部分是为调查人员准备的，还有一部分是为幸存的受害者准备的，如果有幸存者的话。那蓝色部分是要凶手回答的，假如他肯回答的话。粉红色那部分是提问者要问凶手的一组问题，他以此获得凶手的反应及回答。案头活儿不少呢！

案头活儿。克拉丽丝·史达琳出于自身利益，像一头嗅觉灵敏的小猎犬一样在闻着什么。她闻到有一份工作正向她降临——那工作很可能单调乏味，只是往新的电脑系统中输入原始数据。竭尽全力进入科学部对她来说是诱人的，可她知道，女人一旦被拴住做秘书，结果会是什么样——一辈子就在这位置上呆着吧。选择的机会来了，她要好好地选择。

A man can succeed at almost anything for which he has unlimited enthusiasm.

——C. M. Schwab

只要有无限的热情，一个人几乎可以在任何事情上取得成功。

——施瓦布

作者介绍

托马斯·哈里斯，美国通俗小说家，曾任美联社驻纽约记者兼编辑，专门从事刑事案件的采编，积累了丰富的写作材料。他先后出版了《黑色星期五》、《红色龙》、《沉默的羔羊》等多部侦探小说和犯罪小说，其中以《沉默的羔羊》影响最大，曾跃登《纽约时报》畅销书排行榜榜首。

单词注解

flush [flʌʃ] *v.* 涌；涌流

puff [pʌf] *v.* 一阵阵地吹

instructor [in'strʌktə] *n.* 教员；教练；指导者

texture ['tekstʃə] *n.* 组织，结构，质地

marshal ['mɑ:ʃəl] *n.* 元帅；司仪；典礼官

database ['deitəbeis] *n.* 资料库，数据库

flimsy ['flimzi] *adj.* 脆弱的；易损坏的；轻薄的

beagle ['bi:gl] *n.* 小猎犬；密探

名句大搜索

史达琳是那种不求人施恩、不强求他人友谊的人，但克劳福德这种做法还是叫她感到困惑和后悔。

显然是出什么事了。

选择的机会来了，她要好好地选择。

Catch-22

第二十二条军规

[美] 约瑟夫·海勒（Joseph Helle）

故事发生在第二次世界大战期间，美国空军的一支飞行大队驻守在意大利以南地中海上的一个小岛上。主人公约塞连是这支飞行大队的上尉轰炸手。他本来是一个正直勇敢、富有爱国心的青年。起初，他抱着为祖国而战的信念，出色地完成了任务，因而被提拔为上尉，还获得了一枚勋章。后来他发现周围的人都在暗算他，企图置他于死地。他竭力要保全自己的生命，他要逃离这个“世界”。最后，约塞连恍然大悟，第二十二条军规原来是一个骗局，他临阵逃脱，跑到瑞典去寻找避难所。

The Texan

It was love at first sight.

The first time Yossarian saw the chaplain he fell madly in love with him. Yossarian was in the hospital with a pain in his liver that fell just short of being **jaundice**. The doctors were puzzled by the fact that it wasn't quite jaundice. If it became jaundice they could treat it. If it didn't become jaundice and went away they could discharge him. But this just being short of jaundice all the time confused them.

Each morning they came around, three brisk and serious men with efficient mouths and inefficient eyes, accompanied by brisk and serious Nurse Duckett, one of the ward nurses who didn't like Yossarian. They read the chart at the foot of the bed and asked impatiently about the pain. They seemed irritated when he told them it was exactly the same.

"Still no movement?" the full colonel demanded.

The doctors exchanged a look when he shook his head.

"Give him another pill." Nurse Duckett made a note to give Yossarian another pill, and the four of them moved along to the next bed. None of the nurses liked Yossarian. Actually, the pain in his liver had gone away, but Yossarian didn't say anything and the doctors never suspected. They just suspected that he had been moving his bowels and not telling anyone.

Yossarian had everything he wanted in the hospital. The food wasn't too bad, and his meals were brought to him in bed. There were extra rations of fresh meat, and during the hot part of the afternoon he and the others were served chilled fruit juice or chilled chocolate milk. Apart from the doctors and the nurses, no one ever disturbed him. For a little while in the morning he had to **censor** letters, but he was free after that to spend the rest of each day lying around idly with a clear conscience. He was comfortable in the hospital, and it was easy to stay on because he always ran a temperature of 101.

After he had made up his mind to spend the rest of the war in the hospital, Yossarian wrote letters to everyone he knew saying that he was in the hospital but never mentioning why. One day he had a better idea. To everyone he knew he wrote that he was going on a very dangerous mission. "They asked for volunteers. It's very dangerous, but someone has to do it. I'll write you the instant I get back." And he had not written anyone since.

All the officer patients in the ward were forced to censor letters written by all the enlisted-men patients, who were kept in residence in wards of their own. It was a monotonous job, and Yossarian was disappointed to learn that the lives of enlisted men were only slightly more interesting than the lives of officers. After the first day he had no curiosity at all. To break the monotony he invented games. Death to all modifiers, he declared one day, and out of every letter that passed through his hands went every adverb and every adjective. The next day he made war on articles. He reached a much higher plane of creativity the following day when he blacked out everything in the letters but a, an and the. That erected more **dynamic** intralinear tensions, he felt, and in just about every case left a message far more universal. Soon he was **proscribing** parts of salutations and signatures and leaving the text untouched. One time he blacked out all but the salutation "Dear Mary" from a letter, and at the bottom he wrote, "I yearn for you tragically. R. O. Shipman, Chaplain, U. S. Army." R.O. Shipman was the group chaplain's name.

When he had exhausted all possibilities in the letters, he began attacking the names and addresses on the envelopes, obliterating whole homes and streets, **annihilating** entire metropolises with careless flicks of his wrist as though he were God. *Catch-22 required that each censored letter bear the censoring officer's name.* Most letters he didn't read at all. On those he didn't read at all he wrote his own name. On those he did read he wrote, "Washington Irving". When that grew monotonous he wrote, "Irving Washington". Censoring the envelopes had serious repercussions, produced a ripple of anxiety on some ethereal military echelon that floated a C.I.D. man back into the ward posing as a patient. They all knew he was a C.I.D. man because he kept inquiring about an officer named Irving or Washington and because after his first day there he wouldn't censor letters. *He found them too monotonous.*

It was a good ward this time, one of the best he and Dunbar had ever enjoyed. With them this time was the twenty-four-year-old fighter-pilot captain with the sparse golden **mustache** who had been shot into the Adriatic Sea in midwinter and not even caught cold. Now the summer was upon them, the captain had not been shot down, and he said he had the grippe. In the bed on Yossarian's right, still lying amorously on his belly, was the startled captain with malaria in his blood and a **mosquito** bite on his ass. Across the aisle from Yossarian was Dunbar, and next to Dunbar was the artillery captain with whom Yossarian had stopped playing chess. The captain was a good chess player, and the games were always interesting. Yossarian had stopped playing chess with him because the games were so interesting they were foolish. Then there was the educated Texan from Texas who looked like someone in Technicolor and felt, patriotically, that people of means—decent folk—should be given more votes than drifters, whores, criminals, degenerates, atheists and indecent folk—people without means.

得克萨斯人

这可是实实在在的一见钟情。

初次相见，约塞连便疯狂地恋上了随军牧师。约塞连因肝痛住在医院，不过，他这肝痛还不是黄疸病的征兆，正因为如此，医生们才伤透了脑筋。如果它转成黄疸病，他们就有办法对症下药；如果他不是黄疸病而且症状又消失了，那么他们就可以让他出院。可是他这肝痛老是拖着，怎么也变不成黄疸病，实在让他们不知所措。

每天早晨，总有三个男医生来查房，他们个个精力充沛，一本正经，尽管眼力不好，一开口却总是滔滔不绝。随同他们一起来的是同样精力充沛、不苟言笑的达克特护士。她就是讨厌约塞连的病房护士中的一个。他们看了看挂在约塞连病床上的病况记录卡，不耐烦地问了问肝痛的情况。听他说一切还是老样子，他们似乎很是恼怒。

“还没有通大便？”那位上校军医问道。

见他摇了摇头，三个医生互换了一下眼色。

“再给他服一粒药。”达克特护士用笔记下医嘱，然后他们四人便朝另一张病床走去。没有一个病房护士喜欢约塞连。其实，约塞连的肝早就不疼了，不过他什么也没说，而那些医生也从来不曾起过疑心。他们只是猜疑他早就通了大便，却不愿告诉任何人。

约塞连住在医院里什么都不缺。伙食还算不错，每天都有专人送餐，而且还外送一份肉。在下午很热的时候，他和其他病号还能喝到冰果汁或是冰巧克力牛奶。除了医生和护士，没人来打扰他。每天上午，他得去检查信件，之后便无所事事，整日躺在病床上消磨时光，倒亦心安理得。在医院里他过得相当舒坦，而且要这么住下去也挺容易，因为他的体温一直在华氏 101 度。

约塞连打定主意要留在医院，不再上前线打仗，自此以后，他便去信告知所有熟人，说自己住进了医院，不过从未提及个中缘由。有一天，他心生妙计，写信给每一个熟人，告知他要执行一项相当危险的飞行任务。“他们在征募志愿人员。任务很危险，但总得有人去干，等我一完成任务回来，就给你去信。”从那以后，他再也没有给谁写过一封信。

依照规定，病房里的每个军官病员都得检查所有士兵病员的信件，士兵病员只能呆在自己的病房里。检查信件实在是枯燥得很，得知士兵的生活只不过比军官略多些许趣味而已，约塞连很是失望。第一天下来，他便兴味索然了。于是，他就别出心裁地发明了种种把戏，给这乏味单调的差事添些情趣。有一天，他宣布要“处决”信里所有的修饰语，这一来，凡经他审查过的每一封信里的副词和形容词便统统消失了。第二天，他又向冠词开战。第三天，他的创意达到了制高点，把信里的一切全给删了，只留下冠词。他觉得玩这种游戏引起了更多力学上的线性内张力，差不多能使每一封信的要旨更为普遍化。没隔多久，他又涂掉了落款部分，正文则一字不动。有一次，他删去了整整一封信的内容，只保留了上款“亲爱的玛丽”，并在信笺下方写上，“我苦苦地思念着你。美国随军牧师A·T·塔普曼。”A·T·塔普曼是飞行大队随军牧师的姓名。

当他再也想不出什么点子在这些信上面搞鬼时，又将注意力转移到信封上的姓名和地址，随手漫不经心地一挥，就抹去了所有的住宅和街道名称，好比让一座座大都市消失，仿佛他是上帝一般。第二十二条军规规定，审查官必须在自己检查过的每封信上署上自己的姓名。大多数信约塞连看都没看过。凡是没看过的信，他就签上自己的姓名；要是看过了的，他则写上：“华盛顿·欧文”。后来这名字写烦了，他便改用“欧文·华盛顿”。审查信件一事引起了强烈反响，令某些养尊处优的高层将领产生了焦虑情绪。结果，刑事调查部派了一名工作人员装作病人，住进病房。军官们都知道他是刑事调查部的人，因为他老是打听一个名叫欧文或是华盛顿的军官，而且第一天下来，他就不愿再审查信件了。他觉得那些信实在是太枯燥无味了。

约塞连这次住的病房挺不错，是他和邓巴住过的最好的病房之一。同病房里有一名战斗机上尉飞行员，24岁，蓄着稀稀拉拉的金黄色八字须。这家伙曾在隆冬时节执行飞行任务时被击中，飞机坠入亚得里亚海，但他竟安然无事，都没有感冒。时下已是夏天，他没让人从飞机上给击落，反倒得了流行性感冒。约塞连右侧病床的主人是一名身患疟疾而吓得半死的上尉，这家伙的屁股被蚊子叮了一口，此刻正脉脉含情地趴在床上。约塞连和邓巴中间隔着通道。紧挨邓巴的是一名炮兵上尉，现在约塞连再也不跟他下棋了。这家伙棋技极高，每回跟他对弈总是趣味无穷，然而，正因为趣味无穷，反而让人有种被愚弄的感觉，所以约塞连后来就不再跟他下棋了。再过去便是那个颇有教养的得克萨斯人，看上去很像电影里的明星。他有一颗爱国心，他认为较之于无产者——流浪汉、娼妓、罪犯、堕落分子、无神论者和粗鄙下流的人，有产者，亦即上等人，理应获得更多的选票。

We must accept finite disappointment, but we must never lose infinite hope.

——Martin Luther King

我们必须接受失望，因为它是有限的，但千万不能失去希望，因为它是无穷的。

——马丁·路德·金

作者介绍

约瑟夫·海勒（1923–1999），美国小说家，“黑色幽默”的代表作家之一。约瑟夫海勒可谓是多产的作家，主要作品有《第二十二条军规》、《并非笑话》、《悠悠岁月》以及两个剧本《我们轰炸纽黑文》和《克莱文杰的审判》。海勒的幽默、讽刺把荒诞与严肃、夸张与真实、闹剧与正经调和起来，以阴冷的、玩世不恭的幽默来嘲笑一切，表达对现实世界的不满和抗议，使人在震颤中去思索，在喜剧中去悲哀。

单词注解

jaundice ['dʒɔːndis] *n.* 黄疸病；偏见；嫉妒

censor ['sensə] *n.* 审查员

dynamic [dai'næmik] *adj.* 力的；动力的

proscribe [prəu'skraib] *v.* 放逐

annihilate [ə'naiə,leit] *v.* 歼灭，消灭；彻底击溃；毁灭

mustache [məs'tɑːʃ] *n.* 髭，小胡子

mosquito [məs'kiːtəu] *n.* 蚊子

名句大搜索

这可是实实在在的一见钟情。

第二十二条军规规定，审查官必须在自己检查过的每一封信上署上自己的姓名。

他觉得那些信实在是太枯燥无味了。

The Shawshank Redemption
肖申克的救赎

[美] 斯蒂芬·金（Stephen King）

银行家安迪，被当做杀害妻子的凶手送上法庭。妻子的不忠，律师的奸诈，法官的误判，狱警的凶暴、典狱长的贪心与卑鄙，将正处在而立之年的安迪一下子从人生的巅峰推向了世间地狱。而狱中发生的一系列事情迫使忍无可忍的安迪终于在一个雷电交加的夜晚，越狱而出，重获自由。当翌日典狱长打开安迪的牢门时，发现他已不翼而飞，预感到末日来临的典狱长在检察人员收到安迪投寄的罪证之前，畏罪自杀。

There' s a guy like me in every state and federal prison in America, I guess— I' m the guy who can get it for you. Tailor-made cigarettes, a bag of reefer, if you're partial to that, a bottle of brandy to celebrate your son or daughter's high school graduation, or almost anything else... within reason, that is. It wasn't always that way.

I came to Shawshank when I was just twenty, and I am one of the few people in our happy little family who is willing to own up to what he did. I **committed** murder. I put a large insurance policy on my wife, who was three years older than I was, and then I fixed the brakes of the Chevrolet coupe her father had given us as a wedding present. It worked out exactly as I had planned, except I hadn't planned on her stopping to pick up the neighbour woman and the neighbour woman's infant son on the way down Castle Hill and into town. The brakes let go and the car crashed through the bushes at the edge of the town common, gathering speed. Bystanders said it must have been doing fifty or better when it hit the base of the Civil War statue and burst into flames.

I also hadn't planned on getting caught, but caught I was. I got a season's pass into this place. Maine has no death **penalty**, but the district attorney saw to it that I was tried for all three deaths and given three life sentences, to run one after the other. That fixed up any chance of parole I might have, for a long, long time. The judge called what I had done 'a hideous, heinous crime', and it was, but it is also in the past now. You can look it up in the yellowing files of the Castle Rock Call, where the big headlines announcing my conviction look sort of funny and **antique** next to the news of Hitler and Mussolini and FDR's alphabet soup agencies.

Have I **rehabilitated** myself, you ask? I don't know what that word means, at least as far as prisons and corrections go. I think it's a politician's word. It may have some other meaning, and it may be that I will have a chance to find out, but that is the future ...something cons teach themselves not to think about. I was young, good-looking, and from the poor side of town. I knocked up a pretty, sulky, headstrong girl who lived in one of the fine old houses on Carbine Street. Her father was agreeable to the marriage if I would take a job in the optical company he owned and 'work my way up'. I found out that what he really had in mind was keeping me in his house and under his thumb, like a disagreeable pet that has not quite been housebroken and which may bite. Enough hate eventually piled up to cause me to do what I did. *Given a second chance I would not do it again, but I'm not sure that means I am rehabilitated.*

Anyway, it's not me I want to tell you about ; I want to tell you about a guy named Andy Dufresne. But before I can tell you about Andy, I have to explain a few other things about myself. It won't take long.

As I said, I've been the guy who can get it for you here at Shawshank for damn near forty years. And that doesn't just mean contraband items like extra cigarettes or booze, although those items always top the list. But I've gotten thousands of other items for men doing time here, some of them perfectly legal yet hard to come by in a place where you've supposedly been brought to be punished. There was one fellow who was in for raping a little girl and exposing himself to dozens of others ; I got him three pieces of pink Vermont marble and he did three lovely sculptures out of them — a baby, a boy of about twelve, and a bearded young man. He called them The Three Ages of Jesus, and those pieces of sculpture are now in the parlour of a man who used to be governor of this state.

Or here's a name you may remember if you grew up north of Massachusetts — Robert Alan Cote. In 1951 he tried to rob the First Mercantile Bank of Mechanic Falls, and the hold-up turned into a bloodbath— six dead in the end, two of them members of the gang, three of them **hostages**, one of them a young state cop who put his head up at the wrong time and got a bullet in the eye. Cote had a penny collection. Naturally they weren't going to let him have it in here, but with a little help from his mother and a middleman who used to drive a laundry truck, I was able to get it to him. I told him, Bobby, you must be crazy, wanting to have a coin collection in a stone hotel full of thieves. He looked at me and smiled and said, I know where to keep them. They'll be safe enough. Don't you worry. And he was right. Bobby Cote died of a brain tumour in 1967, but that coin collection has never turned up.

I've gotten men chocolates on Valentine's Day; I got three of those green milkshakes they serve at McDonald's around St Paddy's Day for a crazy Irishman named O'Malley; I even arranged for a midnight showing of Deep Throat and The Devil in Miss Jones for a party of twenty men who had pooled their resources to rent the films ... although I ended up doing a week in solitary for that little escapade. It's the risk you run when you're the guy who can get it.

I've gotten **reference** books and fuck-books, joke novelties like handbuzzers and itching powder, and on more than one occasion I've seen that a long-timer has gotten a pair of panties from his wife or his girlfriend... and I guess you'll know what guys in here do with such items during the long nights when time draws out like a blade. I don't get all those things gratis, and for some items the price comes high. But I don't do it just for the money; what good is money to me? I'm never going to own a Cadillac car or fly off to Jamaica for two weeks in February. I do it for the same reason that a good butcher will only sell you fresh meat: I got a reputation and I want to keep it. The only two things I refuse to handle are guns and heavy drugs. *I won't help anyone kill himself or anyone else. I have enough killing on my mind to last me a lifetime.*

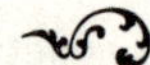

我猜美国每个州立监狱和联邦监狱里，都有像我这样的人物，不论什么东西，我都能弄到手。无论是高级香烟或大麻（如果你有此偏好的话)，或弄瓶白兰地来庆祝儿子或女儿高中毕业，总之差不多任何东西……我的意思是说，只要在合理范围内，我是有求必应；可是很多情况不一定都是合情合理的。

我刚满 20 岁就进了肖申克监狱。在这个快乐的小家庭中，我是少数几个肯痛痛快快承认自己干了什么的人。我犯了谋杀罪。我为大我三岁的太太投保了一笔数目庞大的寿险，然后在她父亲送我们的结婚礼物——一辆雪佛兰轿车的刹车上动了手脚。一切都按我的计划进行，只是没料到她会在从城堡山上下来进镇的路上把邻居太太和她的小儿子载上。结果刹车失灵，车速越来越快，冲到路边的树丛，撞上了一座内战纪念雕像的底座而轰然起火。目击者说，当时的车速足有每小时50英里。

我也没料到自己居然会被逮住，但我却锒铛入狱，在这里长期服刑。缅因州没有死刑，但检察官认为我应为三条人命负责，数罪并罚，判了我三个无期徒刑。这样一来，我在很长一段时间内，都不可能有机会假释了。法官还在判决书上写着：罪行重大，死有余辜。的确如此，不过现在这些事都过去了。你可以去查查城堡岩的旧报纸档案，有关我的判决当时是地方报纸的头条新闻，与希特勒、墨索里尼以及罗斯福手下那些字母开头的特工人员的新闻并列，现在看来，实在有点可笑，也早已成为老掉牙的旧闻了。

你问我，我改过自新了吗？我甚至不知道什么叫改过自新，至少我不晓得那在监狱里代表什么意思，我认为那只是政客爱用的字眼，这个词也许有一些其他的含意，也许有那么一天，我会明白它的含意，但那是将来的事了……而将来是囚犯不愿意去想的。当年的我出身贫穷，但年轻英俊。我让一个富家女珠胎暗结，她出身卡宾街的豪华宅邸，漂亮娇纵、但老是闷闷不乐。她父亲同意让我们结婚，条件是我得在他的眼镜公司工作，“靠自己的实力往上爬。”后来我发现，他真正的用意是要让我随时都在他的监控下，就像管着家里的不太听话、还会咬人的猫狗一样。我的怨恨经年累月，越积越深，终于出手造成了这样的后果。如果再给我一次机会，我绝对不会重蹈覆辙，但我不确定这样是否表示我已经痛改前非了。

不过，我真正想说的不是我自己的事，而是安迪·杜佛尼的故事。但在我开始说安迪的故事之前，还得先说几件关于我的事情，反正不会花太多工夫。

正如我刚才所说，差不多40年来，在肖申克监狱里，我有办法帮你弄到任何东西。除了永远名列前茅的香烟和酒等违禁品之外，我还有办法弄到上千种其他东西，给这儿的人打发时间用。许多东西都是合法的，只是在这样一个惩罚人的地方是弄不到的。例如，有个家伙强暴了一个小女孩，还涉及几十件其他的案子。我给他找了三块粉红色的佛蒙特大理石，他雕了三座可爱的雕像，一个婴儿、一个12岁男孩，还有一个长胡须的年轻人，他称这些雕像为“耶稣的三个不同时期”，现在这些雕像已经成为前任州长客厅中的摆设了。

如果你生长在北马萨诸塞州的话，一定能想起这个名字——罗伯特·艾伦·科特。他在1951年，企图抢劫莫堪尼克弗市第一商业银行，结果那次抢劫演变成血腥事件，死了六个人，包括两个强盗、三名人质，还有一个是一位年轻警察，他在错误的时间把头伸了出去，一颗子弹射中了他的眼睛。科特有收集钱币的嗜好。监狱自然不会准他将收藏品带进来，但在他母亲和洗衣房卡车司机的帮助下，我还是替他弄到了他想要的东西。我告诉他：你一定是疯了，竟然想在这个满是盗贼的石头旅馆中收藏钱币。他笑着对我说：“我知道该把钱币藏在哪里，绝对安全，你别担心。”他说得没错。直到1967年，他死于脑瘤时，他所收藏的钱币始终没有现过身。

我在情人节设法为狱友弄到巧克力；在圣帕迪日为一个叫欧迈利的疯狂爱尔兰人弄到三杯麦当劳的绿色奶昔；我甚至还安排了一次午夜剧场，为20个人放映《深喉》和《琼斯小姐体内的魔鬼》。他们为租这些电影花光了积蓄……虽然我因为这些越轨行动被关了一周禁闭，但要维持“神通广大”的英名，就必须冒这样的风险。

我还能弄到参考书和黄色书刊、会让人发痒的粉末之类的恶作剧新奇玩意儿，甚至替被判长期徒刑的家伙弄到太太或女朋友的内裤……我猜你也知道这些人究竟是如何度过如刀割似的漫漫长夜了。这些东西并非免费的，有些东西代价不菲。但我绝不是光为钱来干这些事。金钱对我又有何用呢？我既无法拥有一辆凯迪拉克，更不能在二月天飞到牙买加去度假。因为与一个好屠夫只卖新鲜肉一样，我想得到个好名声并保持下去。只有两种东西，我绝对不碰，一是枪械，一是毒品。我不会帮助任何人自杀或杀人。在我的有生之年心里缠绕着太多的杀戮了。

The value of life lies not in the length of days, but in the use we make of them.

——Montaigne

生命的价值不在于能活多少天，而在于我们如何使用这些日子。

——蒙　田

作者介绍

斯蒂芬·金是恐怖小说大师的代表。他于 1947 年 9 月 21 日出生于美国缅因州波特兰的一个贫困家庭。后来去州立大学学习英国文学，毕业后开始写作。70 年代中期声名渐起，被《纽约时报》誉为“现代恐怖小说大师”。自 80 年代以来,他的小说总是名列各大畅销书排行榜榜首。1979 年，在他 32 岁时，成为全世界作家中首屈一指的亿万富翁。斯蒂芬·金的作品超越了传统的恐怖小说，他不靠具体的意象来获得恐怖效果，而是通过对事件气氛的营造来震慑读者。

单词注解

commit [kə'mit] *v.* 犯（罪），做（错事）

penalty ['penlti] *n.* 处罚；刑罚

antique [æn'ti:k] *adj.* 古代的，古老的；年代久远的

rehabilitate [ˌri:hə'biliteit] *v.* （使）复兴；（使）恢复原状

hostage ['hɔstidʒ] *n.* 人质；抵押品

reference ['refrəns] *n.* 提及；涉及

名句大搜索

我猜美国每个州立监狱和联邦监狱里，都有像我这样的人物，不论什么东西，我都能弄到手。

如果再给我一次机会，我绝对不会重蹈覆辙，但我不确定这样是否表示我已经痛改前非了。

我不会帮助任何人自杀或杀人。在我的有生之年心里缠绕着太多的杀戮了。

Young Goodman Brown

年轻的布朗大爷

[美] 纳撒尼尔·霍桑（Nathaniel Hawthorne）

在这篇小说里，霍桑写了早年的新英格兰，故事主人公去出席在半夜举行的魔鬼聚会，发现在座的不仅有镇上所有德高望重的人，甚至还有他的妻子费思……

Young Goodman Brown came forth at sunset into the street at Salem village ; but put his head back, after crossing the thresh old, to **exchange** a parting kiss with his young wife. And Faith, as the wife was aptly named, thrust her own pretty head into the street, letting the wind play with the pink ribbons of her cap while she called to Goodman Brown.

"Dearest heart," whispered she, softly and rather sadly, when her lips were close to his ear, "prithee put off your journey until sunrise and sleep in your own bed tonight. *A lone woman is troubled with such dreams and such thoughts that she' s afeard of herself sometimes.* Pray tarry with me this night, dear husband, of all nights in the year."

"My love and my Faith," replied young Goodman Brown, "of all nights in the year, this one night must I tarry away from thee. My journey, as thou callest it, forth and back again, must needs be done 'twixt now and sunrise. What, my sweet, pretty wife, dost thou doubt me a1ready, and we but three months married?"

"Then God bless you!" said Faith, with the pink ribbons ; "and may you find all well when you come back."

"Amen!" cried Goodman Brown "Say thy prayers, dear Faith, and go to bed at dusk, and no harm will come to thee."

So they parted ; and the young man pursued his way until, being about to turn the corner by the meeting-house, he looked back and saw the head of Faith still peeping after him with a **melancholy** air, in spite of her pink ribbons.

"Poor little Faith!" thought he, for his heart smote him. "What a wretch am I to leave her on such an errand! She talks of dreams, too. Me thought as she spoke there was trouble in her face, as if a dream had warned her what work is to be done tonight. But no ; no ; 't would kill her to think it. Well, she's a blessed angel on earth ; and after this one night I'll cling to her skirts and follow her to heaven."

With this **excellent** resolve for the future, Goodman Brown felt himself justified in making more haste on his present evil purpose. *He had taken a dreary road, darkened by all the gloomiest trees of the forest, which barely stood aside to let the narrow path creep through, and closed immediately behind.* It was all as lonely as could be, and there is this peculiarity in such a solitude, that the traveler knows not who may be concealed by the innumerable trunks and the thick boughs overhead, so that with lonely footsteps he may yet be passing through an unseen multitude.

"There may be a devilish Indian behind every tree," said Goodman Brown to himself ; and he glanced fearfully behind him as he added, "What if the devil himself should be at my very elbow!"

His head being turned back, he passed a crook of the road, and, looking forward again, beheld the figure of a man, in grave and decent attire, seated at the foot of an old tree. He arose at Goodman Brown's approach and walked onward side by side with him.

年轻的布朗大爷在落日时分出现在塞勒姆村的街上，他走出去又返回来，跟年轻的妻子吻别。妻子名叫费思，这时她把自己美丽的头伸过来，在她叫布朗大爷时，任风吹拂着软帽上的粉红色缎带。

“亲爱的心肝儿，”等她的嘴唇凑近他的耳朵时，她温柔地、伤感地小声说，“请你把这次旅程推迟到日出以后，今儿晚上还是在自家的床上安歇吧。一个孤独的女人常受到噩梦和忧虑的烦扰。在一年里所有的夜晚中，亲爱的丈夫，今夜请你留下陪着我吧。”

“我亲爱的费思，”年轻的布朗大爷回答，“在一年里所有的夜晚中，我这一夜必须离开。我的往返旅程，如同你所说的，必须在现在和日出之间结束。怎么，我亲爱又美丽的妻子，你是在怀疑我吗，我们结婚才不过3个月啊？”

“那么，愿上帝降福给你！”扎着粉红色缎带的费思说，“愿你回来时，发觉一切顺遂。”

“阿门！”布朗大爷喊了一声，“你祈祷吧，亲爱的费思，黄昏时分就上床睡觉，不会有事的。”

就这样，他们分别了。年轻人启程上路。后来在那个聚所旁边准备拐弯时，他回头看了一下，看见费思仍然带着一种忧郁的神情在注视着他，根本不顾那条粉红色的缎带。

“可怜的小费思！”他想着，因此他心里十分难受，“我撇下她去办这样一件事，是多么卑鄙啊！她还谈到做梦。我觉得她说的时候，很是不悦，仿佛有一场梦事先已经告诉了她今儿夜晚将要出什么事。可是，不，不；想着它会送了她的性命的。嗨，她是世上一位幸运的天使。过了这一夜，我就跟她去天堂。”

对于未来作出了这一美好的决定之后，布朗觉得可以心安理得地赶紧去了结眼下这邪恶的勾当了。他走的是一条沉寂的道路，树林里所有最幽暗的树木把这条路遮得一片漆黑。那些树木长得密密匝匝，简直不容这条羊肠小道穿过，而且总在后面立刻就又合拢了起来。四下里一片凄凉，在这样的落寞中，行路人并不知道那些树和粗枝上可能隐藏着些什么人，所以他迈着孤单的步伐，可能还在经过一大群隐而不现的人哩。

“也许每棵树后面都藏着一个凶恶的印第安人。”布朗大爷暗自这么说。他满怀恐惧地朝身后瞥了一眼，又加上一句：“要是魔鬼本人就在我的身旁，那可怎么办！”

他回头张望着，走到了一个拐弯处，然后又朝前望去，看见一个穿着朴实大方的人，坐在一棵老树的脚下。当布朗大爷走近时，他站起身来，和他并排朝前走去。

作者介绍

纳撒尼尔·霍桑（1804-1864），美国小说家。霍桑是清教徒的后裔，深受道德洗礼。他的作品包括《我的亲属，莫理斯上校》、《罗杰·马尔文的葬礼》、《年轻的布朗大爷》和被列入美国最好小说的《红字》等。他是一位文学艺术家，也是寓言兼象征主义大师，他被称为美国最伟大的小说家。

单词注解

exchange [iks'tʃeindʒ] *v.* 交换；调换；兑换

melancholy ['melənkəli] *n.* 忧思，愁思

excellent ['eksələnt] *adj.* 出色的；杰出的；优等的

decent ['di:snt] *adj.* 正派的；合乎礼仪的

名句大搜索

一个孤独的女人常受到噩梦和忧虑的烦扰。

他走的是一条沉寂的道路，树林里所有最幽暗的树木把这条路遮得一片漆黑。那些树木长得密密匝匝，简直不容这条羊肠小道穿过，而且总在后面立刻就又合拢了起来。

他回头张望着，走到了一个拐弯处，然后又朝前望去，看见一个穿着朴实大方的人，坐在一棵老树的脚下。